CASTOFFS OF CAPITAL

CASTOFFS OF CAPITAL

Work and Love among
Garment Workers in Bangladesh

LAMIA KARIM

University of Minnesota Press | Minneapolis | London

Excerpts from poetry by Lovely Yesmin and Babul are reprinted with permission.

Copyright 2022 by the Regents of the University of Minnesota

All rights reserved. No part of this publication may be reproduced, stored in a retrieval system, or transmitted, in any form or by any means, electronic, mechanical, photocopying, recording, or otherwise, without the prior written permission of the publisher.

Published by the University of Minnesota Press
111 Third Avenue South, Suite 290
Minneapolis, MN 55401-2520
http://www.upress.umn.edu

ISBN 978-1-5179-1335-9 (hc)
ISBN 978-1-5179-1336-6 (pb)

A Cataloging-in-Publication record for this book is available from the Library of Congress.

The University of Minnesota is an equal-opportunity educator and employer.

Dedicated to the garment workers killed in factory fires and accidents in Bangladesh

I am so small I can barely be seen
How can this great love be inside me?

—Jalal ad-Din Muhammad Rumi, *On the Turn*

CONTENTS

PREFACE AND ACKNOWLEDGMENTS   xi

Introduction: Toward an Ethnography of Older Factory Women   1

1. The Disorder of Work and Life   23

2. The Age of Excitement: The Rise of the Garment Industry in Bangladesh   53

3. The Arc of Change: Factory, Family, and Class   77

4. Changing Norms of Romance, Marriage, and Sexuality   123

5. After Work: Life in the Shadows of Capital   165

Conclusion: Politics of the Precariat   199

EPILOGUE. AFTER DEATH: A BODY WITHOUT A HOME   213

APPENDIX I: SIXTEEN GARMENT WORKERS IN 2017–2018   219

APPENDIX II: FOLLOW-UP ON SIXTEEN GARMENT WORKERS IN 2020   221

NOTES   225

INDEX   243

PREFACE AND ACKNOWLEDGMENTS

On April 24, 2013, the eight-story Rana Plaza factory collapsed, killing 1,134 workers and injuring another 2,500. It was the most significant apparel factory accident since the 1911 Triangle Shirtwaist Factory fire in New York City. Cracks had appeared in the Rana Plaza building a few days prior, leading several other businesses to close their operations and remove their personnel. After seeing the cracks, garment workers did not want to go inside the factory, but their managers forced them to start work. In less than an hour, the building collapsed, burying thousands of workers in the rubble. The industrial accident finally brought global attention to the unsafe conditions inside factories in Bangladesh that were producing clothes for multinational brands like H&M, Walmart, Gap, Target, Zara, Old Navy, KIK, Tchibo, C&A, Primark, and many others. It led Western governments and labor rights organizations to demand factory safety upgrades in the garment industry in Bangladesh.

The following year, I presented my initial research on the accident at the Annual Women's Conference at Lewis and Clark College. When I asked the students what they would like to know about the garment workers in Bangladesh, they replied unanimously, "Tell us their stories. We want to know about the women who make our clothes." At the Osher Lifelong Learning Center in Eugene, Oregon, a group of retired people heard my talk on the accident and told me that they wanted to know about these women workers' lives. In academic and nonacademic settings, people have asked me to write about the women who make their clothes.

Throughout the research and writing of this book, one question haunted me: How do I portray these women's lives in all their human dimensions? Trapped within capitalism, these women are not "cheap" workers, nor are their lives reducible to capitalism or poverty, patriarchy or modernity. All these structures shape who they are and who they can be, but they do not capture the essence of what it means to be human. Being born poor is a matter of circumstance; buying too many clothes is a choice we consumers make in the First World. My objective here is to contextualize the life stories of female workers in all their aspirations, grittiness, and complexities, focusing on older and aged-out workers. These women are not only workers; they are also thinking, feeling, and acting agents. Yet, most of the voluminous research produced about female factory labor in Bangladesh refers to them in terms of cold statistics—the lowest-paid workers in the world, the most impoverished workers working in hazardous situations, the cheapest of the cheap. While these statements are factually accurate, they do not reveal much about what life means for these women. *Castoffs of Capital: Work and Love among Garment Workers in Bangladesh* seeks to humanize these women through their stories and make their lives intelligible via the prism of their wants and desires.

Many people have assisted me over the years to complete the research for this book. There are far too many to thank each individually. My deepest thanks are to the garment workers who shared their life stories of hard labor and aspirations for a better life. My thanks also go to my terrific research assistants, especially Al-Zahid, Atia, Shahid, Tithi, and the staff at Kormojibi Nari. Without their assistance, I would not be able to complete the research. My appreciation to my colleagues and friends for their support and comments as the manuscript went through revisions: Yvette Alex-Assensoh, Michael Allan, Suzanne Bergeron, Louise Bishop, Jim Faubion, Melissa Fisher, Michelle Gamburd, Sangita Gopal, Eileen Otis, Carol Stabile, and Lynn Stephen. In Bangladesh, my thanks go to Aharar Ahmed, Kalpona Akter, Nazma Akter, Firdaus Azim, Ahmed Kamal, Anu Muhammad, Rokeya Rahman, Sahanaj Sadin, Binayek Sen, Sunzida Sultana, and Lovely Yesmin. Thanks to Elise Hanson for her copyediting, to my sister Yasmin Hagen for kindly reading my work, and to the two anonymous readers whose close reading helped clarify the manuscript.

For financial assistance, I am grateful to the Work and Human Life Cycle in Global History/re:work, Humboldt University (Berlin, Germany), for a 2016–17 fellowship that allowed me to analyze my materials and ask new questions of women's labor and aspirations that finally turned the research into a manuscript. Most important, through the weekly seminars, my colleagues at re:work pushed me to go beyond the traditional narrative of work and female labor. At re:work, I wish to thank Andreas Eckert, Felicia Hentsche, and Susan Zimmermann. My thanks are also due to the Wenner-Gren Foundation for Anthropological Research for a postdoctoral grant that allowed me to conduct research on aged-out workers. At the University of Oregon, my research was supported by an Oregon Humanities Center VPRI Project Completion Fellowship, a Faculty Research Award, Division of Equity and Inclusion, and a Center for the Study of Women and Society research grant. In addition, I am grateful to my department for providing me with the time I needed to finish the book. Finally, all faults and errors that remain are mine alone.

INTRODUCTION
TOWARD AN ETHNOGRAPHY OF OLDER FACTORY WOMEN

HALIMA'S ASPIRATIONS

"All my life, I have felt like an orphan. My father remarried after my mother died, so as a child I lived in my uncle's house, where they treated me as a domestic worker. I was the last to get any food, and often the food was rotten. I always wanted to go to school, but they never sent me to primary school. By age fifteen, I was married off. Once I married, I thought I would have a better life, a husband who would care for me, plenty of food, and a roof over my head. My husband lost his land to river erosion, and we came to the city in 1995 in search of work. Soon I joined a garment factory as a helper at taka 300 per month [$7.50 at the 1995 exchange rate].[1] Nevertheless, my husband would take away my wages, and I couldn't save a penny. He would often beat me in his anger over my ability to earn money, which he called his own. After the birth of our two daughters, he left me for a younger woman. Unable to take care of my children in the city, I took them back to the village to be raised by my parents."

I met Halima, a forty-five-year-old former garment factory worker, on a winter evening in Mirpur, an industrial area within greater Dhaka, Bangladesh. We were sitting at a labor rights office, having tea and discussing her work life. Within the four white-washed and drab walls of the office, Halima, in her brightly colored sari, was like a sliver of sunlight. She was small in stature. When she spoke, her voice was soft and nearly inaudible. Her work life spanned almost twenty-two years between 1995 and 2017. It was only in the last seven years that she had secured some financial stability. Over the years, she had risen through the ranks to become a senior sewing operator making taka 7,500 ($93.75 a month at the 2018 exchange rate). From long-term work, Halima developed an infection in her lungs that required taka 40,000 for medical care. She had to borrow the money to pay for her medical expenses. Like the majority of garment workers, Halima went into debt to pay her living costs.

Halima hoped that her daughters would not become garment workers like her. However, facing financial insecurity, the older daughter joined the garment industry at age sixteen. At the time of our interview, the younger daughter was enrolled in grade 10. I asked Halima why she did not want her younger daughter to work in a factory. She replied that the factory is an inhospitable environment for women. Pointing to her hands, she said, "I suffer from constant pain in my hands, headaches, and a general sense of malaise. Once I fainted in the factory." Sighing, she added, "I worked hard, never missed a day of work, so my daughters could have a better life than me. The older one I could not help, but the younger one will hopefully get into government service."

Halima had expected to receive taka 90,000 from the factory when she retired, but she only received taka 63,000. She did not complain about it to the union representative at her factory. Halima confided that she believed this was what "Allah had decreed for her." After years of work, she was physically and mentally weary of fighting factory bureaucracy. Unlike the younger generation of workers that I met, Halima had not been socialized to fight for her rights. She joined the workforce in 1995 at a time when trade-union activism was virtually nonexistent in this industry, but she was acutely aware of workplace injustices. She explained, "Those workers who speak back are fired by factory management."

As for her future, Halima wanted to buy a small piece of land in the village. However, she did not have the cash to purchase the property. She had heard that many workers were going overseas to Mauritius to work in factories owned by Chinese and Indian businessmen. The pay in Mauritius was much higher. If she could go there, she would be able to save enough to build her house. She described her dream home as a brick house with a few rooms, piped gas for cooking, and electricity, all the accoutrements of modern life she had experienced in the city. There would be a vegetable patch and chickens and ducks in the yard, reminiscent of a rural upbringing. It sounded whimsical and beautiful—the small imaginings that offer women like Halima the resilience to wake up every day to go to work. What remained unsaid was, who would hire a forty-five-year-old worker? Several months later, in a follow-up phone call, I learned that Halima's younger daughter had begun working at a garment factory. Halima said, "We had run out of money. But my daughter has a grade 10 education, and she may soon become a line supervisor." Halima's life was a tapestry of the human need for security, nourishment, care, and love, elements that were absent from her life as an older worker.

Castoffs of Capital: Work and Love among Garment Workers in Bangladesh is an ethnographic study of how female workers in the global apparel industry experience their work and nonwork lives. Inspired by the raw and powerful stories of workers' encounters with capitalist modernity, the book introduces a new dimension to the making of a precariat female-headed workforce in Bangladesh that numbered approximately four million in 2018.[2] The book focuses on the lives of garment workers with a special emphasis on older and "aged-out" female workers. I examine the relations between work, gender, and age, on the one hand, and these factory women's search for the good life of love and care against the backdrop of neoliberalism and industrialization, on the other. *Castoffs of Capital* analyzes how global capital targets poor women to advance its neoliberal agenda of market penetration and labor flexibility, and it shows how women also navigate these spaces to increase their and their families' well-being. Informed by the scholarly works of Carla Freeman on neoliberal aspirations, Lauren Berlant on cruel optimism, Arjun Appadurai on globalization, Guy Standing on precarious labor, and Bangladeshi anthropologist Nurul Momen Bhuiyan's notion of "residue of hope," the book is a study of these older women's quest for a good life as human subjects with rights, dignity, and desire.[3]

A Google Scholar search with the words "Bangladesh garment industry" on April 10, 2022, returned over 34,500 scholarly articles. While a plethora of articles have been written about the garment industry in Bangladesh, the significance of *Castoffs of Capital* lies in bringing these older women's lives into the discipline of feminist labor studies. If we are to write the history of apparel manufacturing, what happens to older women workers after they leave factory work is particularly important for scholars to know. Female workers who are aged out of factory work are largely ignored in labor history, because they cease to be part of the labor force. This book fills this lacuna and foregrounds these women not only as workers but also as mothers, wives, sisters, lovers, friends, and political agents—that is, in their full humanity. Through ethnographic case studies, it examines the making and unmaking of these women's wants and aspirations, loves and tribulations, hopes and despairs, and triumphs and struggles. Furthermore, the book explores the intergenerational changes between the older and younger workers; assesses the multiple subject formations induced by industrial work, migration, and globalization; and analyzes these women's often ill-fated aspirations around love, marriage, and children.

After China, Bangladesh is the largest producer of apparel for the global market, ahead of Vietnam, Cambodia, and Sri Lanka. Its garment labor force is 80 percent female and 20 percent male. The workers are predominantly recent rural-to-urban migrants with low skill and literacy levels. Female workers enter the workforce around the average age of fifteen years, and they are aged out of factory work between thirty-five to forty years of age by management. After twenty-plus years of working on an assembly line, these older women have broken bodies and shattered dreams. The book challenges their invisibility by showing their lives, labors, and aspirations and by learning what those lives can teach us about the reproduction of patriarchy and capitalism as well as women's agentic roles within those bounds. In writing this book, I asked the following questions: What aspirations structured these older women's lives, and what were they able to achieve by the end of their work lives? What compelled these women to leave the security of their rural homes and journey into the belly of the beast—the city—a place of dangers, provocations, pollution, chaos, and indifference to human suffering? Was it money alone?

Capitalism and modernity are coterminous processes that depend on similar "rationalities and orientations focused around the simultaneous re-making of personal life and society in pursuit of control over nature, material improvement, and the belief in a more inclusive society and polity."[4] In what Paul Kennedy calls "vampire capitalism," certain kinds of bodies are deemed valuable, others not. These older women are considered worthless and disposable by factory management once they are around thirty-five to forty years of age, even though they still have another fifteen years of work life left. In contrast, male garment workers exit factory work between forty-five and fifty-five years of age, and the retirement age for public servants in Bangladesh is fifty-nine. As they age, these female workers are replaced by a younger generation of workers who cost less and are less likely to defy their managers. However, age is not the sole determinant in the global economy. Age and the knowledge economy operate differently for various categories of workers. In European and American contexts, a new dynamic is emerging called encore careers, in which older workers reinvent their work lives by training in new skills.[5] However, the workers I studied were poor and had low literacy skills. Their tragedy was capitalism's refusal to invest in them beyond rudimentary assembly-line work, and thus they fell outside of the encore economy.

During my research, I found that there were very few women over the age of thirty-five working in the factories. Trade union leaders and the more than one hundred workers I met told me that female factory workers over age thirty-five are rare. Factory management confirmed that older women workers leave "due to changes in life circumstances," which is a disingenuous statement, since most of them are aged out when deemed to be less productive workers. I found that no institution—the Bangladeshi state, the apex organization of factory owners known as the Bangladesh Garment Manufacturers and Exporters Association (BGMEA), the Bangladesh Institute for Labor Studies (BILS), the International Labour Organization (ILO), and labor rights NGOs—was concerned with tracking these women once they ceased to be labor. When I asked a longtime labor activist about what happened to older workers once they exit out of work, she said, "That is a good question. We do not track them once they leave the factory."

The exploitation of women as industrial workers has led labor scholars and activists to construct them as subjects who seek decent work conditions through trade unions, labor rights nongovernmental organizations (NGOs), and the courts to adjudicate for their rights.

The ILO defines "decent work" as work that provides "fair income, security in the workplace, and social protection of families," as well as "freedom for people to express their concerns, organize and participate in the decisions that affect their lives."[6] It is a term that is used widely by labor rights groups. This study goes beyond these stereotypical notions of the worker as a rights-bearing subject. Instead, it examines these workers as human subjects with aspirations and desires, helping us to understand these women not only as workers trapped in the global supply chain of commodity production but also as agents who strive to create the good life (*shundor jibon*).[7]

As thinking/acting subjects, these women navigated their lives by making choices within their limited social world. Workers sought the good life through improvements in the material conditions in their lives, better diet, housing, and education for their children that would lead to upward mobility. They also sought the good life in terms of affect—their desire to be seen as women who love and can be loved. As one woman said to me, "For more than eight hours a day, I stitch clothes. My body embraces the sewing machine. At night, an emptiness enters my life. There is no embrace waiting for me." It is this striving for a good life of material comfort and loving companionship that undergirds these women's humanity and engenders future political possibilities not only as workers but as full human subjects with rights, dignity, and desire.

My research indicates that there is no clear demarcation between these women's work life and their life after the workday ends; their life stories disrupt this distinction between the private (home) and the public (factory), creating a weave of aspirations where the private/public distinctions collapse and merge. As Freeman noted in her work on Barbadian entrepreneurial subjects, these lives are about how affects around "care, interest and joy . . . are conjured up, desired, repressed and unleashed."[8] Paying attention to Freeman's work on neoliberal aspirations, the book follows the aged-out women's life trajectories and compares the intergenerational changes between a group of older workers who are over forty-five years of age and a younger generation of women workers who are below thirty-five years of age. By comparing the intergenerational differences, it explores the shifting aspirations among these factory women.

Taking all these aspects into account, *Castoffs of Capital* is about multiple levels of betrayal against these working-class women—by factory owners defrauding them of wages; by Western buyers enforcing rock-bottom pricing that keep wages very low; by the state, trade unions, and political parties manipulating them as pawns to advance their agendas; and finally, by the men in their lives, who use them instrumentally for financial and sexual gratification. It is about the life cycles of garment workers trapped between patriarchy and global capital, between their aspirations for a better life and the brutal conditions of work, between their desire for romance and the betrayals by the men they fall in love with. It is about the lack of sovereignty of the worker over her life.

ORGANIZATION OF THE BOOK

Castoffs of Capital is organized in five chapters along with this Introduction, a Conclusion, and an Epilogue. Each chapter has the women's case studies woven in to illustrate the dynamic changes occurring in their lives through garment industry work, migration, neoliberal sentiments, and globalization. After a brief chapter outline, this Introduction concludes with a detailed examination of my methodological approach.

Chapter 1 locates this study within the broader landscape of feminist studies on female labor and capitalism. This scholarship has focused primarily on employed workers and has neglected workers who have left factory work. These older workers are the missing piece in the history of apparel manufacturing. The chapter also explores the localized meanings of the good life for garment workers. Next, the chapter covers the theoretical architecture, beginning with Standing on precariat labor, Freeman on neoliberalism, Berlant on cruel optimism, Appadurai on globalization, and Bhuiyan on hope as residue in these women's lives. Their theoretical insights have shaped my interpretations of the ethnography. Next, the chapter covers the five subject formations—economic, moral, aspirational, legal, and political—emerging among the workers through their encounters with capitalist modernity. Finally, it addresses the question of modernity and the making of the modern subject within the cultural landscape of Bangladesh.

Chapter 2 provides a brief history of the rise of the ready-made garment (RMG) industry in Bangladesh. First, the chapter examines the international treaties that incorporated women into development schemes. Next, it covers the structural adjustment policies of the World Bank and the Multifibre Arrangement, which offered quota-free status to goods produced in Bangladesh, and how these policies facilitated the growth of the garment industry. Next, it considers the privatization policies of the military state, which encouraged multinationals to use Bangladesh as a cheap source of labor. The chapter covers the workers' strikes over low wages and inhumane work conditions, and the 2006 Labor Act, which provided some safeguards to workers. Finally, it discusses the factory upgrades and inspections implemented through two agreements that Western buyers and factory owners signed. The chapter ends with changes to factory routines after the collapse of the Rana Plaza industrial factory 2013, and the effect of these changes on workers.

In chapter 3, I draw on my interviews with older and younger garment workers to explore the changing dynamics of their work and nonwork lives. I adopt a comparative frame in analyzing the lives of older and younger workers, showing how work, age, and employment have shaped their lives. First, I briefly sketch the landscape of garment work using data from a survey of one hundred workers that I conducted to underscore the changes that have occurred in the lives of these factory women. The survey is followed by an examination of the dynamics around factory work routines, changing social and family dynamics, and the ideas of middle-classness and consumerism that are on the upswing among garment workers. In the last section of this chapter I discuss how work and globalization have informed two young women's lives, creating new horizons of graduated possibilities.

Chapter 4 addresses one of the key questions that shaped my research: How do younger and older women experience the intimate sphere of love, marriage, and romance in their lives? To ethnographically study their private lives, I discuss a range of themes—romantic love, sexuality, changing marriage and divorce norms, causes of marital discord and abandonment, family courts, and older male and female workers' attitudes toward female sexuality. I also analyze women's toxic relations with their spouses/lovers. Female garment workers are challenging deeply held social attitudes not only toward woman's work but toward women's sexual autonomy as well. The chapter ends with two brief case studies:

first, a garment couple who had found love and mutual respect and lived a happy life; and second, an older woman whose love and sexual longings were brutally crushed by a patriarchal society.

Chapter 5 is the focal point of the study. One question that guided the research was, what did these women seek to gain through industrial work, and what did they achieve at the end of their work lives? The chapter is based on my interviews with sixteen older and aged-out workers. From these sixteen I have described three women's life stories in detail, providing the reader with a rich ethnography of their life trajectories. Each case study covers these women's childhood, married life, children, factory life, and old age/aspirations. These women's life stories reveal a shocking array of betrayals from the factory to their homes, portraying how Berlant's "cruel optimism" and Freeman's "aspirational subjects" intersect in the lives of aged-out workers. These women lived in the interstices of these opposing sets of impulses: desire that beckoned with false promises and then crushed them with betrayals. Despite all the insecurities the women faced, their lives offer us lessons in human resilience, imagination, and dignity.

In the Conclusion I return to the question of politics in the garment industry. Garment workers have developed an insurgent identity that factory owners have stoked through their inhumane behavior. These insurgencies occur when years of bottled-up anger spills over and workers take to the streets to demonstrate. I argue that, because of the lack of a robust labor movement in the country and the fact that workers themselves reject the "working-class" position, this insurgent identity does not necessarily translate into a wider workers' movement. These workers seek middle-class respectability and economic comfort that the left-identified trade unions have failed to recognize. I argue that these working women are multidimensional subjects with aspirations for upward mobility that have thwarted the future of a radical politics rooted in a wider workers' struggle.

The Epilogue circles back to an older worker and her violent death from poor health brought on by exploitative work conditions and spousal abuse. I explore the necropolitics of gender when her corpse is denied burial by her village community. Her poignant story represents the facelessness and namelessness of older garment workers, and their inability to find dignity even in death.

METHODS

Our knowledge of the women who make our clothes extends primarily to wages, workers' rights, and trade unions—practices that are extremely important for creating a decent work environment. Nonetheless, they fail to capture the full human dimensions of these women's lives. While their lives undergo a qualitative change in material circumstances once they become wage labor in the garment industry ("I could not eat in the village, but now I can eat"), there is a profound sense of emptiness in the after-work lives of these older women. These women live in the empty spaces of modernity that are created by global capital, factories, state, families, and their intimate partners, spaces that they try to fill through aspirations brought on by globalization that beckons them with new concepts of the good life. The life histories of these women reveal how urban living and factory work had changed their circumstances after they migrated to the city at a young age, some as young as eleven. Industrial work, wages, and urban living have touched every aspect of these women's lives—from rural–urban connections, to whom they marry and how they raise their children (do they keep them in the city or send them to the village?), to their relationship with their absent husbands and families, their living arrangements, workers' protests and demonstrations, and their relationship with factory bureaucracy—in creating social knowledge that was previously absent in their rural lives.

I conducted my research from 2014 to 2018, making multiple trips that ranged from two weeks to three months. During 2016 and 2017, I took time off while I was a fellow at a labor research center (re:work) at Humboldt University in Berlin. I am a Bangladeshi woman who has conducted research in Bangladesh since 1995. I am fluent in Bengali and can communicate with my research subjects directly. My familial contacts and my long-term research in Bangladesh have provided me with access to a range of local scholars and activists who assisted me with the research.

My research assistants—three women (Atia, Tithi, and Sahanaj) and two men (Al-Zahid and Shahid)—facilitated my access to the garment workers and worked with me in staggered phases over the course of my study. A labor rights NGO based in Mirpur, an industrial hub of garment factories, provided four of the five research assistants. This labor organization has worked with garment workers for more than twenty-five years and built a relationship of trust and solidarity with them. Apart from their workers' advocacy and training workshops funded by multilateral and bilateral organizations, the NGO helps both institutional and independent researchers with research projects. Most of their employees who work as research assistants come from a leftist political ideology where workers' rights and social justice issues are considered critical. My interlocutors were both the garment workers and the employees of the labor rights organization. These employees had long-term immersion with factory women, and they helped fine-tune my questions and answered many of my queries. My research assistants were my most trusted allies in this research. Two trade union leaders, Lovely Yesmin and Najma Akhter, met with me and also facilitated meetings with garment workers.

In my research plan I adopted what George Marcus termed "following the story."[9] The story is the map that takes the researcher to new ideas to consider and new sites to explore. Ethnography teaches careful listening and observation strategies. The story is not only in the spoken words, but is contained in physical movements, pitch, eye movement, gestures, and silences. Speakers adopt a range of tactics in telling their stories, and the craft of the ethnographer is to search for hidden maps within the spoken words. The ethnographer also locates the ethnography within a broader cultural landscape and identifies other relevant issues to frame and analyze the conversation with the interlocutors. That is, the anthropologist speaks not only with a person but also with other individuals associated with the person's lifeworld. The major critiques of anthropology from social scientists are its small study population (economists often ask how big the sample group was), its textual orientations, the recognition that ethnography is based on "the notion of the heroic individual ethnographer and her or his interpretation of the lifeways of another culture," and so on.[10] The list is long, the debates ongoing. It is necessary to point out here that all research has its blind spots and that all researchers have their biases and preferences of what they consider important to study.

I follow a particular formula in conducting my ethnographic research. I develop a network of insiders and trusted people who come from the community that I wish to engage with. Since Bangladesh is a face-to-face society, knowing the person who is introducing the researcher is of paramount importance to members of the community. Trust was a key factor in conducting this ethnography, and four of my research assistants were invaluable in facilitating my introduction to the garment workers. Without their ongoing assistance and elaborations on the material collected, this research would not have been possible. Yet at every step of my research I was brutally reminded of my limits in capturing these factory women's essential desires for being. One day I went to a coffee shop with a friend. As I was sipping my coffee, the young female server came up to clean the table. Knowing that many garment workers who were fired from factory work found employment in the service sector, I asked her, "How do you like working here?" I had asked this question in the anticipation that it would lead to a conversation about work in the restaurant business. Instead, the young woman replied, "What is there to like? I have to survive and feed myself and my children." Her refusal to answer my question stopped me in my tracks. An interlocutor's refusal to speak is an essential part of ethnography; it teaches the ethnographer to reexamine her questions and positionality. Not only was I confined in my middle-class subjectivity, but the discursive limits of its discourse also imprisoned me. While I cannot exit out of my subjectivity, I can reposition my queries from different perspectives. Since the research was staggered over several years, I had time to reflect on the material and rethink my questions and approaches.

The first phase of my research focused on trade unions and workers' rights. Later I moved away from that topic, because that is what is mostly written about. As I listened to the women's stories, I realized this was not what was most revealing about their lives. So, I let their stories take me to other sites—to their private lives, to their intimate desires, their toxic relationships with spouses and lovers, their unrealized dreams, their successes, and their adult sons who often abandoned them in their old age. Their lives became a kaleidoscope of betrayals, but I also found "residues of hope." Listening to their life stories, I realized what they were saying was, "I am human. I am like you with feelings and desires. See me in my entirety."

The women I studied were all Muslim. I did not have any Hindu or Chakma (an ethnic minority) women in my study group. A small number of Hindu women primarily from the caste known as Namasudras work in the garment industry, but none showed up in my survey or in the

Figure 1. Labor rights training workshop conducted by the NGO Kormojibi Nari in Mirpur.

interviews I conducted. It is rare to find Chakma women in the RMG industry in Dhaka, although many of them work in Chittagong, the second-largest city in the country, which has a substantial garment sector. I worked in three areas: Mirpur, Savar, and Ashulia. Mirpur is within greater Dhaka, and Savar and Ashulia are in an industrial belt approximately twenty miles from the city. During this time, I met with over one hundred female and male workers—some one-on-one meetings, others in focused group gatherings. I recorded the life histories of multiple workers. I visited workers in their homes, walked with them in markets while they shopped, attended labor rights training sessions, and observed them while they worked inside factories. (The factories I observed were all compliant with safety upgrades that were required after the 2013 Rana Plaza industrial factory collapse.)

In tracking the lives of all these workers, whether young or old, I found that various forms of violence occurred in their quotidian lives. These women continually faced physical violence, financial fraud, and multiple forms of betrayal from factory owners and their male partners.

In order to elucidate how violence manifested in the lives of these women through global flows of industrial work, I interviewed both the women and the men in their lives. I interviewed men who were employed in the garment industry and those who were not. Overall, I found that men from this social class had intense gender-based class envy. They had lost their ability to be traditional breadwinners, and that had made them feel emasculated, since the women now controlled the purse strings. Unable to fulfill their expected roles as providers, the men became bitter toward the women who were now preferred for factory jobs.[11] It is important to recognize that these men too were silently beaten down by an economic system that saw hiring women preferable because it could pay them less and expected them to be more docile.

These pent-up frustrations in men found expression in violence against the women in their lives over whom they exercised social control. The men I met needed support systems to develop nontoxic masculinities, but such training opportunities were not available to them. That is, women and men were both victims of rapid industrialization that appropriated their labor for economic growth. As neoliberal subjects, they were expected to build their lives without external support systems. The women endured these hardships because their gendered roles as caregivers had conditioned them to a life of sacrifice for others. My intention here is not to pathologize these women as victims of domestic violence who should be pitied or to view all poor Bangladeshi men as abusers. My intention is to show how these women's new industrial lives have created a space for the expression of emotions and a human need to respond to those emotions within toxic environments. The emotional lives of these women are important to underscore, because in Bangladesh, female sexuality remains obscured and shrouded in moral panic. I also want to push against the idea held by many middle-class people and researchers that if the garment industry shrinks and workers are let go, then in all probability these women will become sex workers. To think of these working women in such degrading terms because they are poor is disrespectful. Bangladeshi rural women have a strong sense of dignity. All the women I met had a profound sense of morality shaped by customary beliefs and Islamic ideas of proper conduct.

After the Rana Plaza industrial catastrophe in 2013, trade unions, factory owners, global buyers, and the state reached an agreement to reduce the workday to eight hours a day for six days a week from the excessive fourteen to sixteen hours that factory managers forced on the workers to meet overseas orders. The workers in my research area in Mirpur worked nine hours a day with an unpaid hour for lunch (8 a.m. to 6 p.m.) six days a week, with Friday the only day off to do their weekly chores. So, our meetings were held in the evenings in the offices of the labor rights NGO. I met workers in individual interviews that lasted for three hours. When I interviewed women, a female research assistant was with me. When I interviewed men, a male research assistant helped me. I interviewed husbands of garment workers, working mothers with young children with and without day care, and the adult sons of female workers. I also interviewed women and men who worked in the shadowy subcontracting profession of the garment industry as suppliers for factories, and I met a few women who were independent subcontractors. In analyzing the older women's lives, I asked a series of questions: What did these women hope to accomplish from industrial work? What did they eventually achieve at the end of their work lives? Did the women acquire new skills and knowledge that translated into income-generating opportunities when they were forced to enter the informal economy in their old age? What were their social safety nets after they exited work?

At the beginning of my research I conducted a survey with the help of one of my research assistants, Atia, to get some baseline data. The survey covered questions regarding marital status, years worked at factories, the number of children, what these women liked and did not like about their new urban/factory lives, what benefits they saw from factory work, and so forth. Each question listed a set of options that the respondents could tick off. They were not asked open-ended questions. The survey was done in the early phase of my study when I was focusing on women employed in the factory instead of those aged out or on the cusp of being aged out. It was a randomized survey, and Atia conducted it in the industrial belt of Savar. The survey was conducted during workers' lunch breaks and in some cases in their homes after work. Each intake lasted approximately thirty minutes. The only requirement was that the workers surveyed were currently employed at a garment factory.

The survey was one method among several (case studies, individual and group interviews) that I used in my research. The female workers surveyed were as young as fourteen and as old as fifty-two, and the majority were under thirty-five. While we did not intend to include workers below age eighteen, a few underage workers showed up on the survey. Even when workers claimed to be eighteen years of age, which is the official minimum age for factory work, it was often evident from their physical appearance that they were underage workers. These underage workers are coached by their families not to reveal their age to outsiders, because they could lose their factory employment. While the survey gave me some specific data, it also highlighted the difference between what people say and what they do. In weaving together the survey results and the ethnographic observations, I turned to Sherry Ortner's understanding of practice theory, according to which the world is made and unmade through the actions of ordinary people. This, as Ortner notes, opens the path to political possibilities, because the constructed world can also be remade by thinking/acting agents.[12] These garment workers were thinking/acting agents within the unfolding of neoliberal possibilities through globalization and factory work. However, what is less identifiable are the unpredictable paths that these neoliberal subjects may follow.

There is very little research on the life circumstances of these older women after they leave factory work. I found that if they had some savings, the women remained in the city and searched for another factory job. Failing that, many of them became domestic workers or helpers for fruit/vegetable vendors. In the early stages of unemployment they maintained a circular relationship between the city and the village. If they had a place to stay in the village, they moved there but then returned to seek employment in the city. These women had developed a wage-earning identity that enabled them to provide for their upkeep, and they no longer wanted to live on the charity of others. This shift in identity, "I can work and provide for myself," was a new subject formation among most of the women I met. It increased their sense of self-worth. Once all their resources dried up, however, they returned to their village to live out the remainder of their lives. Those without financial resources or familial support networks disappeared into the anonymity of the urban landscape and became untraceable. For the aged-out workers, I initially met with twenty women over the age of forty. I took their case histories following historian Tamara Hareven's life-cycle approach.[13] In her approach to the study of family and life cycles, Hareven noted that since the 1970s the scholarly study of family has moved from a discrete, often static approach to one in which the family is dynamic, interacting "with the worlds of religion, work, educational, correctional and welfare institutions, and with processes such as migration, industrialization, and urbanization."[14]

Two important factors concerning industrial workers warrant elaboration. First, in the Euro-American context that Hareven studied, industrialization made men and women leave the rural economy for the industrial towns where workers created new lives tied to manufacturing. In contrast, Bangladeshi workers maintain circular ties to their rural roots and return to their village multiple times during their life cycles for marriages, births, deaths, and religious holidays. Rather than breaking the rural–urban distinction in Bangladesh, industrialization has integrated these two locations through telecommunications and fast travel facilitated by highways that link the periphery to the metropolitan center. Part of this attachment is due to the strong kinship structure that defines life in Bangladesh, where one's membership in society is determined by family, regional origin, education, and religion.

Second, Hareven showed that European and American female workers left work to raise children and reentered the workforce after their children were older. That is, social production interrupted the work life of female workers and also reduced their income compared to men. In Bangladesh we found that garment workers live in extended families and that a majority of women do not exit the workforce for social reproduction. In the extended family structure, parenting is not the sole responsibility of the birth mother. Grandparents, aunts, uncles, and older siblings all participate in the raising of children. This relationship of reciprocity ties several generations together in the reproduction of the family. While this economy of care has been stretched and weakened by the migration of family members, it is still available to the migrant workers as a viable option. These garment workers' relationship with rural society is renewed through kinship, remittances, telecommunications, and travel between the migrant worker and her family.

The women I met created new families in the city, although they remained deeply tied to their kin group in the village. Children were often raised by grandparents in the village while the women worked in the city. Family life often became fragmented as husbands abandoned their wives, making women into heads of households. The large number of women who, as single heads of households, were working and raising children on their own was remaking family life in a conservative Muslim society and also endowing women with new ideas of self and responsibilities.

To understand attitudinal changes among male children toward women's work, I also interviewed twenty adult sons of garment factory women and five adult sons of stay-at-home mothers. I also met with trade union leaders and labor rights activists, visited several factories, and met with officers of the BGMEA. To protect the identities of all the workers, I have only used their first names and have not identified the factories where they worked. I have kept the names of activists anonymous unless they agreed to their names being used or their names and activities were part of the public record in newspapers and court documents. All interviews were recorded in Bengali, then transcribed into written Bengali by my research assistant, and later translated into English by me. This ethnography then is a thrice-written tale.

In the last year of my research, I focused on the aged-out workers. The twenty workers lived in various slums in and around Dhaka city. All the workers interviewed gave verbal consent to their stories being used. Over the next six months we conducted this research following the case study approach, conducting several follow-up interviews. During the research, four women left the city without leaving any contact information. That left me with sixteen women, and each was contacted for subsequent interviews. In August 2020, during the Covid-19 pandemic, one of my research assistants contacted all sixteen workers for updates on their life circumstances (discussed in chapter 5). Almost all the workers interviewed at that time described their living conditions as "dire."

My procedure in the interview was as follows. I would begin with an open-ended question such as "Tell me about your life." Framed as such, the workers would speak about their private lives over their work lives, because their private life mattered the most to them. They worked to live a better life, that is, work was a means to an end. Then I would probe further: "What were your expectations from working in a factory? Were you able to achieve those goals?" Every time, the workers would answer, "In the village, I could not eat. After working in the factory, I was able to feed my children and myself." When I pushed them to say more about what they hoped for through work, they would eventually open up and say, "A good life." Pushed further to explain what a good life meant, they would talk about the ability to provide a better education for their children so they would not have to end up working in the factory. "Good life" here referred to a moral compass, of being a pious, dutiful daughter and a good mother and wife. In Bangladesh, these are the gender roles that constrain what women can expect from life. As I pushed the boundaries of our conversation, I asked what other things made them happy. Beyond fair wages and better work conditions, food and shelter, and education for their children, what else did they want in life?

As our conversations became more intimate and intense, we went into new and unanticipated territories. I began to see these women through a new lens, not primarily as industrial workers but as full human

Figure 2. Poet and trade union leader Lovely Yesmin with a young worker outside the worker's living quarters.

subjects in which industrial work was just one aspect of their being, and not what they valued the most. In the 1980s and 1990s these rural and illiterate women had very few options. If they did not find work in the factory they would most likely become domestic workers in middle-class homes in Dhaka. By the late 1990s factory work had lost its earlier stigma, and women saw it as more respectable than domestic work. Although factory work was not seen as desirable, these women wanted something better for themselves and their children. Neoliberal ideas of self-improvement and universal primary education had freed their imaginations to entertain alternative ideas of self and opportunities that had been previously lacking for this older generation of workers.

SEEING WORKERS THROUGH POETRY

My goal in this research is to write against the dominant narrative of reducing these women into one-dimensional working machines. Poetry offers a unique medium through which to see these women from humanistic dimensions. I was curious to know if some garment workers wrote poetry and what that poetry would be like. In searching for that, I came across Lovely Yesmin, a former garment worker who is now a trade union leader and poet. She heads the Bangladesh Readymade Garment Workers Federation. She prefers to be called by her first name, Lovely. As a poet, she was an anomaly among garment workers. Her poetry helped to open the door to a new way of seeing these women. Because of their lack of education and the child care they had to provide after the workday ended, very few female garment workers wrote poetry. Almost all of the garment worker–poets I met were men. Lovely had not studied beyond grade 8. She entered factory work at age twelve due to dire family circumstances. Seeing the exploitation of workers in the factory, she joined trade union politics at an early age to fight for their rights. She said, "If we did not fight for our rights, we would be dead." She recently completed a book of poems called *Nari Sramik* (Woman Worker).[15] Her poetry is woven through this book as a commentary from the subaltern space of workers' lives.

Her prose is simple; it is not the high Bengali of the literati, and that is its power. She communicates her emotions directly in a rudimentary form. She does not engage with poetic devices or enhance her language with meter, sound, rhyme, rhythm, or figurative speech. She writes in the language of the workers, and her imagery is visceral. Commenting on her work with garment workers, Lovely said, "I do not want TV, car, a house. I want workers to be respected by the state and society and that we should get our fair wages and rights. That is my dream." In her poem "I Am a Machine Operator," she notes the forgotten worker in Bangladesh. Her poetry speaks to an intensely globalized world where garment workers are bouncing around like pinballs inside a global work machine. With her permission, I have translated several of her poems into English for the book.

> I Am a Machine Operator
>
> Working twelve hours a day
> Often I work overtime
> Sometimes even through the night.
> We are workers in the assembly lines.
> We make shirts, jeans, jackets, sweaters, bras, panties and whatnot!
> What is it that we do not make?
> From a Third World country, we send our clothes to Europe and America
> Our clothes dominate the Asian markets too
> Even the U.S. president wears our clothes.
> Our sweat helped to grow the country.
> But we are "cheap" workers.
> We do not get subsidized food, we do not get living quarters.
> Eight thousand takas
> Do not cover our expenses.
> Education and health care are expensive too.
> But we have not given up.
> Is anyone listening to us?

These older factory women are the "debris" of capital: mined for their labor, then forgotten and assigned to capitalism's dusty closet. Laid off from work due to factory management's attitudes toward older female workers as no longer productive, they are unable to provide much-needed financial resources to their extended families. As such, they are no longer objects of desire in conventional terms or useful in capitalism's utilitarian terms. A worker is an entangled subject existing on multiple social scales and identities. Life is about human dignity and the desire to live life beyond bare existence. My task in this book is to stitch these women's stories together from what they have shared with me. *Castoffs of Capital* is about small acts of freedom, occasional pleasures that make life meaningful, and the choices people make as they navigate the factory and urban landscape under the stranglehold of global capital. These life stories reveal the ways in which global capital, patriarchy, and workers' work and nonwork lives intersect in devastating ways, conjuring and repressing their feelings about the good life.

1

THE DISORDER OF WORK AND LIFE

IN FEMINIST ANTHROPOLOGY and across fields of academic production, there is a singular absence of studies of women who have been aged out of the industrial workforce by factory management. While scholars have studied why older female workers are deemed less productive and hence are pushed out of work by factory management, less attention has been paid to these female workers once they left factory work. The feminist research of the 1980s and 1990s focused on the glaring absence of women's reproductive labor in Marxist literature and analyzed capitalism's peripheral relationship to young female labor as disposable bodies. Feminist scholars have noted the importance of recognizing women's unpaid work in social reproduction and the feminization and racialization of low-skilled manufacturing jobs.[1] In highlighting some of the recent approaches to the study of women and factory work, Dina Siddiqi notes:

> Much of this early scholarship—path breaking for its time—located the new global order literally in the body and labour of the woman worker. . . . The effect was to reduce the woman worker to the emblem rather than the subject of multinational exploitation. Reduced at times to archetypal victim of capital and male domination working in collusion, the woman worker's body was multiply appropriated: for global feminists, she stood for the universal subordination of women; for critics of imperialism and capitalism, she

was the embodiment of exploitation by (western) predatory capital; and for human rights activists, she represented the violations of the dignity of labour that occur in the absence of regulation and accountability.[2]

My study builds on this research and adds a new dimension by focusing on the life cycles and aspirations of older and aged-out women workers. I situate my study selectively and not exhaustively from the vast and growing literature on women and work, focusing on two broad categories of writing on female factory labor—anthropologists and feminists writing on female factory labor globally and on female factory labor in Bangladesh in particular. There are three major strands of work in this field—oppression of workers by capitalism, resistance by workers against capitalism, and identity formations among workers through capitalism.

In the first category, oppression of workers, studies show the exploitation of women for their positional vulnerability and the browning of low-skilled industrial work.[3] These studies indicate how poor women as "nimble fingers" bear the costs of the feminization of industrial work from low wages, stigma, gender disparity in income, and exposure to occupational hazards.[4] Feminists have also addressed the question of women's workplace security under capitalism. Helen Safa noted that in developing countries women's social status must be strengthened to limit harm when mainstreaming them into export-processing factories.[5] Naila Kabeer found that Bangladeshi male factory managers preferred women for their docility, not their nimble fingers. Although men performed at higher levels of productivity, she notes that "one factor that overrode all others in explaining their preference for female labour: men made trouble."[6] Speaking of how capitalists have preferred female workers in colonial India, a process that continues to this day, Samita Sen writes that "capitalists have favored women's labor in three different ways."[7] First, recruiting women kept wages low and so offset the cost of hiring them. Second, women's reproductive functions ensured that the labor force was self-reproducing. Finally, capitalists maintained that women's wages were supplementary to male wages and that therefore these wages could be kept low. While feminist scholars have also challenged the myth of the breadwinner argument by offering empirical evidence to the contrary, less attention has been paid in the Bangladeshi context to income disparity between male and female workers in the garment industry.[8]

Furthermore, scholars have maintained that free-market ideologies and corporate capital have contributed detrimentally to workers' rights, forcing them into dangerous work in the absence of factory oversight and regulations.[9] Other authors have argued that the garment industry created employment for rural women, giving them some autonomy over their lives. Carla Freeman, in her study of pink-collar female workers in Barbados, shows how women started small enterprises from skills acquired from the gig economy.[10] Similarly, Sandya Hewamanne found that Sri Lankan women who exited work after their marriage had acquired skills from factory work that helped them earn money for their affinal families.[11] In my study, I found very few Bangladeshi factory women who had the skills or capital to start entrepreneurial activities once they were laid off from work.

In the second category, resistance to capitalism, scholars have analyzed the forms of opposition adopted by female workers against factory-level oppression. Aihwa Ong challenged the idea of the docile female worker and documented various strategies women use, including spirit possession, to contest factory-based patriarchy in Malaysia.[12] Writing on the labor politics of postmodernity, Ong has noted that "workers' struggles are often not based upon class interest or class solidarity, but comprise individual and covert acts against various forms of control."[13] Diane Wolf studied how female factory workers used household dynamics to resist factory discipline in rural Javanese society.[14]

The third category is identity formation of workers through capitalism. Johanna Lessinger, in her study of garment factory workers in Madras, India, found that "women are making certain decisions which put individual needs above household needs and stress their independence of their elders."[15] Hewamanne analyzed how Sri Lankan garment workers in the Free Trade Zones cultivated "an overarching identity for themselves as a gendered group of migrant workers who are different from other women and from male industrial workers."[16] Caitrin Lynch's study of the garment industry in Sri Lanka shows how female workers carefully crafted identities as good and obedient girls to avoid the moral panic around factory women that was overtaking rural society.[17] Kabeer has raised the interplay of cultural factors such as class, gender, and ethnicity in shaping garment workers' lives and identities.[18] All these studies indicate workers not as victims of globalization but, as Priti Ramamurthy argues, "active participants in the processes of imagination," thereby recognizing workers' agency.[19]

Studies on the Bangladesh garment industry have followed the roadmap established by this scholarly tradition by focusing on these women's identities primarily as workers. The literature on the Bangladeshi garment industry is extensive and focuses largely on socioeconomic studies of trade unions, social compliance in factories, workers' wage struggles, and their health issues.[20] Four important books on the garment industry in Bangladesh are Kabeer's *The Power to Choose: Bangladesh Garment Workers in London and Dhaka* (2002); Sanchita Banerjee Saxena's *Made in Bangladesh, Cambodia, and Sri Lanka: The Labor behind the Global Garments and Textile Industries* (2014); Saxena's edited volume *Labor, Global Supply Chains, and the Garment Industry in South Asia: Bangladesh after Rana Plaza* (2019); and Shahidur Rahman's *Broken Promises of Globalization: The Case of the Bangladesh Garment Industry* (2013). Kabeer has written extensively on the socioeconomic status of female garment workers.[21] Nazli Kibria has shown that Bangladeshi garment workers form a diverse group of rural migrants, thereby complicating the causal connection between women's new roles and social change. Instead, she draws attention to the macroeconomic changes that are reshaping the patriarchal family.[22] Saxena has done a comparative study of the working conditions of workers in Bangladesh, Cambodia, and Sri Lanka and has empirically argued that workers' changing relationship with factory management through domestic coalitions has led to improvements in the industry.[23] Siddiqi has written comprehensively on the labor struggles in the industry and on the complexities informing the garment worker as a subject of transnational human rights discourses.[24] In a recent article she offered a historical perspective by situating garment workers' politics in the *longue durée* of workers' struggles in former East Pakistan (now Bangladesh) since 1947.[25]

The most comprehensive study of the Bangladesh garment industry is the edited volume *Labor, Global Supply Chains, and the Garment Industry in South Asia: Bangladesh after Rana Plaza*. Organized into five parts, the volume's thirteen chapters look at the factors leading to the 2013 Rana Plaza industrial catastrophe, its aftermath, rethinking labor solutions from Bangladeshi and international perspectives, and ideas for a way forward for the industry. Saxena notes in her introduction that the volume is an interdisciplinary study addressing "the crisis of labor rights from the perspective of workers, brands, international protections, community organizations, and governments."[26] To solve the problems of low wages and worker oppression, she argues for a multistakeholder and multipronged approach.[27] Shelley Feldman and Jakir Hossain argue for stronger government participation in regulating the garment industry, without which the small improvements made in compliance to the industry post-2013 would soon wither away.[28] In the same volume, Chaumtoli Huq writes that the Accord on Building Safety (2013), designed to upgrade factories to international factory standards, was a corporate model that failed to deliver workers' progressive demands.[29] Siddiqi explores the dangers faced by autonomous and left-identified labor rights organizations in increasing workers' rights against a state that is complicit with global capital and local industrialists. These labor organizations are hamstrung by the political environment within which they operate.[30] Kabeer identifies the global buyers and their lust for extreme profits as the key reason for keeping workers continuously at risk.[31] Saxena and Dorothee Baumann-Pauly explore in their article the hidden role of the subcontracting garment industry and the urgency for regulation and transparency in this industry that continues to operate under risky work conditions, worker exploitation, and the use of child labor.[32]

The research that comes closest to my study of aged-out workers is the 2019 study on the afterlife of garment workers in Bangalore, India, by Alessandra Mezzadri and Sanjita Majumdar. Their work focuses on the economic aspects of afterlife such as heavy debt burdens, whereas mine examines the relationship between work, age, and the aspirational and erotic lives of older women workers. While there are significant similarities, our work also diverges in some critical areas. Mezzadri and Majumdar found that workers exited between thirty and thirty-five years of age, a pattern similar to my study. "Our findings also suggest that the processes whereby women accumulate debt and face an early exit from garment factories are linked to the needs and demands of social reproduction. In fact, reproductive needs are a central consideration for the women as they assess the trade-offs between factory and other forms of (informal) work."[33] However, I found very few women who had withdrawn from factory work for social reproduction. Most women relegated social reproduction, the raising of small children, to family members while they continued to work. It could be that the Bangladeshi women had stronger familial ties in the rural economy because Muslim families have a greater tendency to maintain cohesive bonds.

All these studies, while extremely influential in shaping our views of feminist labor studies, focus on the female worker as industrial labor. Once she ceases to be labor, she is no longer a subject of scholarly inquiry. This is where my study makes a critical intervention. In contrast to these studies, my book decenters the woman as a worker, opening new ways to reconceptualize older women's agency as age diminishes their social value. *Castoffs of Capital* opens new modes of inquiry into the lives of this female-headed workforce operating under neoliberal ideas of individual work ethic, global aspirations around class mobility, and the intimate sphere of erotic love.

PRECARIAT LABOR

Since the 2008 Great Recession, the term *precariat* has been widely used in scholarly writings. The term comes out of the neoliberal economic movement of the 1970s engineered by a handful of influential economists at the University of Chicago. Neoliberalism promoted ideas around free markets, deregulation, and labor flexibility for economic growth and development. At the core of neoliberalism is the idea that "labor was to be freed from regulatory and institutional restraints," thereby allowing corporations to move around the world in search of cheap labor.[34] This labor flexibility led "to the creation of a global precariat, consisting of many millions around the world without an anchor of stability" and the transferring of risks and insecurities from corporations to workers and their families.[35]

The factory women in Bangladesh are part of a global precariat workforce; they often work without hiring documents, no job security, coerced overtime, wages routinely withheld, and numerous other workplace irregularities. These are lives trapped inside the global supply chain of commodity production, and their rights are violated in every step of the work routine. But they are not unfree labor similar to modern-day slavery, migrant workers, and domestic workers.[36] Unfree labor is forced labor against one's will; it refers to the employer's arbitrary domination over the worker. A migrant domestic worker can be deemed unfree labor because of the total control that the recruiting family exercises over her life, from taking away her passport to physically restricting her indoors. The work routines of garment workers exhibit complexity, because they cover a range of restricted forms of freedom and do not fit neatly into this paradigm. The relationship between the conditions of work and one's ability to have a fulfilling life are intertwined. In factories, wages are often paid late, and wages are regularly reduced based on management's discretionary power over what counts as low productivity, work interruptions, late arrival at work, "too many" toilet breaks, talking on the job, and so forth. But as industrial wage labor, these women live outside factories that give them limited autonomy over their nonwork lives. Thus, garment workers, while unfree to some degree, are better defined as precariat labor informed by unstable global labor conditions where "income insecurity is uncertainty" as factories close down, and owners relocate factories to Mauritius, Jordan, and Ethiopia.[37]

In analyzing the women workers' lives, I am indebted to Guy Standing's theorization on precariat labor. Standing writes about the seven forms of labor security offered to workers under industrial citizenship that the precariat labor force lacks:

> *Labour market security*—Adequate income earning opportunities . . .
> *Employment security*—Protections against arbitrary dismissals . . .
> *Job security*—Ability and opportunity to retain a niche in employment . . .
> *Work security*—Protection against accidents and illness at work . . .
> *Skill reproduction security*—Opportunity to gain skills . . .
> *Income security*—Assurance of an adequate stable income . . .
> *Representation security*—Possessing a collective voice in the labour market.[38]

The Bangladeshi garment factory workers operate in an environment where all seven of these work-related industrial citizenship securities are violated. Writing about precarious lives in a different vein, Judith Butler notes that precarious lives are not individual lives. It is the failure of institutions, the state, and the church to protect specific populations from injury and harm that creates these dystopic lives. To Butler, precarity is a "politically induced condition in which certain populations suffer from failing social and economic networks of support more than others and become differentially exposed to injury, violence, and death."[39] Taking Standing's and Butler's viewpoints, I argue that capitalists and the Bangladeshi state colluded to create a socioeconomic environment where millions of young rural women were mobilized into a precariat workforce to serve the interest of capitalism. As industrial workers, they make one of the lowest industrial wages in the world. They have no employment security; they have few protections against workplace injuries. Their representation by trade unions was restricted through harsh tactics of factory owners until the Rana Plaza industrial catastrophe in 2013 led to the implementation of minor labor safeguards in the industry. As assembly line workers, their ability to learn new skills to reenter the economy is nil. Similarly, the Bangladeshi state failed to invest in their welfare and has ignored ongoing workers' deaths from fires in substandard factories.

THEORETICAL FRAMEWORK: WORK AND LOVE

These garment factory women worked for more than eight hours a day, often seven days a week. The women were mentally stressed, their bodies depleted, their lives made precarious. Yet within that precarity, they cultivated a life force that animated them for instantaneous pleasures, small acts of freedom, and excitement. Their lives existed on a spectrum between the desire for something and the emptiness of that desire: from Lauren Berlant's notion of cruel optimism, our deep attachment to objects that injure and harm us although we believe that they will liberate us from present conditions, to Freeman's notion of affects among pink-collar workers in Barbados who sought middle-class status by starting small businesses from skills they had acquired from the gig economy, to Arjun Appadurai's modern subjects of globalization, and finally to Nurul Momen Bhuiyan's perception of how hope existed as traces in their lives, giving them the mental strength to move on.[40] These authors have helped me to think through the aspirations around work and love in the lives of these garment workers.

For all the garment workers I met, whether young or old, the affective life—care, love, affection—was a vital structuration and an aspect of their lives that was often invisible in academic research. What was the meaning of love to these women? Within capitalist oppression and exploitation, love was one emotion that gave meaning to their lives. It was an emotion that intimately belonged to them and could not be taken away by capitalist forces. The majority of research done on industrial work fails to capture the amorous desires of older factory women and their quest for the embrace, an embrace denied to them by global capital that exploited them as working machines, by the men in their lives who used their bodies for sexual pleasure, by the state that saw them as a revenue source, by a society that viewed them as "fallen" women, and by the NGOs and activists who wanted to ensure their security through legal means. In all these domains, these women's desire to be held and be loved was absent.

Love here in the broadest sense meant recognition from the state as its citizens; love from their families as a valued and recognized family member; respect from their employers as workers; and finally, affection and care from their husbands/lovers. The staggering betrayals in their lives were not only about being defrauded of wages and bonuses (an ongoing issue in this sector) but also about the impossibility of being fully human. In their life histories, loss of their attachments was always imminent, yet they strove to make meaningful lives. One such cruel attachment was from the nuclearization of family life in the city. These women, abandoned by their spouses, often raised their children as single mothers. The women invested in their children, particularly their sons, in the hope that they would be taken care of in their old age. However, as the sons grew up, many created nuclear families with women they met in the city and moved away, often leaving their elderly mothers to fend for themselves. Thus, at every step of their lives, the women encountered attachments that were betrayals.

Given the social and economic precarity of their lives, it is extremely difficult for these factory women to be prudent subjects who can calculate emotional and social risks. Unlike the Bangladeshi middle-class woman who decides on her mate based on a set of calculations—is he educated, will he offer me a comfortable life, does he have social status, and so on—these factory women live in a zone of instantaneity. Their new work life does not allow for emotional durability. Their happiness, their love, their embraces do not stick to their lives, but they leave traces that injure them in a way that is on a scale different from work-related injuries or physical abuse. They are stuck within the oppressive structures of industrial work where factory owners, the state, global retailers, their husbands, and families all make demands of their labor, their income, and their bodies. But the deeper scars are the invisible, emotional scars that they carry with them every day. As one woman said to me, "My broken arm may mend one day, but no one sees my broken heart."

In thinking about these women's attachments, I turned to Berlant's notion of cruel optimism. According to Berlant, one becomes attached to "a problematic object in advance of its loss." "All cruel attachments are optimistic," but she also notes that the subjects may not always "feel optimistic." Berlant defines "the object of desire" as a "cluster of promises" that brings us close to an encounter with its "promises." The object of desire overwhelms, enchants, and momentarily makes one forget its potential injury and its lack of durability. For the garment workers, the notion of cruel optimism manifested in the attachments they form to the (imagined) good life—a brick house with the accoutrements of modern life, their children educated into middle-class status, and a caring and loving husband who holds them in a tight embrace at night. These were their "objects of desire." These attachments are fragile and impossible in the lives of the women I encountered, and they leave lethal scars on their bodies and psyches. Yet they continued to strive for them "in the operation of optimism as an affective form."[41]

One is "optimistic" because the future can replicate the imagined past. For example, in the imagination of mainstream white Americans, the 1950s was a time of economic prosperity when postwar reconstruction had created well-paying manufacturing jobs and the GI Bill had allowed many Americans to get a college degree and move into the middle class. The reality of 1950s, however, was that it was a time of racial segregation with Blacks and whites having unequal opportunities. Berlant's notion of cruel optimism is also an idea constructed on an imagined past of the good life that its adherents believe to be true and think is attainable in the future:

"Cruel optimism" names a relation of attachment to compromised conditions of possibility whose realization is discovered either to be impossible, sheer fantasy or too possible, and toxic. What is cruel about these attachments, and not merely inconvenient or tragic, is that the subjects who have x in their lives might not well endure the loss of their object or scene of desire, even though its presence threatens their well-being; because whatever the content of their attachment is, the continuity of the form of it provides something of the continuity of the subject's sense of what it means to keep on living and to look forward to being in the world.[42]

In contrast to Berlant's construction of a false optimism in the U.S. context, for the Bangladeshi garment worker there is no imagined happy past. These women construct their possibilities in the present in terms of a durable marriage, a husband who will love them, and children who will care for them in their old age. Marriage, husbands/lovers, and children—these are their primary "cruel attachments" that break their emotional lives multiple times. Their marriages, even when they are romantic alliances, do not stick. Their children as adults often do not fulfill their expectations of elder care. These women have spent their lives caring for others, but at the end of their lives there is no one to care for them.

There is a secondary cruel attachment to an imagined good life that the women display. They want to return to their "idyllic" village at the end of their work lives. Yet these women remember growing up in the village as a time when "we could not get enough to eat." They recall village life as a tsunami of annual floods, food scarcity, and increased economic deprivation due to a lack of government investment in the rural economy. So, where did these ideas of a good rural life awaiting them in old age come from? The answer lies in what these women saw in their childhood—the prosperous farmers, schoolteachers, and small rural businessmen who enjoyed material comforts and whose lives showed possibilities within the rural landscape. If they could earn more, they too could graduate to that life, or their children could. As industrial wage labor, they now believe that a brick house is a possibility, although it will not materialize for most of them. In that respect, they are forward-looking in terms of Freeman's "aspirations," and they approximate Appadurai's modern subjects where globalization shapes imagination.[43] Appadurai notes that "ordinary people have begun to deploy their imaginations in the practice of their everyday lives. This fact is exemplified in the mutual contextualizing of motion and mediation. More people than ever before seem to imagine routinely the possibility that they or their children will live and work in places other than where they were born; this is the wellspring of the increased rates of migration at every level of social, national, and global life."[44] These forward-looking aspirations place these women temporally within the instantaneous. Their rewards, when they occur, are immediate—getting wages and a good meal, sending their children to school (only later to put them to factory work due to a lack of funds), the joy of being held and loved if only for a day. These are instantaneous and circumstantial optimisms that are sadistically present in their lives. This optimism breaks down numerous times, as their stories reveal in this book.

In writing about women in Barbados seeking middle-class respectability in *Entrepreneurial Selves,* Freeman notes that

> while the explicit lexicon of love that I was looking for was absent, the strong desire for a newly imagined intimacy, self-understanding, and new ways of feeling and expressing emotion figured throughout the entrepreneurs' testimonies. I found an ever-increasing swirl of affects, whose display and exchange was demanded most visibly in the mushrooming service sector, but that resonated across all spheres of life. . . . It is in the combined longings and labors such affects entails, and the cultural specificities of these desires, feelings, and practices, that I see some of the most powerful and dramatic implications of neoliberalism today.[45]

Freeman's study of aspirations about an emergent class of Barbadians seeking respectability through middle-classness resonated with these garment workers, particularly with the younger generation of women who had higher levels of education and wages compared to the older women. The older workers saw themselves as a bridge to the middle class for their children ("They will not work in the factory; they will have office jobs"). The younger workers, whether they were children of older garment workers or new entrants into factory work, considered themselves middle-class people who had moved out of the economic deprivations of their rural life. The term *middle class* is difficult to define, because it signifies different meanings to different categories of people. In rural Bangladesh it has a specific meaning: "These families may live in pukka (brick) houses and have land, but they are cash poor. Not necessarily sharecroppers but the managers of sharecroppers, they are only too conscious of the narrow boundary that separates them from the rural underclass. While they can never become aristocrats, the rural middle class feels that, at all costs, the social distance from the poorest peasants must be maintained."[46] The factory women, whose families were landless farmers, call themselves "middle class" because they have graduated from their former socioeconomic status in rural society through factory work. The term *middle class* allowed them to differentiate themselves from those who were "lower than them on the social scale, whom they would designate as lower class," and to finally breach the margin between them and the rural middle class.[47]

Berlant defined cruel optimism as "an object of desire" that is "a cluster of promises that we want someone or something to make to us

Figure 3. A mother and her teenaged daughter are both garment workers. The daughter had a well-developed sensibility of her new middle-class status, whereas the mother considered herself lower economic class.

and make possible for us." As she notes, "Cruel optimism . . . is an incitement to inhabit and to track the affective attachment to what we call 'the good life,' which is for so many a bad life that wears out the subjects who nonetheless, and at the same time, find their conditions of possibility within it."[48] That is, the world of imagined happiness is through the gates of hell, and yet one is drawn toward this object that seduces and then betrays and chars one's hopes. How do we understand the aspirational/affective field of a (brutalized) subject who closely guards her feelings of intimacy that this new world has opened to her? In response to cruel optimism enfolded in neoliberalism, Freeman poses a provocative question: "Shouldn't a feminist theory of affect be capable of imagining possibilities that are not reductive to false consciousness and a seemingly closed system of neoliberal cruelty?"[49] The women I met did not suffer from false consciousness, nor were they imprisoned in "neoliberal cruelty," although there were traces of both in their lives. They knew the limits of the good life they sought, yet they strove to find "their conditions of possibility within it." Juxtaposing Freeman's provocation with Berlant's notion of cruel optimism opened a way for me to analyze these women's subjectivities in formation.

In an interview, anthropologist Bhuiyan pointed out that "while their lives were battered by precarity, factory labor had created new forms of support networks; these were not the hyper-alienated lives of Western, industrialized societies. These women received monetary and mental support from their kin in times of distress. When a woman could not raise her child in the city, she left her child with her family members who fulfilled their kin obligations. When a woman lost her job, she found accommodation with an adult child or a sibling. Their lives contain these residues of hope." He indicated that these social obligations were built on kinship relations of reciprocity that exist as a patchwork of support for these women. Returning to the village for the Muslim high holidays, births, weddings, and deaths of family members remain a vital belonging in these women's lives. These working women's lives existed in the interstices between cruel optimism and fulsome aspirations, where hope as residue ran through their veins. With Bhuiyan's permission, I have developed his idea of a "residue of hope" into a working concept to think through these women's life stories.[50]

FIVE SUBJECT FORMATIONS

Sherry Ortner has defined subjectivity as "the ensemble of the modes of perception, affect, thought, desire, and fear that animates acting subjects."[51] She also examines "the cultural and social formations that shape, organize, and provoke those modes of affect, thoughts, and so on." I have followed Ortner's definition of the human subject as an acting/thinking/reflexive and creative actor. Actors are also partially knowing subjects. "They have some degree of reflexivity about themselves and their desires," and they have some insight "into the ways in which they are formed by their circumstances."[52] Subjectivity gets formed at the intersection of external and internal processes. Subjectivity is not static; it is on a spectrum of movement that is constantly being made, unmade, and remade. Ortner mediates between two scales of subject formations: "in the more psychological sense, in terms of the inner feelings, desires, anxieties, and intentions of individuals," and at the "large-scale cultural formations."[53] The women in this ethnographic study have encountered a new world of sights, sounds, pleasures, people, lifestyles, and behaviors that widened their existential realities, but they are also aware of the limits of their social possibilities.

From my research, I identified three categories that shaped these women's lives and sentiments: (1) emergent middle-class sentiments among female factory workers; (2) new family dynamics as wage earners and increased gender-based violence between spouses; and (3) aspirational subjects who are on a spectrum from rural to global movements. All these transformations are culturally specific. These dynamics are expressed through five subjectivities that are in formation—economic, moral, aspirational, political, and legal—that exist discursively in the lives of these women. Sometimes they are pronounced; at other times they are more obscure. The women demonstrate the making of these subjectivities through their speech, beliefs, behaviors, choices, attire, habits, and nonverbal communication. The subjectivities are formed through the disciplinary mechanisms that the women are subjected to—family life, factory discipline, rural–urban dynamics, workers' protests, police brutality, courts, labor workshops, and trade union activism.

The economic subjectivity is the most developed in these rural migrants as wage-earning industrial workers. Prior to the expansion of the garment industry, poor women primarily worked in the informal sector in low-paying and non-unionized jobs. With the advent of the garment industry, millions of women now work in this sector, and an estimated twenty million (their family members) are beneficiaries of their wage labor. The economic subjectivity has introduced notions of autonomy and self-worth among the women, and along with it, ideas of class mobility. At the end of each month, the women receive their wages. They described their feelings in the following words: "The happiest day of my life is when I receive my wages," or "The feel of the takas [unit of currency] in my hand makes me feel proud." Similarly, the idea of value has entered their discourse; their labor is valuable, and that makes them valuable as capable human beings. They make products that are prized by their factory managers and society. Families now value daughters who have high income potential as garment workers. Workers make comments like "I am respected as a worker," "I can now help my parents and siblings," "I can educate my children," "I do not have to ask my husband for money," "I will not take domestic abuse; I can earn a living," and so on. These are profound changes in the lives of these women, whose earning potential was close to zero when they lived in the villages. This economic subjectivity runs through the discourses of the older and younger women, indicating that they have found a new identity that has earned them respect that they previously lacked.

In *The Moral Economy of the Peasant,* James Scott writes that "the problem of exploitation and rebellion is not just a problem of caloric intake and income but is a question of peasant conceptions of social justice, of rights and obligations, of reciprocity."[54] His comment surfaces in the ideas around justice and obligation that form a vital core in these women's moral lives. The women I met with were all Muslim, and hence I refer to their moral subjectivity within an Islamic moral compass. For these women, who migrated at a young age to work in the city, migration added layers of stress to their moral subjectivity. In villages, children are raised within the moral code of rural society, which is shaped by religion and customary beliefs. These beliefs and attitudes weaken when women are thrust against the vicissitudes of urban and factory life, and they are reflected as anxieties among men as women leave home for the city. As Sarah White notes, "Bangladesh is experiencing considerable challenge by gender and generation, in both material arrangements and social norms of authority, respect, deference, or proper behavior between older and younger, men and women."[55]

In the new environment of factory work and urban living, rural notions of justice and comportment were destabilized, and factory women were often taunted as "shameless" women for working outside the home with non-kin men. The women fought the assault of these indignities by conceptualizing themselves as "pious Muslims" who followed Allah's guidance. Their reputation as faithful Muslim women was of paramount importance, and their piety was expressed in a range of sentiments within an Islamic moral order. In the city of ill-repute, they were forced to work outside the home, but they were honest ("We do not steal or beg"); they sent their children to Islamic religious schools so they would become good Muslims ("We are pious Muslim women"); and they cared for their elderly parents as dutiful daughters. Outwardly, many of them adopted the Islamic attire of head-to-toe covering (burqa) as a symbol of their morality.[56] While it is true that many women pursued their amorous desires in the city, they still adhered to their morality by marrying the man, even if it was a sham marriage. White, in her study of rural Bangladesh, found that "conformity with the moral order extends even to the level of emotions. . . . The love of a husband for a woman is unique, as is women's love for their husbands. All women feel tenderness for their husbands. This has come from God, and it cannot be questioned."[57] The women's moral integrity was an identity that neither the factory nor society could take away. Allah heard and saw their pain; Allah saw them as ethical beings who remained true to their faith despite their situational vulnerabilities. When all else failed, Allah was their final protector.

The aspirational subject is desirous of a good life made up of higher wages, freedom of association, commodities, improved housing and food, quality education for children, and the opportunity of romantic love and hypergamous marriages. Going from "I could not eat in the village" to "Now I can eat and provide for my children and move around town" made the women feel that they had entered zones of increased mobility and possibilities. This aspirational subject believes that a better life is possible for her children, and that is why she endures factory work. The aspirational subject is also an affective subject; she seeks love and affection in her private life, as these women's life stories reveal. The affective subjectivity is caught between a woman's exhilaration over the possibilities unleashed by capitalism and the profound sadness when those possibilities are brutally thwarted.

Hewamanne, in her study of Sinhalese Buddhist women in the Free Trade Zone (FTZ) garment factories in Sri Lanka, notes, "The process of FTZ women workers becoming desiring subjects who are able to more openly express desires is intimately connected to the process of constructing new senses of self and building an identity as a gendered group of migrant industrial workers."[58] Similarly, garment factory women in Bangladesh now cultivated new selves, explored forbidden love, and enjoyed intimacy by living on their own in the city, but the outcomes of these trysts were unpredictable and often injurious. Unlike the "moral panic" that has accompanied the freeing of women's sexual desires among garment workers in Sri Lanka, in Bangladesh, factory women no longer generate similar moral panic among the professional middle class who view them as development actors who are helping to grow the economy.[59]

Attaining a higher socioeconomic status was a powerful goal among these women. As industrial wage labor, they went from having no income to taka 8,000 ($90) per month at the time of my research in 2018. Appadurai's and Freeman's ideas of globalization were evident in the consumption patterns of the younger generation of workers. These young women wore lipstick, went to beauty parlors, bought new clothes, had smartphones, and went on outings with their boyfriends—activities that the older generation of women did not have access to because they had entered the job market when wages were much lower. Although industrial wages minimally covered their living expenses in the city, new ideas and commodities were entering their world, creating in their wake a "swirl of affects," a feeling that a new world of possibilities had arrived at their doorstep.[60] Suddenly, what was not previously possible was becoming somewhat possible, and this had a definite impact on these women's emotional lives. I found that the younger workers more vividly displayed Freeman's affects, and their encounter with globalization had unleashed an exhilarating joyousness. The older women were weighed down by cruel optimism, yet they also possessed Bhuiyan's "residue of hope" that helped them navigate this terrain of injury and loss.

As women employed as industrial workers, they demonstrated a latent political subjectivity that revealed itself in workplace injustices, such as work interruptions over the nonpayment of wages and holiday bonuses. This subjectivity expressed itself in spurts of bottled-up anger when workplace injustices crossed the threshold of tolerance and workers came out to the streets to demonstrate. To address their grievances, workers have demonstrated through a range of tactics, from strikes to lockouts to blockades and factory-level work disruptions. In the absence of a formalized labor movement, these disruptions have remained episodic and have not translated into a broader workers' movement. Beyond fighting wage injustices, the workers were not inclined to struggle for prolonged periods due to a lack of financial resources (they lived from paycheck to paycheck), along with the absence of a viable trade union movement in Bangladesh that could have facilitated a broader workers' movement. In my analysis, the aspirational subjectivity overlaid the political subjectivity. These workers formed a precariat class, but they did not form what Standing has termed "a dangerous class," whose politics are unstable and can potentially undermine the social order. My ethnographic observations about the garment workers suggest that their desire for middle-class status has impeded their transition to radical political activism, a point I discuss in the conclusion.[61]

This latent political subjectivity was overwritten by a legal subjectivity—the citizen–worker, a subject who is produced by legal discourses, "who is armed with the knowledge of laws and rights" and can redress her grievances through the juridical process.[62] This citizen–worker is a result of global human rights discourses that have entered political life through various treaties and conventions since the 1980s.[63] Increasingly, international NGOs (Solidarity International, for example) and local NGOs train workers about their rights. They also identify leaders from the workers and train them on how to negotiate with management over workplace issues. These pedagogical workshops also depoliticize workers by inducting them into a managerial subjectivity that can operate successfully in boardroom settings. But this success comes at a cost. The workers gradually move away from their public stance through strikes about workplace injuries to moderated boardroom negotiations as disciplined subjects.

The legal subjectivity also emerged from workers' introduction to family courts through NGOs. I found that hardships caused by multiple abandonments and divorces had already introduced many women workers to the family courts. Through legal aid offered by NGOs and trade unions, workers presented their cases to judges in family courts. Through this process, the rights-seeking subject transitions from a political subjectivity to the arena of laws and courts. Thus, we see that the aspirations of the workers intersect "with the culture of legality" where the discourse has shifted with a neoliberal twist from the Comaroffs' observation of the political movement from "class struggle to class action."[64] Instead, here we see individual actions where a lone worker pleads to the judge to adjudicate her case either for unpaid wages from factory management or alimony from her husband who has abandoned her. What one begins to witness then is a complex structure of transformations occurring through migration and industrial work that disrupts and displaces bedrock attitudes around women's roles, marriage, family, and social relations.

Ultimately, what came through in these women's stories was the lack of intimacy and love in their private lives and the sexual violence that marked their everyday existence, yet they longed for intimacy as a tango dancer who longs to drown her sorrows in the arms of an unknown dancer. In *Paper Tangos*, Julie Taylor writes about the violence coded in the tango and notes that "this embrace can be danced to enact and exaggerate not inclusion but exclusion, objectification not intimacy, difference not sameness."[65] Similarly, capitalism excluded the women from its profits, objectified them as workers, and separated them from the factory owners and global apparel buyers. For the women, the intimate world of touch and feelings, arousals and excitement was also lost in a labyrinth of emptiness. Private thoughts and feelings, one's desire for love, an embrace, a husband who loved them—these were profoundly complex and discursively hidden in these women's discourses. It is not that they did not desire the intimacy of touch, feelings, sexual arousals. They did, and they deeply missed them. Time and again, they tried to rewrite life, as Lovely Yesmin wrote in the poem "Krishno, the Lover" (discussed in chapter 4), "Against the empty pages of the past / Let life begin afresh," and repeatedly, they failed. Shorn from the life of the village and thrust into the hustle and bustle of the city of crime, corruption, and indifference, where trickery and treachery ruled the day from the home to the factory floor to the world outside, their lives felt like a void in modernity.

A SMALL QUESTION OF MODERNITY

This female-headed workforce is not only helping to grow the Bangladesh economy; it is also propelling women into a sphere of modernity with new ideas, aspirations, social identities, and lifestyles. So, what is this modernity unfolding in Bangladesh?

A little over two hundred years ago, fueled by the rise of scientific and technological knowledge coupled with wealth earned through colonialism, Western nations began to industrialize their economies. This unleashed a range of changes in societies, from the economic and technological to the social, political, and cultural. Alongside the project of industrial modernization came the idea of a modern subject, a subject rooted in the European history of Renaissance and Reformation. In theory, this abstract subject denoted modernity and transcended parochialism and religious dogma by embracing science, reason, and Enlightenment ideas of democracy, freedom, rule of law, due process, and rights of the citizen. These are all aspects of the Western project of becoming modern.

Recent cultural theorizations have questioned the unitariness of the modern subject and ideology, pointing to multiple modernities that are operating within the same temporality.[66] Dilip Gaonkar writes of modernities as "bearing colonial inscriptions" in the *longue durée,* and notes that although modernities have proliferated worldwide, the "West remains the clearinghouse of global modernity."[67] If there is not one modernity but multiple modernities, then its subjects are also multiple and unevenly positioned on the spectrum of modernity leading to diverse outcomes. Unequal access to education and opportunities, whether in the rural West or in the Global South, have also shaped how subjects dwelling in uneven modernities think of possible futures, of who they are, and who they can be. What we are witnessing, then, is a rapid expansion of the horizon of expectations that far exceeds the horizon of possibilities ushered in by modernization.

Partha Chatterjee, in his essay "Our Modernity," grapples with the question of colonial modernity in undivided Bengal under British rule. Chatterjee writes that "the forms of modernity will have to vary between different countries depending upon specific circumstances and social practices."[68] Tani Barlow widens the scope of differential modernities by positing the following: "'Colonial modernity' can be grasped as the speculative frame for investigating the infinitely pervasive discursive powers that increasingly connect at the keys points to the globalizing impulses of capitalism."[69] She goes on to add that "colonial modernity can also suggest that historical context is not a matter of positively defined, elemental or discrete units—nation states, stages of developmental, or civilizations for instance, but rather a complex field of relationships and threads of material that connect, multiply in space time, and can be surveyed from specific sites."[70] Heeding Barlow's and Chatterjee's calls to specificity, we can turn the attention to analyzing the unfolding of modernity in Bangladesh.

In Bangladesh, the English words *development* (*unnayan*) and *progress* (*progoti*) have displaced the term *modern* (*adhunik*). Ask any Bangladeshi, "What is your modernity?," and they will respond, "Women's empowerment," followed by development indicators such as GDP growth, higher literacy rates, lower birth and mortality rates, and higher per capita income. This can be termed GDP (Gross Domestic Product) modernity and refers to assessing the well-being of a population by looking at indicators such as the rise in per capita income instead of the distribution of wealth in the country.[71] This new lingua franca—that modernity equals growth, freedom, and empowerment—is nestled in Western notions of development and progress. The notion of women's empowerment is told through development scripts highlighting courageous Muslim women who have come out of their homes as market subjects. Nationalists take the Bangladeshi woman as the hallmark of modernity for a Muslim-majority country. They point out that rural Bangladeshi women can now run for public office and vote in national elections, activities they could not engage in under Pakistani rule (1947–71). For middle-class Bangladeshis, then, the idea is to become like the West in terms of free speech, free assembly, the right to vote, free and fair elections, rule of law, due process, and the rights of the citizen.

If women's social and economic empowerment is one mark of modernity, then one has to address the contributions of the foremost Bangladeshi feminist author and educationist, Begum Rokeya Sakhawat Hossain (1880–1932). Begum Rokeya advocated education for Muslim women in colonial Bengal, opening the first school for girls in her village of Bhagalpur (1909) with only five girls. In 1916 she established Anjuman-e-Khawatin-e Islam, a society for Muslim women's welfare that taught women about their political and legal rights.[72] In Begum Rokeya's time, the issues facing women were child marriage, lack of education, and limited employment opportunities. Under the project of modernization in Bangladesh in the 1970s through the early 2000s, some of those issues have been partially met. Birth and mortality rates have fallen, and primary and secondary education has become universal, although poverty prevents many children from getting an education. At the same time, new domains of struggle have emerged with globalization and increased poverty, and as women become industrial wage earners, men now demand money and commodities from their working wives. This has resulted in increased domestic violence, demand for excessive dowries, and high rates of marital insecurity for factory women. Simultaneously, sexual exploitation at work has increased as more women have come out to work. While it is true Bangladeshi women have come a long way from their mothers and grandmothers, it is equally true that their emancipation remains a distant reality from the rhetoric of Western-inspired development that is full of promises of freedom.

Bangladesh remains primarily an agrarian society, with more than 70 percent of the population residing in rural areas. These questions of modernity have to take into account this vast swath of society. The women working in the garment industry come from this demographic group. However, neither the Western donors nor the Bangladeshi elite evaluate modernity by taking into account the perspectives of the ordinary Bangladeshi as a sharecropper, rickshaw puller, or garment worker. In a critical assessment of the Bangladeshi elite identity that is nestled within Western notions of progress, Ahmed Sofa's 1992 essay "On the Issue of Bangladesh's Upper Class and a Social Revolution" is instructive. According to Sofa, a small segment of society represents the majority through a myopic vision of westernization and progress that is often at odds with local interpretations of the good life: the urban elites "are more foreign than the foreigners themselves . . . they identify and aspire towards a global cultural existence which has no roots in the realities of the millions in this country."[73] Sofa does not engage with questions of modernity and does not offer an alternative paradigm. Instead, he offers a caution of the impending backlash that will eventually come if this vision of development continues to ignore vast segments of society.

Since Sofa wrote his essay in 1992, notes Ahmad Ibrahim, "the chasms have grown wider even as the proliferation of technological apparatuses like social media and the Internet bring a virtual proximity to the lived experiences of the people of this country. In short, it has become much, much easier to virtually experience these differences in culture and lifestyles and add to the anxieties accumulating on both sides of the cultural and economic divide."[74] The marking of vulnerable women as the agents of change also marks them as the objects of backlash from equally vulnerable men who feel threatened by the forces of change. In many ways, Appadurai's modernity at large has taken on unexpected visages.

Speaking of the modern middle-class woman in Bangladesh, Firdaus Azim, professor of English at Brac University, linked women's increased autonomy to higher levels of education. She attributed the change to the lively movement for women's rights in the country, which has made women more conscious about their rights and opportunities and these ideas have trickled down to the garment workers.[75] Economist Binayek Sen framed modernity for women by equating it with employment, saying, "With the garment industry, a certain autonomy has come to the woman as a wage earner." But he also noted that "this industrialization takes place in a barren space of uneven development, so the results are ambiguous for women. This modernity does not guarantee safeguards for women."[76] Ahrar Ahmed, a political scientist, enumerated modernity more broadly by moving it away from work and consumerism to the domain of rights:

> The question of our modernity can be looked at in two ways. The more popular form is the capitalist/consumerist form where modernity is equated with readily available consumer goods and services. Access to commodities becomes the marker of modernity/change. The second and perhaps more complex form of modernity is its intellectual and moral form. This needs more rigorous evaluation. What does it mean to be modern? In the moral and intellectual domain of modernity, one looks at the question of the human subject. Who is this subject and what are its rights? Modernity has to provide justice, individual rights, inclusion, rule of law, security. A woman in order to be a modern subject must feel safe

inside and outside of her home. Without security, she cannot exercise her rights as a modern subject.[77]

Bangladesh is a highly polarized society. One segment of the population endorses Western notions of the rights-bearing modern subject as the hallmark of economic and social progress. Another segment turns to the clergy as the guiding force through the maelstrom of globalization when so many feel anchorless. Thus, how the clergy view women's work and the ideas they promote among their adherents are equally important to consider. One hard-line counterpoint to the project of modernizing women comes from the clergy.[78] In their congregations, the clergy use questions around women's work and female autonomy to excite their followers against the West and women who have joined the industrial labor force. The clergy operate within a globalized world, and their ideas of what it means to be Muslim are derived more from their contact with Saudi Arabia and the Middle East. They take women's role in Saudi Arabia as the model of Islamic womanhood—that is, women should adhere to Islamic dress code and remain inside the home. These days the clergy use social media to reach a diasporic audience. Many of their adherents have left their wives and daughters behind to travel to the Middle East and Malaysia in search of work, and these men feel anxious over their loss of control of their women. When members of their congregation ask the clergy to explain the Islamic viewpoint of women working in factories with non-kin men, the clergy have to offer plausible answers within their Islamic framework.

In a famous instance, Maulana Ahmed Shafi, the leader of a religious movement named Hefazat-i-Islam (the caretakers of Islam), mentioned in a video that "You women should stay within the four walls of your houses. Sitting inside your husband's home, you should take care of your husband's furniture and raise your male children; these are your duties." He asked his followers not to send their daughters to work in garment industries, adding that they go to work early in the morning and return home late at night. He accused garment women of committing *zina* (unlawful sexual activities) and earning money through prohibited sexual practices.[79] Yet he did not exhort his followers to attack garment factories and workers, because fatwas and religion-identified attacks are struggles over symbolic and political capital for the parties concerned rather than "a struggle over the expansion of women's work."[80] When I spoke to some garment workers about his comments, they rejected them. One woman said to me, "We come because of poverty. Our village homes do not even have four walls. What is he talking about?"

While women are condemned for working outside the home, the clergy do not speak about the rights of workers and their wages in the jute mills, shipyards, and the agriculture sector, which primarily employ male workers. In defense of workers' wages, the clergy routinely cite a hadith, "Wages must be paid before the sweat dries on a worker's body."[81] If the question is posed to them, "What if the wages are not fair, then what?," they often answer with a counter hadith, "What you eat, you should give the same to those working under you." But beyond that, there is no critique of economy, capitalism, and development other than misogynistic and anti-Western diatribes. There are a few outliers within the clergy who are thinking about labor rights from a critical perspective, but their social imprint is negligible, if not invisible.

As Bangladeshi society goes through rapid social and economic transformation, different categories of people representing diverse ideological perspectives—from secular human rights to ultra-orthodox religious viewpoints—are bringing their worldviews to bear on the bodies of women. Modernity and modernization are separate processes that get entwined in these conversations. Modernity is a way of acting and being in this world; modernization is about the social and economic processes of industrial change. Modernity is experienced in the quotidian. The Bangladeshi garment worker experiences modernity by walking the city streets and encountering its sounds, smells, images, excitements, and possibilities. When a new road connects the village to the city, people, goods, ideas, media, fashion, and styles of being all travel along this route, opening ways for people to reconsider their positions and possibilities within a rapidly transforming landscape. In today's technologically driven world, ideas about the modern come through multiple vectors from physical interconnectivity and virtual reality—social media, Facebook, Instagram, TV shows, and movies. Modern technology has enabled people to experience modernity without even leaving their villages. In rural Bangladesh, the wide usage of cell phones has wired people to a global world of migrants living in different parts of the world, and their contact with these new worlds is changing their lives.

During my research I met women who had never set foot outside their village, but they spoke of traveling to Jordan or Mauritius because someone from their village worked there. They were wired into Appadurai's notion of globalization where they experienced the world without leaving their home. Their sons living in the slums of Dhaka played video games on their cell phones and maintained a global network through these games. Many of them played a game called Players Unknown Battle Ground with players from all over the globe—Hong Kong, Japan, Australia, Germany, and so on. The young men called the global players their "friends," although they would never meet them in person, but there was a connectivity that they experienced and enjoyed through the Internet. The players did not share a common language, but they communicated through the vernacular of the game. The video game played on the small screen of their cell phone made them feel much bigger than their restricted environment in the slum. This increased virtual mobility has energized people to think beyond their shores and imagine alternative futures regardless of whether those futures are feasible. This is what Appadurai has termed "modernity at large" and "diasporic public spheres."[82] Yet, how people consume these new ideas is specific to their cultural histories.

Taking all these into account, I define modern life as the increased possibility of being and living where new models and ideas become available, though not necessarily fully or substantially, to subjects who were previously denied those possibilities. Can the child of a sharecropper or a garment worker in Bangladesh hope to become a doctor? In almost all instances, the answer is no. These subjects are not on the highway to economic liberation. But the fact that these actors can imagine new worlds, however compromised, is a mode of thinking/being—that is, a new habitus—that should be carefully studied. I can become *x*. If I cannot, then my child can become *x*. The idea that the sharecropper can become an industrial wage laborer, that the wage laborer's child can hope to become a doctor or a schoolteacher, is an important shift in consciousness. The needle has shifted from the lament of the poor, "What else can I do?," to perhaps a maybe, and better yet, "Yes, my child can be something more than I." Universal education, a marker of modern life, has opened new doors of imagination. The modern subject imagines more possibilities than the previous generations of small-scale farmers and sharecroppers under feudalism. Thus the modern, as an idea, can begin to chafe away at the chains of patriarchy and feudalism to some degree. The needle is moving—not teleologically to a triumphant end where we are all free subjects, but to uneven futures.

Formed within consumer capitalism, the Bangladeshi woman as a new subject of capitalism is desirous of a better life. There are small changes in her life—wages, living in a small brick room in the squalid slums of Dhaka with piped water and gas for cooking, the ability to purchase a new set of clothes every few months, small outings on her day off, and watching television serials about lifestyles of middle-class women living in upscale high-rise apartments with beautiful clothes, rich food, expensive cars, and fancy objects. These shimmering lives beckon pleasure and excitement. Viewing these images makes her believe that this world is arriving at her doorstep. But the modern subject is also critical of the limits of her possibilities. As a worker, she knows that all this may not happen, but she has sacrificed her young life at the altar of fast fashion to make a better life for her parents, her siblings, and her children. In the words of a recent garment worker who had returned to Dhaka after working in Jordan:

> I had expected to be happy, live in a clean house, eat well, have nice clothes, go to the zoo, shops, and cinema halls. I have seen pictures of these foreign countries. Their roads are clean, their houses gleam, there is electricity, everything looks new and shiny. In Dhaka, I lived in a small room that I shared with several garment workers. Our living quarters were dingy, drab, and dark. In Jordan, we lived inside the factory compound. We could not go out. We were paid more, but most of our wages were deducted for room and board. I did not get any of these things I had seen on TV and had hoped for in my new life.

Then she stopped and thought for a while. "Yes, I was able to send money home to my parents, so they could build a new roof, pay for my younger brother's and sister's education, and set some money aside for my marriage. They got something by my working overseas, but I did not get anything. That world, if it exists, it is not meant for women like me."

In the 1950s, Syed Waliullah, one of Bangladesh's preeminent authors, lamented the poverty of rural society that pushed people off their ancestral lands. He wrote: "There are too many of them on this land, this piece of raped and ravaged land which yields no more. . . . Yet some do escape, some do manage to leave their homes. Once away they move quickly and their eyes burn fiercely with hope."[83] The life stories of the women I document in this book replicate Waliullah's lament and Berlant's cruel optimism, but at the same time, they are about Freeman's neoliberal fantasies and Lovely Yesmin's excitement when they first come to the big city, a place of possibilities, perils, and romance. They are like shards of glass. On one level, their lives are splintered. On another level, they emit possibilities of joy and partial fulfillments because glass also reflects light.

2

THE AGE OF EXCITEMENT
THE RISE OF THE GARMENT INDUSTRY IN BANGLADESH

> When the day breaks
> My eyes take in a vision
> Of a tide of garment workers on the streets.
> ....
> Have you seen so many women's faces together?
> Have you heard the thunderous sound of a thousand women walking?
> This surge is the force behind our economy.
> —Lovely Yesmin

ON ANY GIVEN DAY AT DHAKA AIRPORT, one sees long lines of migrant workers returning from Middle Eastern and Southeast Asian countries. These are lines of weary travelers who appear to be fatigued and in poor health. One can tell from their faces and bodies that they are migrant workers. Their bodies are lean and thin, their clothes shabby, their eyes tired. Yet, most of them have a happy smile. They are coming home to see family after many years. This migrant labor force, primarily male and young, works in construction, agriculture, hospitality, food processing, and related industries in these countries. If one looks carefully, one sees young female workers who are also returning home. They too are migrant workers who work as nannies, household help, cleaners, and garment workers. In recent years, a new trend has started as Bangladeshi female workers are taken as contract workers to work in garment industries that are starting in Mauritius and Jordan with Chinese investment.[1]

If one turns the gaze from the long lines of workers, one sees another novel feature. In the 1980s and 1990s Bangladesh was hailed for its innovative NGOs, and Western diplomats and donors would arrive in multitudes at the airport. By the early 2000s these development bureaucrats were replaced by a new demographic consisting of large numbers of Chinese, Indian, and Korean business people who represent investors in the garment and construction industries as the Bangladesh government attempts to advance into an economic boom. The fact that Bangladesh, famously hailed as a "basket case" by a U.S. diplomat in the 1970s, has transitioned from aid to trade is a significant development for a country that was long seen by economists as aid-dependent, a failed state, a place of natural calamities of Malthusian proportions.[2] Today Bangladesh is famous for its innovative NGOs, including the 2006 Nobel Peace Prize winner, the Grameen Bank, and BRAC, the world's largest NGO, with worldwide operations in impoverished and conflict-ridden countries of Asia (Afghanistan, Myanmar, Nepal, Philippines) and Africa (Rwanda, Sierra Leone, South Sudan, Tanzania and Uganda).[3] The country has also garnered worldwide recognition as the second-largest apparel-producing country in the world.

On a visit in 2019, the World Bank's chief executive officer, Kristalina Georgieva, praised the achievements of Bangladeshi women as the key element of the country's economic growth, noting that the "per capita income has gone up from $100 to $1,500, and Bangladesh is well on track to bring poverty down to under 3 percent. It is a country with high population density. It has managed to bring down population growth primarily through empowering women."[4] The World Bank now hails Bangladesh as a country on its way to reaching upper-middle-income status by 2025 (a stalled project due to the Covid-19 pandemic).[5] Noting this evolution, David Lewis, a long-term researcher of development policies in Bangladesh, wrote:

> Bangladesh remains an important focus for the international-development industry. It has long attracted high levels of aid and been a testing ground for development ideas and approaches. Recently, Bangladesh has gained international respect as a country that has made significant progress towards at least some of the Millennium Development Goals (MDGs) developed by the United Nations, which focuses on meeting targets by 2015 for, among

other things, poverty eradication, reduction of child mortality, improved maternal health and primary education. Bangladesh's extensive NGO sector increasingly commands international media attention.[6]

In the liberalization of the Bangladesh economy, women have been upheld as model citizens in the microfinance and garment industries. The appropriation of rural Bangladeshi women as agents of change is tied to UN/World Bank mandates over women's new roles in development that successive Bangladeshi governments were able to capitalize on. The following pages cover these changes, from global decrees concerning women's role in development, the privatization policies adopted by successive Bangladeshi governments from 1975 on, and the role of the Multifibre Arrangement (MFA) in facilitating the growth of the garment industry. Finally, the chapter covers the changes that occurred in the ready-made garment (RMG) industry following the 2013 Rana Plaza industrial catastrophe.

WOMEN AND DEVELOPMENT

At the heart of the story of industrial apparel manufacturing are poor women from developing counties. Ester Boserup's influential book *Women's Role in Economic Development* (1970) showed how the 1960s Green Revolution in Africa had failed to consider women's actual economic activities. Boserup analyzed how large-scale economic development projects had closed off common lands, areas where women had traditionally gathered firewood and other resources to feed their families and livestock.[7] Boserup, along with the rise in second-wave feminism in the West, positioned women as a central part of development practice.[8] In 1975, at the International Year of the Woman Conference in Mexico City, participants agreed on increasing women's economic and decision-making roles not just to help women but to accelerate national development. Following the conference, a program officer at the Ford Foundation wrote in the *New York Times* that "hundreds of thousands of women in Bangladesh and Indonesia have lost their only source of income (rice husking) because machines can do the job better."[9] The 1970s heralded not only neoliberal ideas of free market and individual enterprise but also well-intentioned ideas of helping women in developing countries.

The 1970s through the 1990s were marked by a series of conventions that targeted women's issues at a global level. Foremost among them were the 1994 International Conference on Population and Development, held in Cairo, and the 1995 Fourth World Conference on Women, held in Beijing. At the Cairo conference, representatives from 179 countries came together to address the impediments that were preventing women from realizing their full potential. The signatories agreed that gender equality "implies a society where both men and women enjoy the same opportunities, outcomes, rights, and obligations in all spheres of life." They also agreed on guaranteeing women access to reproductive health care (although some countries refused to sign off on abortion rights), natural resources, and economic, educational, and political empowerment.[10]

Conversations around the inclusion of women in development programs raged among policy makers working in the UN, the World Bank, and international organizations, leading to the UN's declaration of 1975–85 as the Decade for Women. The new mandate for development organizations was to come up with models that included women as participants. Aid officials working in different countries identified women as resources for donors and nations. By the 1980s the idea that women's economic participation amounted to progress was firmly entrenched in global discourses and practices. The 1995 World Conference on Women in Beijing further advanced issues regarding women's economic, political, and legal rights. The women's empowerment model of the 1990s, which grew out of these initiatives, also coincided with worldwide changes in economic restructuring and the opening of markets in many countries, as well as the implementation of neoliberal policies that reduced the role of the state in key areas such as development, education, health care, and rural credit. On the one hand, the new model of development encouraged states to work as partners with NGOs, charitable organizations, and donors aligned with UN and World Bank development policies; on the other, it sought to open markets in developing countries through structural adjustment policies.

To bring capitalism into developing countries, researchers and consultants hired by development organizations wrote reports that conceptualized the "Third World" woman as a wannabe sovereign individual who made rational choices in the marketplace. She was resourceful, entrepreneurial, and a disciplined worker. These agencies targeted women for their industry and worked to bring them outside the home into the formal job market. This was a highly successful policy that developing countries adopted. Liberal notions of women's employment focused on integrating women as low-skilled wage labor in manufacturing and as microcredit entrepreneurs in the informal economy. Remarking on this point, Meena Khandewal and Carla Freeman argued, "If liberalism pushed for flexibility in global workplaces via women's cheapened labor, then neoliberalism's innovation is to valorize entrepreneurship and thus, implicitly, the informal economy, which is the most flexible of all spheres."[11]

The integration of women into development programs has its share of detractors. Feminists have critiqued this model as an "add and stir" approach that did not address the root causes of gendered inequality and the social constraints within which women operated. Sandra Harding termed this trend "dedevelopment."[12] To Harding, "Development has often meant incorporating women into work that benefits others but not themselves; that destroys the environment upon which their daily subsistence often depends; that leaves them with no time or resources to provide for their children and others who are dependent on them."[13] What remained unsaid in these policy documents was how men were losing their traditional role as breadwinner as capitalism entered markets in the developing world, privatized common lands and resources, and began to rip apart families from their traditional sources of livelihood.[14]

In these policy debates, "Third World women's" empowerment operates as a vague "catch phrase that crops up uncritically in the service of today's one-size-fits-all development recipes."[15] The World Bank, a strong advocate of promoting women's work outside the home, defines empowerment in the following terms: "In its broadest sense empowerment is the freedom of choice and action. It means increasing one's authority and control over resources and decisions that affect one's life."[16] Naila Kabeer clarifies the term *empowerment* by noting that it is the "ability to make choices."[17] According to her, for the idea of empowerment to work, there must be feasible choices. In this definition, a formerly disempowered person must be able to exercise her choice in a manner that increases her well-being in a positive direction. Turning the lens to garment workers in Bangladesh, Chaumtoli Huq has argued that workers' empowerment comes through labor organizing. She writes that "worker participation in labor organizing has been empowering because it increases their awareness of rights, allows them to use organizing and the trade union space to bring about measurable changes and outcomes, and has motivated them to take on leadership roles in their factory level unions, and in some instances, national unions."[18] While I agree with both Kabeer and Huq, I examine empowerment as a discursive rhetorical device that domesticates women into the neoliberal economy as low-paid workers or self-employed entrepreneurs, both of which are precarious occupations. Thus, while the female body was made visible in these global endeavors as a model worker–citizen, her work conditions and wages remained invisible because her cheaply sourced labor supplied enormous profits to multinational companies.

NEOLIBERALISM IN BANGLADESH

"Neoliberalism has provided a kind of operating framework or 'ideological operating software' for competitive globalization. Crucially, its premises also established the ground rules for global lending agencies operating in the crisis-torn economies of Asia, Africa, Latin America, and the former Soviet Union, where new forms of 'free-market' *dirigisme* have been constructed. Indeed, proselytizing the virtues of free trade, flexible labor, and active individualism have become so commonplace in contemporary politics—from Washington to Moscow—that they hardly even warrant comment in many quarters."[19] In this scenario, neoliberal ideas of "pull yourself up by the bootstraps" have shifted the care of the citizen from state and welfare agencies to individual actors, families, and non-state institutions (religious organizations, for example).

Bangladesh entered the global community as an independent state on December 16, 1971. At its birth it posed a massive and intriguing challenge to development institutions and policy makers. The question that plagued policy makers was how to rebuild this war-torn country with a huge population pressure of 75 million on 56,577 square miles in the Bengal Delta with annual flooding of the plains. A third of the country is covered by rivers, restricting the acreage of arable land, putting Bangladesh at the forefront of climate change with an estimated 25 to 30 million people who are at risk from rising sea levels. In a study of the 1974 famine that killed 1.5 million people, economists Just Faaland and John Parkinson noted the need for a "continuing massive injection of aid" to stimulate the country's economy. According to them, the importance of Bangladesh was in its "availability as a test bench for two opposing systems of development, collective and compulsory on the one hand, and a less fettered working of the private enterprise on the other."[20] These economists argued that if the problem of poverty could be solved in Bangladesh—a land facing a Malthusian catastrophe with very high levels of population density, poverty, and illiteracy—then that model could be used in other contexts to alleviate poverty. Ultimately, it was the free-market approach that won over the collective approach to development in the 1970s with the installation of military rule in 1975.

Between 1972 and 1975, the first democratically elected government of Sheikh Mujibur Rahman of the Awami League nationalized all the privately held large industries. But the military came to power on August 15, 1975, and assassinated Sheikh Mujibur Rahman along with members of his family. Military rule was welcomed by the West, for the military readily adopted the market liberalization polices of the World Bank. The first military dictator, General Ziaur Rahman, made significant changes to industrial policy known as the 1975 Revised Industrial Policy, promising that "the state would never nationalize private enterprise."[21] The military's cozy relationship with the World Bank's structural adjustment policies allowed them to stabilize their rule and receive funds for development initiatives. The role of the military rulers was crucial in cementing neoliberal policies of privatization, deregulation, foreign direct investment, and the withdrawal of state subsidies in the agricultural economy.[22]

In the rural economy, the military allowed Western development organizations to funnel money directly to the embryonic NGO sector to work with the rural poor. By the 1980s the NGO sector took on many of the functions traditionally reserved for the state in microcredit, primary education, health care, immunizations, rural road reconstruction, and development training programs that they offered to their subscribers. The NGO sector also became a conduit through which liberal ideas about entrepreneurship, human rights, voter education, and women's new roles circulated in society. By the 1990s the NGO sector had developed into a formidable force, with millions of rural subscribers who depended on the NGOs, and not the state, for much of their sustenance.

General Ziaur Rahman took measures to "reduce the budget deficit, reform the public sector, withdraw subsidies on such items as food, fertilizer, and petroleum, and liberalize the trade regime."[23] The defunding of agricultural inputs (fertilizers, seeds, irrigation water) hurt the subsistence farmers, "whose cost of production has increased without compensatory gains from higher prices available to bigger farmers with a marketable surplus. The rise in prices has thus become a tax on small farmers."[24] Unable to provide for their children, rural families were forced to send their young daughters to work in the city. Thus "the feminization of the working-class is . . . a result of the withdrawal of state subsidies in agriculture that has resulted in a reduction in the purchasing power of rural people."[25] Many of these migrant women went to work in the garment factories that were being set up under generous incentives provided by the government to factory owners.

The military also consolidated its urban base by building alliances with an emergent business class in Bangladesh. For example, in the 1979 national elections, 28 percent of the newly elected members of Parliament were industrialists and traders, and 33.5 percent of the executive committee of Ziaur Rahman's new political party, the Bangladesh National Party, were business elites who helped shape government policy.[26] The second military ruler, General Hussain Muhammad Ershad (1982–90), accelerated the pace of economic liberalization to court more development resources from the World Bank. He introduced the New Industrial Policy (NIP) in 1982 (it was revised in 1986). "Within a year of NIP, the military transferred ownership of 60 jute and textile industries to the private sector," and while 32 percent of industries were privately held in 1981, by 1985, 78 percent of industries were in private hands.[27] This process of privatizing and defunding the public sector has continued under democratic rule that began in the 1990s. In describing these changes at the macro level, Anu Muhammad wrote, "The export-oriented garment factories became the mainstay of manufacturing and permanent jobs in factories were replaced by a system of temporary, part-time, outsourced, and insecure work," what Guy Standing has called precariat labor.[28] In the energy sector, resources were privatized by the state with a corresponding rise in the cost of production, forcing many farmers to seek employment in the informal and formal labor markets at home and abroad. Today, many rural families have at least one daughter in the garment factory and one son as a migrant worker overseas.

In Bangladesh, it is difficult to disarticulate the state and the private sector; they are different faces of the same set of economic interests. The state and the capitalist class collude to maintain their profits by restricting trade union activities, deploying industrial police to discipline workers, jailing labor activists, and appropriating female labor at cut-rate wages. For example, in the 2018 general elections, 182 members elected to the 300-seat Parliament were drawn mostly from the garment industry.[29] The gap between the state and the capitalist class is increasingly shrinking, jeopardizing the welfare and safety of workers and making it radically difficult to monitor the garment industry. And as Muhammad has argued "In Bangladesh, neoliberal programs and the model of (Marx's) primitive accumulation work as twins: they help each other, rationalize each other, and strengthen each other."[30]

THE RISE OF THE GLOBAL GARMENT INDUSTRY

The rise of the garment industry in Bangladesh occurs within this terrain of labor flexibility and the outsourcing of manufacturing from the United States and Europe to low-cost countries of Asia, Africa, and Latin America. For example, "In the late 1950s, only one of every twenty-five garments purchased in the US was manufactured abroad."[31] By the 1970s, as U.S. wages rose and neoliberal policies of market deregulation gained traction, U.S. garment manufacturers began to look for lower production costs in the Asian markets of South Korea, Hong Kong, and Taiwan.[32] These countries, which were rapidly expanding their manufacturing base, offered flexible solutions to the specific characteristics of the garment industry, from fast changes in trends, abundant supply of affordable labor, and increasingly complex supply chains as multiple sites were combined in the manufacturing of textiles and ready-made clothes.[33] Identifying this transformation, Aihwa Ong wrote, "Since the early 1970s, mixed systems based on free-trade zones, subcontracting firms, and sweatshops have come to typify industrialization in Asia" that kept the cost of production low.[34]

However, these countries soon came under the regulation of the Multifibre Arrangement (1974–94; replaced by Agreement on Textiles and Clothing, 1995–2004), which was an agreement between the United States and European countries to regulate textile production. The MFA restricted the import of manufactured clothing from middle-income countries in the mid-1970s as the main exporters of textiles to the U.S. and EU markets. These middle-income countries were Hong Kong, South Korea, and Taiwan. Instead, the MFA allowed unrestricted access to garments produced in the least developed countries (LDCs) like Bangladesh, Sri Lanka, and Vietnam to help build these countries' economies. South Korean exports were severely curtailed by the MFA quota restrictions. To circumvent the restrictions, the South Korean company Daewoo, a major apparel producer, partnered with Desh Company of Bangladesh in 1978.

The two Bangladeshi men who started the first joint venture between Bangladesh and South Korea were Abdul Majid Chowdhury and Noorul Quader. They were young businessmen who focused on textiles to create employment in a war-ravaged economy that had only jute as its primary export commodity in the 1970s. In a National Public Radio interview, Chowdhury said that after touring a South Korean garment-manufacturing firm that employed Korean women, he realized that rural Bangladeshi women could do the job equally well and would be a much cheaper source of labor.[35] Desh and Daewoo signed a five-year contract that covered collaborations in key areas like "technical training, machinery, fabric, plant set-up, and marketing, in return for a specific marketing commission on all exports by Desh during the contract period."[36]

The Desh–Daewoo collaboration occurred at a crucial juncture in the economic restructuring of global markets in deregulations and labor flexibility. The Bangladeshi government under military dictatorship provided lucrative incentives for the setting up of private industries. This opportunity enabled many Bangladeshi garment factory managers who had gone to South Korea to train in industrial production to start their own factories. The Desh–Daewoo partnership spurred the growth of the garment industry and eventually "brought Bangladeshi garments to doorsteps all over the world."[37] By the late 1980s the industry began to slowly take off, and Bangladeshi policy makers left the industry to market forces for capital to develop. Factories were set up in three tiers: the first tier was foreign-owned factories or joint foreign–Bangladeshi ownership that were in the export-processing zones where trade unions were not allowed to operate; the second tier was outside the export zones and owned by Bangladeshis with minimal trade union representation; and the third tier was the subcontracting factories that had no trade unions. Of these three, labor and work conditions were the worst in the subcontracting factories.

Shelley Feldman and Jakir Hossain noted that the growth of the industry was reliant on incentives provided to Bangladeshi entrepreneurs by the government, such as bonded warehouses and back-to-back lines of credit. These lines of credit gave easy access to credit for the factory owners so they could hire workers and import the required raw materials for manufacturing. Under the rules of the "bonded warehouse facility, no custom duty had to be paid," lowering the cost of production for factory owners.[38] Both the United States and the EU were influential in the growth of the garment industry by giving apparel exports from Bangladesh preferential access to their markets. In 2018, 60 percent of

Figure 4. Garment factories in Mirpur.

apparel produced in Bangladesh went to the United States, although it is only 6 percent of the U.S. apparel market, and 40 percent went to the EU, with Germany as the largest buyer. By the 1990s, Korean, Chinese, and Indian factory owners were operating alongside Bangladeshi owners, taking advantage of quota-free status, extremely low wages, no oversight of factories, and the benefits of a non-unionized labor force. All these conditions helped to keep production costs depressed in the garment industry.

By the early 2000s, Bangladesh had become a significant producer of RMGs for the global market, but the MFA under which it received tariff-free patronage, expired in 2004. Instead of losing its market share, the Bangladesh garment industry began to surge, and it did remarkably well during the global economic recession of 2007–8. In 2005, RMG exports were $6 billion. By 2008, exports rose to $10 billion; that is, exports nearly doubled during the recession.[39] There are several reasons for the phenomenal growth of the garment industry during the economic crisis. The first is called the Walmart effect. Analysts found that "when purchasing power is under pressure, consumers forsake more expensive products for the cheaper ones offered by discounters such as Walmart and that US retailer happened to be Bangladesh's largest clothing buyer." Second, Bangladeshi factory owners who had made high profits in previous years "were willing to reduce margins so as to reinforce relationships with buyers" who were demanding lower prices due to the economic crisis.[40] Another feature was that "factories often accept abnormally low prices in an effort to attract buyers . . . and in order to maintain a profit, low-cost suppliers often avoid safety measures and reduce worker's real wages through increasing working hours, cutting their benefits, not spending on other facilities."[41] Third, the expiration of the quota restrictions coincided with rising wages in China. Chinese factory operators wanted to exit out of apparel manufacturing, and they saw Bangladesh as a golden opportunity where they could relocate many of their garment factories. By 2005, China became a lead investor in the garment industry, reaping the benefits of an unregulated industry and rock-bottom wages.

But this rapid growth of the garment industry came at the expense of labor rights that the World Trade Organization failed to protect. While the WTO introduced patent rights protections for pharmaceutical companies and agribusinesses, it did not protect workers with a social clause, which would have ensured minimum labor standards, including "prohibition on child labor, forced labor and discrimination, and with union rights as the key measure for addressing all working conditions."[42] Within the WTO, EU countries advocated for higher labor standards for workers, whereas developing countries argued that onerous labor codes would handicap their manufacturing advantage and stymie their economic growth. Feminist scholars were similarly divided over the absence of the WTO social clause for textile workers. One group supported the clause for improved protection of workers' rights, while another group looked on garment jobs as the best available option for poverty-stricken women in non-industrialized countries.[43] It was the latter group of feminists, economists, and policy makers who successfully defeated the inclusion of the social clause in WTO trade agreements in the 1990s.

For garment workers in Bangladesh, the absence of a social clause has been horrific, as the ongoing work-related accidents in the industry have established. For the global market in apparel, these Bangladeshi workers are the cheapest workers worldwide, making it possible for global retail giants like H&M, PVH, Tchibo, C&A, and Walmart, among many other brands, to make huge profits by ignoring the ongoing labor violations in the factories from which they sourced the clothing. Without the social clause, global buyers exercise enormous power over setting prices, because it is a buyer's market. By the end of 2018, garment exports had reached over $30 billion. The WTO's lack of a social clause for garment workers, MFA incentives, government subsidies, and the interest of global buyers in finding low-cost production sites converged to make the Bangladeshi garment industry second to China in apparel production by 2005, overtaking Vietnam and Sri Lanka. According to industry experts, Bangladesh may even replace China as Chinese garment laborers migrate to higher paying jobs.[44]

The growth of the garment industry was also enabled by the availability of a large labor force of female migrants that was a result of the World Bank's structural adjustment policies and the government's disinvestment in the rural economy. The factory owners targeted these young women who could be coerced to work long hours at very low wages in substandard and hazardous conditions. "According to the

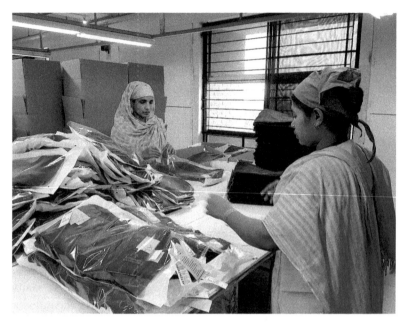

Figure 5. Garment workers pack merchandise in a factory that has met the safeguards required by Western buyers after the industrial catastrophe in 2013.

BGMEA website, four million women worked in the garment industry in 2012–14. Around 15 per cent of Bangladeshi women aged 15–30, it is estimated, work in the garment industry."[45] Were Bangladeshi women chosen as factory workers for their nimble fingers? In her study of workers, Kabeer discovered the interesting fact that factory managers viewed male workers as more productive, but men were considered troublemakers. Hence, male workers were replaced by female workers, who were considered less productive but more subservient. This displacement of men by women had diverse effects on society and gender relations. Prior to the global garment industry, men had worked in the local garment-manufacturing sector. But when export-oriented apparel manufacturing took over, it flooded the local markets with overflow reject products from the garment factories that were sold at deeply discounted prices. These products cut into the profitability of the indigenous shirt- and trouser-making industry, which traditionally employed men, and many lost their jobs. Today only 20 percent of the garment labor force

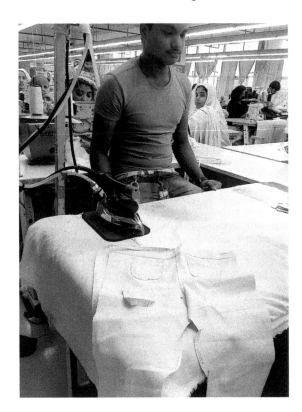

Figure 6. Male worker in the ironing section of a compliant factory.

is male. The loss of their economic power has led to heightened anxieties among men, a dynamic I discuss in subsequent chapters.

FACTORY UPGRADES AFTER THE 2013 RANA PLAZA INDUSTRIAL CATASTROPHE

While the garment industry expanded exponentially in the early 2000s, it remained an unregulated sector with labor code violations and weak building infrastructure. Between the 1980s and 2013, the sector had factories with faulty electrical outlets; no fire escapes, fire doors, or sprinklers; crowded stairwells; and padlocked doors and windows with iron grills to reduce pilferage and prevent workers from leaving. Not only had management cut off exits, but factory owners illegally locked workers inside factories and often forced them to work twelve-to-fourteen-hour shifts to meet quotas. As a result, accidents and workers' injuries and deaths have been an ongoing feature in this sector. Workers were not docile; they have routinely protested workplace injuries, deaths, and low wages. As early as 1990, workers came out in the thousands to protest the deaths of twenty-seven workers at the Saraka garment factory fire, but their agitation failed to provide them with Standing's industrial citizenship (discussed in chapter 1).[46] For example, between 2006 and 2009, 414 workers were killed in 213 factory fires. After 2013 the number of deaths had jumped to 1,660, which includes 112 deaths in the Tazreen Fashion fire in 2012 and 1,134 deaths in the 2013 Rana Plaza catastrophe.[47]

Given the high number of factory fires and deaths, and workers' demonstrations for higher wages and better work conditions, global apparel buyers were fully aware of the dreadful conditions inside these factories but chose not to lower their profits by acknowledging them. In November 2012, a fire at Tazreen Fashion gutted the nine-floor building and killed 112 workers who were trapped inside locked rooms. Four months later, on April 24, 2013, the eight-story Rana Plaza building collapsed, killing 1,134 workers and injuring another 2,500. A few days earlier cracks had already appeared in the building, and several offices located in the plaza had evacuated their personnel. But the garment factory managers forced the workers to work to meet their shipment. Less than an hour after the shift began, the entire factory collapsed, burying hundreds of bodies in the rubble. It was the spectacle of dead bodies that became the watershed moment in the history of the garment industry. Given the global outcry over the images of the workers killed, neither the global buyers nor the local factory owners could hide behind deception any longer. Following the collapse, the United States suspended its Generalized System of Preferences, which granted preferential tariffs to Bangladeshi products, and the EU issued a statement that as the largest trade partner with Bangladesh, it was concerned about labor conditions in the factories and the government had to improve work conditions if it wanted to continue to do business with EU companies.[48]

In the aftermath of the 2013 Rana Plaza catastrophe, the United States and EU governments, global apparel buyers, factory owners, trade unions and NGOs finally came together to solve the problem of unsafe work conditions. They adopted two separate treaties, known as the Accord on Fire and Building Safety in Bangladesh (the majority of EU

Figure 7. Line supervisor in a compliant factory. The room is airy with good lighting and sufficient space for workers to exit in case of an emergency.

and other major retailers as signatories) and the Alliance for Bangladesh Worker Safety (Walmart, Target, and Gap as signatories), to monitor the industry through factory safety upgrades that included fire escapes, fire doors, water sprinklers, and stairs free of boxes so workers could exit in case of fire. Moreover, workers could not be made to work in rooms with locked doors and windows. Changes were made to daily work hours, breaks, and so forth.[49] Inspectors representing Accord and Alliance agreements inspected factories for compliance, and nearly two hundred factories were shut down for safety violations and their workers laid off. Of these two treaties, the Accord is considered more pro-worker. It is a unique binding agreement that oversees factories where mostly European companies source from. The Alliance is a nonbinding agreement with several U.S. retailers with little accountability for buyers. The Alliance agreement expired on December 31, 2019, after it had completed five years of factory inspections, and the Accord agreement was extended for another five years to continue its monitoring of the industry. The

Accord has kept a relatively transparent website listing the number of factories inspected for safety compliance, whereas the Alliance project did little to improve worker safety. Michael Posner, a professor of ethics and finance at the Stern School of Business at New York University, praised the agreements, commenting, "The accord was a trailblazer for global worker safety and auditing, which made genuine on-the-ground improvements in Bangladesh. . . . Reacting to public outrage, both it and the alliance set a precedent that forced rival Western companies to work together, improve supply chain transparency and take greater responsibility for a system in which they have long reaped the bulk of profits."[50]

The Accord and Alliance agreements have been received ambivalently by labor rights groups and scholars. Huq has critically refuted the claim that the Accord is more pro-labor: "At its essence, it is a private agreement for services between brands and unions to conduct safety inspections, and if owners do not comply, the brands will not purchase from them. The inspections are limited to inspection and remediation, but not to wages and organizing that are central issues for workers."[51] Similarly, Ashraf Hasan and Rebecca Prentice have argued that "the intention of the Accord is to make Bangladeshi garment factories safe from fire and building collapse . . . in ways that depoliticize the issue by rendering it a technical matter devoid of labor politics. . . . This approach neglects the profitability of precarity itself: that the low manufacturing costs that draws multinational companies to Bangladesh are a function of the lack of labor voice that itself leads to unsafe conditions."[52]

A major shortcoming is that the Alliance and Accord websites do not show the number of subcontracting industries that continue to operate in very dangerous and exploitative conditions, often using underage children to work in their factories. While importation of items produced by child labor was abolished by the 1999 U.S. Child Labor Deterrence Act, children are still employed in factories, especially in the subcontracting factories. It is very difficult to measure the use of child labor, because even in the compliant factories, workers are trained by management to say that their age is eighteen years, the legal age for factory work. As for the subcontracting industry, workers are "off the radar," and purposely so.[53] In the aftermath of these factory upgrades, the low wage/cost competitiveness in the Bangladeshi garment industry now falls heavily on the unregulated subcontracting industry, where costs can be cut by undermining labor safety issues.[54]

In another positive move, Western governments pressured the Bangladeshi government to remove prohibitive restrictions on trade unions, so workers could have freedom of association. Prior to the 2013 industrial catastrophe, trade union registrations were mired in bureaucratic obstructions. The labor ministry routinely delayed registration of trade unions causing enormous backlogs of applications. Moreover, union representatives had to register 30 percent of all workers in a factory before they could form a union. Thus, unionization was restricted to the smaller factories with five hundred to fifteen hundred workers. For example, the Ha-Meem Group, one of the largest garment-manufacturing companies in Bangladesh, has over fifty thousand workers and twenty-six garment-manufacturing factories. It would be next to impossible to register 30 percent of that labor force.[55] Although trade union restrictions have been eased since 2013, most workers remain non-unionized through a range of tactics operationalized by factory management that include hiring their own people to act as fake union representatives.[56]

Wages

The most contested issue between workers, factory owners, the state, and trade unions is the abysmal wages in the industry. The government of Bangladesh sets the wage scale for workers through a board that it appoints. All factories associated with the apex organization representing factory owners, the Bangladesh Garments Manufacturers and Exporters Association, are required to pay their workers the wages set by the government board. Factories that fall outside the BGMEA jurisdiction have their own wage policies. While the government sets the minimum wage scale, it does not monitor factory compliance with its guidelines.

Each wage increase has occurred only after massive protests by workers in 2006, 2010, and 2013. Inflation and rising food and housing costs have forced workers to the street to demand a living wage. However, each time the wages fell far below what was demanded by workers, labor activists, and economists as the minimum living wage. When the first garment wage board was appointed in 1994, wages were set at $11 a month, and it remained unchanged until 2006. During this period, the Bangladeshi currency was devalued multiple times, making

Bangladeshi products cheaper for global buyers while workers were left to cope with rising inflation. The next wage increase came in 2006 after massive workers' protests. Five thousand workers demonstrated for better wages, and after a worker was killed, angry workers burned sixteen factories, vandalized fifty factories, and ransacked two hundred vehicles and turned the city into a "battlefield."[57] Given the widespread unrest, BGMEA officials and government officials met with Sramik Karmachari Oikya Parishad, the national federation of labor unions, to mediate a settlement. At the 2006 wage negotiations, several leftist trade union leaders had demanded $30 as the monthly wage, but they were defeated through a coalition of union representatives who were bought off by factory owners. In the negotiations, one trade union leader, a former female garment worker, acted as agent provocateur and argued against higher wages for workers.[58] The final wage agreement was set at $22 a month (taka 1,662).

Following the 2006 workers' strike, the government passed a Labor Act (also called labor law) that provided garment workers with some economic safety nets. One key outcome was a sector-wide Minimum Wage Board for garment workers that replaced the ad hoc process of the government creating a wage board at its caprice. Importantly, the Labor Act required that all workers had to be provided identity cards, timecards, and hiring documents. It also mandated that after a year of work at a factory, a worker would get permanent status. The act required employers to create individual provident (savings) funds for workers into which both employer and employee would contribute monthly. Employees invest between 7 and 8 percent of their monthly wages into the fund, a figure that is matched by the employer, although employers can develop their own plans for maintaining such a fund. The act does allow employers the right to terminate work due to a pandemic or an unforeseen situation, but all permanent workers had to be paid an additional thirty days of wages for each year worked in a factory (this is called a "gratuity"), plus the provident fund they have contributed to. These are *paper laws,* and as the case studies in chapter 5 reveal, most workers, particularly the older workers, are regularly defrauded of their provident funds.[59]

Despite the Labor Act, low wages and nonpayment of wages have continued to plague the industry. On June 30, 2010, more than twenty thousand workers protested in the streets over low wages and the rising cost of living. In the ensuing clashes between police and workers, witnesses saw children beaten by the police. Child labor is prohibited in the industry under the 1999 U.S. Child Labor Deterrence Act, but children can be found working in various factories. After months of negotiations, wages were raised to $30 (taka 3,000) per month in November 2010.[60] After the 2013 Rana Plaza factory collapse, over fifty thousand workers took to the streets demanding $100 a month as a fair living wage. The workers' protests over low wages and poor factory conditions, widely covered in the media, forced the government to finally set the new wage at $67 (taka 5,300) per month in November 2013. At that time, an agreement was made that wages would be increased every five years. In December 2018, wages were raised to $90 a month. The next wage increase is due in 2023.

These wage negotiations are complex affairs. The wages are set through a mechanism known as basic pay plus benefits for housing, medical, food, and transportation expenses. Any wage increase is calculated on the basic pay rate. For example, in 2013 when wages were set at taka 5,300 per month, the breakdown was as follows: taka 3,000 as basic pay rate plus 1,200 (housing), 250 (medical), 200 (transportation), and 650 (food). Any future pay increase would be calculated on the monthly basic pay rate of taka 3,000, not on taka 5,300. For example, a 5 percent monthly pay raise on taka 3,000 is 150, versus 265 on taka 5,300. This is a devious mechanism instrumentalized by factory management with the government's consent to keep wage increases depressed.

The wages earned by Bangladeshi garment workers continue to be a global low, although Ethiopia is now ranked the lowest for garment workers at $26 a month. Table 1 shows a comparison chart of the 2019 monthly minimum wages in U.S. dollars for ten Asian apparel-producing countries that was compiled by Sheng Lu, an associate professor in the department of fashion and apparel studies at the University of Delaware.

The Effect of Wage Increase on Workers

The 2013 wage increase came with a set of new factory regulations that reduced the work week to forty-eight hours and two hours overtime per day for a total of sixty hours per week. Workers had to be given a day off from work. Prior to the regularization of work hours in 2013, workers often worked twelve- to fourteen-hour daily shifts to meet seasonal

Table 1. 2019 monthly minimum wages in U.S. dollars for ten Asian apparel producing countries

Name of Country	Monthly Wages (USD) in 2019
Jordan	$131
Mauritius	$240
China	$217
Cambodia	$176
Vietnam	$151
Pakistan	$111
Myanmar	$94
Bangladesh	$64
Sri Lanka	$55
Ethiopia	$26

Source: www. shenglufashion.com.

demands. Factory managers would coerce workers to work seven days without a day off during the peak seasons. The shortening of the work schedule to eight hours per day adversely affected workers' income, because overtime pay provided them much-needed supplemental income. The rise in wages to $67 a month in 2013 came with an increased workload for workers. For example, the workload increased from 60 to 120 pieces per day per worker. If a worker failed to meet her target, she was called "lazy and unproductive" by her managers. She had to stay at work without overtime pay to finish her target. In many factories, helpers were eliminated or their numbers drastically reduced to maintain rock-bottom production costs. Helpers work with sewing operators by handing them pieces of cloth and cutting off threads sticking out of stitched clothes as the operators work on the machines. Overall, the pay increase to $67 for workers was more demanding on them physically and reduced their income, since their overtime hours were curtailed.

Workers are not the only ones who were affected by these factory upgrades. In speaking with me, several factory owners complained about the upgrades that were imposed on them by global buyers as financially onerous. These upgrades came with the buyers' mandate that factory

The Age of Excitement   75

Figure 8. Female worker in a compliant factory.

operators buy equipment from their recommended manufacturers, who did not offer the most competitive prices. One factory owner mentioned how his German buyer had insisted that he buy sprinklers from a German company that would increase his expenses by a million dollars when he could buy the same equipment from a Chinese company for a lot less. However, such comments should be evaluated carefully, since factory owners often buy inferior-grade equipment at a lower cost. Another factory owner who walked with me through his factory complained about how the European buyers had insisted that the space between the assembly lines must be exactly a certain number of feet so that workers could exit safely in case of emergency. This, he claimed, was an undue economic burden on his factory because they had to rearrange the assembly lines according to buyers' specifications, adding enormous cost to his expenses. He added, "The people who really benefit from our low cost of production are Western buyers. Why don't researchers write about them?"

A correlate of the garment industry that has not received much attention in the media or scholarly research is industrial waste and pollution. The older model of apparel production was four seasonal styles annually. In recent years, the Spanish company Zara took the lead in introducing new fashion trends every two months, sometimes turning styles over in two weeks, drastically shortening the production cycle. Known as fast fashion, brands now release "between eight to ten cycles per year," and this places enormous pressure on both suppliers and the workforce.[61] At the global level, the manufacture and disposal of cheap clothes also produces enormous waste and pollution that are not being addressed by manufacturers, global buyers, and consumers. At the local level, the industrial washing of manufactured clothes creates a massive amount of pollution from dyes and chemicals that is released by factories into nearby streams that people use for washing and cooking. Bangladesh does not have the infrastructure in place to handle the pollutants that are released into the environment, nor does it have effective regulatory agencies to monitor the proper disposal of waste. The workers live in the slums that have grown next to these factories. They frequently complain of headaches and chronic upper-respiratory problems from the environmental pollution that surrounds their work and living situations.[62] Given these conditions, one could term the overall result of the garment industry on workers as a zero-sum game. The case studies in the following three chapters detail these effects on their lives.

Within this cycle of industrial production, capitalist patriarchy uses women instrumentally to increase profits. Kabeer, in her interviews of male factory owners, found that they employ women because "they go home after work. . . . Women listen better and they don't talk back. And women are cheaper because they have fewer choices—in terms of physical location of work and in terms of their physical ability to do different kinds of work."[63] Thus, as long as the female garment worker is able to fulfill the utilitarian goals of capital, she is eulogized by the state and capitalist forces as a skilled worker helping to grow the national economy. She is, as the saying goes, "Made in Bangladesh." As she grows old and exhausts her utilitarian function for capital and the state, she is cast off as a useless remnant.

3

THE ARC OF CHANGE
FACTORY, FAMILY, AND CLASS

IN THIS CHAPTER, I draw on my interviews with older and younger workers to explore the changing dynamics of their work and nonwork lives. First, I briefly sketch the landscape of work using data from the survey of one hundred workers that I conducted to underscore the changes that have occurred in the lives of these factory women. The survey is followed by an examination of dynamics around factory work routines, changing social and family norms, and the ideas of middle-classness and consumerism among garment workers. In the last section, I discuss how work and globalization have informed two young women's lives, creating new horizons of graduated possibilities. The first woman, Happy, embarked on an entrepreneurial activity by becoming a subcontractor servicing the garment industry. The second woman, Rabeya, went overseas to work in a garment factory in Jordan. Their lives show the risky journeys that younger workers embark on in search of a good life. If life is a canvas where we construct our lives through practical acts, then these young women workers offer us a tableau of possibilities that are unlike the lives of the older female workers discussed in chapter 5. The stories of older and younger women read in unison reveal some of the sentiments and contours of lives lived in the shadows of capital.

From my research I found that industrial work and city lights have seduced and deceived these rural women into believing that a good life that represented middle-class aspirations was possible for them and their children.[1] This aspirational good life has opened hitherto restricted experiential worlds of independent living, consumerism, and class mobility for these women workers. For the female workers I met, the door to a world of enhanced opportunities had opened slightly, but the world of affects remained brutally closed to them. New experiential domains of work and independent urban living had also opened their eyes to amorous possibilities, but their amorous desires were simultaneously unleashed and repressed by the forces at play in their lives. Their aspirations for the good life of warmth, care, and love were pitched between Lauren Berlant's "cruel optimism," especially for the older and aged-out women, and Carla Freeman's "swirl of affects" among the younger workers who were excited by the opportunities introduced by globalization. That is, their lives fused neoliberal optimism with cruel optimism, and were in the interstices of these frameworks. Each sentiment contained within it threads of other sentiments and possibilities, making their life stories into a weave of aspirational subjectivities. These lives were a cascade of seductions and betrayals, but it would be an error to read their lives primarily as exploited labor with unmet desires. Their lives also contained what Bangladeshi anthropologist Nurul Momen Bhuiyan called "residue of hope." Hope as residue is a trace that underlies many of the conversations that I had with the women. They were caught inside the neoliberal development project of rapid industrialization, which did not provide them with any solid anchor of job security. Instead, they floated like buoys in the ocean with the horizon of distant possibilities alluring and disappearing from their vision. In my ethnographic endeavor, I sought to excavate these traces of hope, resilience, and disenchantments that were continually buffeted by the winds of globalization.

THE CHANGING LANDSCAPES OF WORK AND LIFE

In Bangladesh, women work primarily in the agricultural sector as non-paid workers, and they conduct "80% [of] pre- and post-harvest activities in addition to their daily household chores."[2] Prior to the emergence of the garment industry, poor rural women worked primarily as domestic workers, cooks, cleaners, mud-cutters for rural road constructions, and brick-breakers in real estate development.[3] These are low-paid and nonunionized jobs, and compared to men, women are paid less in all these sectors. In the formal sector, women's participation is the largest in the ready-made garment sector, which had approximately four million workers in 2018. As discussed by Sarah White, "Over the past twenty years, however, rates of women's economic activity have rapidly increased, through a combination of push factors of household poverty and rising expectations of consumption on the one hand, and the pull factors of mushrooming garment factories, micro-credit schemes, and female-coded white collar jobs in health and education on the other."[4]

Migration is a complex mixture of push and pull factors. On the one hand, migration has pushed women and men out of their homes due to lack of employment, family debt, demographic pressure, and environmental degradation. The river erosion in the Bengal Delta, an age-old phenomenon in Bangladesh, has been exacerbated by deforestation in recent times. It has led to the destruction of arable lands and forced many people off their ancestral lands. In addition, Muslim inheritance laws, which entitle sons and daughters (in unequal portions) to a share of parental property, have led to the breaking of land into small parcels. These small pieces of land cannot sustain the average rural family of five to six members. On the other hand, migration's pull factor has widened the scope of people's everyday activities and brought them closer to Appadurai's notion of a world mediated by movements. Nowadays, highways, bridges, and widespread cell phone usage connect Bangladeshis internally and globally. In the city, almost every adult person has a cell phone; in rural communities, practically every family has one as well. Internally, many migrants work in a town distant from their domicile and return by bus to their homes at night, a possibility that did not exist thirty years ago. Even when rural men are absent from their homes due to migration overseas, they remain connected through cell phones. They use FaceTime and recorded videos to share their lives lived away from family. Thus, the out-migration of men has not eroded male authority in the home; rather, it has reworked how patriarchal power is exercised over women, property, and family. These minute changes are essential to our understanding of how working women's lives are changing through their encounters with globalization.

The out-migration of men has loosened the patriarchal family's strict control over its women to some degree, enabling millions of young women to migrate to the city to live on their own, but it has come with unfavorable outcomes.[5] The shrinking of agrarian opportunities has made many men abandon their spouses and children in recent years. Men's mobility has facilitated spousal abandonment, since men can move away but women cannot. My focus in this study was not on the men who had abandoned their wives but on the women who were working in garment factories in the city, many of whom had been abandoned by their spouses. The few men I spoke with who had abandoned their wives did not take personal responsibility for their actions. Instead, they all claimed that they left their wives because they were "bad women" who were disobedient. This was a characteristic male ruse that masked their lack of spousal responsibility. A more nuanced explanation of such behavior was their emasculation, since these men could no longer fulfill their expected roles as breadwinners. In interviews, men asked why they should pay for household expenses when factories hired women at high wages. The shame associated with their failure as primary providers for their families created intense gender-based envy toward the women whom they saw as the beneficiaries of development (the garment industry, for example), and that resulted in multiple forms of domestic abuse that I have recounted in the pages of this book. Undoubtedly, these changes have profound sociological implications for family and gender relations in society that need further study.

The women who worked in the factories came from low-income families that depended on subsistence farming. They were not from the traditional artisanal families of weavers, potters, and carpenters. In artisanal families, women and men work collectively on production, with each member performing a specific task. Among weavers, for example, women and children wash, color, and spin cotton; men work the looms. The artisanal families remain together, since their livelihood depends on working collaboratively. In contrast, the vast majority of women in the garment industry came from landless, agrarian families. Marjina, a forty-five-year-old worker in a sweater factory, came to Dhaka after the 1998 floods had washed away her home. She moved to the city to save her children's lives. Speaking of the positive effects of factory work, she said, "If I didn't have this factory job, we would not have any place to stay, money for food; we would have all died." Mahmuda, a fifty-two-year-old aged-out worker, said that they ate a gruel of broken wheat and rice for two weeks of the month in the village. Laila, a fifty-year-old aged-out worker, said that her family had come to the city because her father lost all his land to debt. Thus, life was divided between rural life without work, wages, or food, on the one hand, and urban life with factory work, wages, and food, on the other. This division was a dire reflection of their material conditions. For these older women, factory work was a Hobson's choice. It was not what they desired, but it was their only option for survival. Unable to feed or educate their children, these poverty-stricken rural families sent their daughters to the city.

SURVEY AND CHANGING LIFE PATTERNS

As mentioned in the introduction, I did a short survey of one hundred workers to get some baseline data on the changes in workers' lives. The survey was conducted at the early stage of my research, and a majority of the workers interviewed were young, with nearly half between fourteen and twenty-four years of age. Almost all the workers interviewed worked as sewing operators; a few worked as helpers. Most workers enter the factory as helpers, and if they can pick up the skills fast they are promoted to sewing operators. Beyond that, there is no upward mobility for these women. On average, 50 percent of the older women I met had changed factories two times, largely due to getting laid off from work or the birth of a child. The husbands of these women mostly worked as day laborers, construction workers, rickshaw pullers, three-wheel scooter drivers, vegetable vendors, small dry goods store owners, security guards, and in similar low-income jobs. Based on the survey results, I created four pie charts that show age, literacy levels, marital status, and education levels of the workers surveyed. The first pie chart shows the breakdown of the ages of the women surveyed: 48 percent of the women were 14–24 years old, 33 percent were 25–34, 11 percent were 35–44, and 8 percent were 45 or older. If we consolidate the workers between the ages of 14 and 34 years, the largest number of workers — 81 percent— fall below thirty-five years of age, which corresponds with my observation that it is rare to find workers over age thirty-five in garment factories.

The second pie chart shows the literacy levels of the surveyed workers: 21 percent are illiterate, 30 percent are grades 1 through 5, and 27 percent are grades 6 through 8. Thus, 51 percent of the workers fall

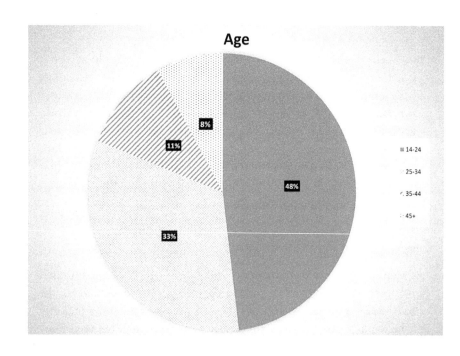

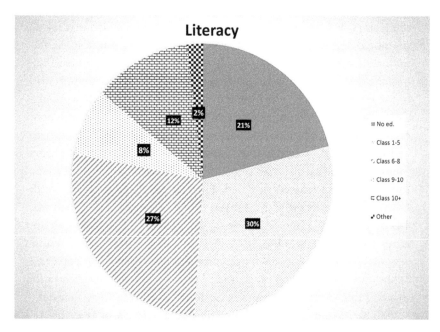

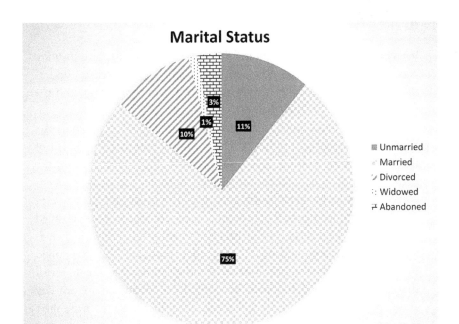

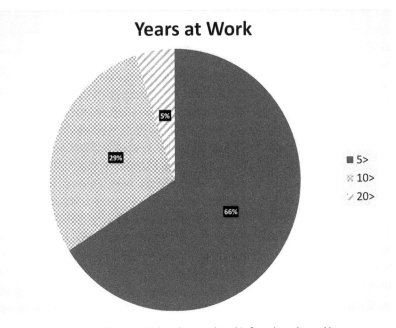

Figure 9. Results of a survey of one hundred workers conducted in Savar by author and her research assistant.

between no education and grade 5 (rural primary school). This primary education is basic literacy (the ability to read simple sentences, understand elementary arithmetic such as addition and subtraction, and the competence to write their names).

The third and fourth pie charts illustrate marital status and years of work in the garment industry. The former shows that 75 percent of the women were married. It was an unusually high number given the high rate of divorce, abandonment, and multiple marriages prevalent among garment workers. Marital status is a foundational principle of social status for women in Bangladesh. I found that many women claimed to be married because they were ashamed to admit to outsiders (such as my research assistant and myself) that their husbands had abandoned them, although once rapport is developed they are more willing to reveal that they had been abandoned. Bangladeshi rural women are not coy about personal matters; they will speak candidly once they trust their interlocutor. During the initial survey, my research assistant had not developed that rapport with the women, since the focus was on gathering some baseline data. When I compared the survey findings on marriage with my ethnographic research, I found that 70 percent of the women in my ethnography, whether young or old, had been abandoned by their husbands. While marital abandonment was more common than divorce among older workers (it is financially less onerous for a man to abandon his wife than to seek a divorce through the courts), divorce was on the rise among young women. Younger workers were more emboldened to file for divorce and seek alimony due to their exposure to NGOs that teach women about their marital rights. I would simply posit here that many of the women who claimed to be married in this survey may have been abandoned or divorced. Only 1 percent were widowed, which is not surprising, because the workers surveyed were young and employed. The final pie chart shows the years worked at a factory. Of these workers, 66 percent had worked for five years, 29 percent for over ten years, and 5 percent for over twenty years. Again, we find very few workers have worked for longer than twenty years.

The survey revealed that, on average, workers' work life is approximately twenty years. Most of the workers have only functional literacy and therefore could not read the hiring and firing documents used by factory management, putting them at risk from employers who could lay them off without following labor laws. While their marital status was very insecure (high levels of domestic violence, spousal abandonments, living with co-wives, multiple marriages of their husbands), the survey could not capture that information. While a survey yields essential data, it is also restricted in terms of deeper understandings of people's lives. For example, the survey indicated that a woman entered work at a certain age and worked for a certain number of years—important data, but it failed to capture the hermeneutics of work. What did work mean to her? Did it offer her what she had hoped for? Did it provide her with an opportunity for happiness? For answers to these and other questions, I turned to my ethnographic interviews conducted with workers over several years.

The survey also yielded some data on what the women saw as the advantages and disadvantages of urban living and factory work. Of the women surveyed, 59 percent lived in nuclear family settings, and in those families, husbands and children helped the mother with housework. These women viewed this as a positive outcome of factory work. Fifty-eight percent saw their ability to purchase consumer goods as an affirmative aspect of factory work. Women who lived in nuclear family settings were the same women who said that they could spend their money on consumer goods without the interference of husbands or families. Thus there was a direct correlation between living in a nuclear family and a woman's ability to make decisions about small purchases. The women identified two major disadvantages of factory work. Sixty-six percent noted the high cost of living in the city, and 60 percent said that they were unable to save because of the high cost of living. Again, there is a correlation between the high cost of living in the city, low factory wages, and one's inability to save for a rainy day. Only 8 percent of the women saw schooling for their children as a positive outcome of factory work, and this was due to the young age of the majority of the respondents surveyed. That is, a very small number of women could avail themselves of urban school facilities. While tuition is free in government schools, these schools cannot accommodate the number of students seeking enrollment. Many garment workers send their children to local madrassas (Islamic religious schools) or to the substandard private schools that have sprung up all over the city. Others have left their children in the village to be raised by grandparents or close kin.

Figure 10. A garment worker purchases a snack with Sahanaj, a labor rights organizer, on a Friday evening.

The most interesting finding was that 86 percent of the women saw freedom of movement as the most positive outcome of factory work. In contrast to the city, women's sexuality and physical movements are strictly regulated in the village, where they are under constant surveillance by older family members when they venture outside. City life and factory work have enabled women to move about in ways that were previously denied to them. A woman could now walk around, sit at a restaurant with a friend, or talk to a non-kin man without her intentions being scrutinized by family. The women enjoyed this new freedom of mobility. In Dhaka, people say that one knows a garment worker by how fast she walks in the street. Traditionally, women are expected to make their bodies and voices invisible, because a woman who is loud and visible is considered a shameless person. These garment women now stride quickly and purposefully with confidence. They speak loudly when necessary. Some of them are confident of themselves and their movements. If anyone says to them, "Why are you walking around like a man?," they say, "It is none of your business." These are significant changes in women's attitudes and comportment in public spaces.

Take the example of Sahana Begum, a forty-eight-year-old aged-out garment worker. "I could not speak easily with strangers before, now I can. I walk alone from the factory to home, nobody says anything to me, nobody touches my body. I could not do any of these things before in the village." Had Sahana remained in the village, her father, husband, or a male member of her extended kin would be responsible for her physical security and the protection of family honor. In Bangladeshi society, non-kin men cannot touch another man's daughter or wife. In the new urban environment that these women were moving to, these forms of familial protection disappeared, leaving women like Sahana to fend for themselves. The factory culture had shifted responsibility from the family to the individual, creating increased excitements and insecurities for the newly arrived women in the city. Overnight, their lives changed from living within the four walls of their rural homestead to an urban jungle without boundaries. These are dramatic changes in these women's lives.

In the next section I discuss the factory routines and workplace harassment faced by these women. In Mirpur, where I conducted my research with workers, a majority of the factories did not have more than two thousand workers, and these factories were owned by Bangladeshis. After 2013, many noncompliant factories closed down following inspections mandated by the Accord agreement, and thousands of workers were laid off. In 2018, the smaller factories in my research area were not getting regular orders from overseas buyers, and most of the workers complained about a lack of overtime work. In contrast, some of the larger factories continued to get orders, and the workers were coerced to work long hours. Many factory owners evaded monitoring despite their agreement with EU governments and buyers that they would limit overtime work to two hours per day. Six months after the Rana

Plaza industrial catastrophe, a *Wall Street Journal* investigative report showed that at Next Collections, which is owned by one of the country's largest garment producers, Ha-Meem, company records indicated that workers worked from 8 a.m. to 6 p.m. Inside the factory, however, the owners violated that condition and forced many of their forty-five hundred workers to work as late as 5 a.m. to stitch clothes for Gap and Tommy Hilfiger. They did this by keeping two sets of records, one for monitors from Accord and another for their private use. Also, the inspections by Accord officials do not occur late at night, when one would see workers working excessive overtime. In most instances, factory owners know when their factories will be inspected, allowing them time to rearrange their work operations to fit the stipulations of the Accord treaty.[6]

FACTORY ROUTINES AND WORKPLACE HARASSMENT

Since the 1990s, the influx of millions of young women into the urban areas of Dhaka has begun to transform the city's landscape and social dynamics. The city—with its high crime rates, gambling, drug use, pollution, and traffic congestion—encloses these women's everyday existence. Between the hours of 6 a.m. and 8 a.m., and again between 6 p.m. and 8 p.m., young women in brightly colored saris and *shalwar kameezes* (long, shift-like attire with pantaloons) occupy the streets of Dhaka on their way to and from work, challenging the male-dominated gender dynamics of the city. These workers marry and reproduce the second generation of workers in the city, creating an infrastructural challenge in terms of housing, day care, and schooling for their children that the factory owners and the government have failed to deliver.

As the garment industry has expanded and as wages have increased from the early days of factory work, social attitudes toward women's work have also changed. In the 1980s and 1990s, women who worked in factories were considered women of ill repute, and families were reluctant to allow their unmarried daughters to work in the garment industry. An older factory worker mentioned that when her neighbor suggested to her impoverished sharecropper father that he should send his daughters to work in the garment industry, he had replied that he would rather throw his daughters into the river than let them become factory workers.

Finally, unable to bear the poverty of her family, she ran away to the city to seek employment in the garment industry where she worked for twenty years. Once she began to send money to her parents, it appeased her father's attitude toward factory work. The discourse of women's factory work has changed as families began to recoup the benefits of industrial wages paid monthly to their factory daughters. The pay in the factories is higher than what these young women could earn as domestic workers in the city, which was the only option available to poor migrant women prior to the establishment of the garment industry.

In the factories, women primarily work as sewing operators. The men tend to work in stretching bales of textile rolls, ironing, cutting, washing, packing individual pieces into plastic wrappers, and boxing clothes for shipment—activities that require more physical strength. In all factories, a small number of men work as sewing operators and women as packers. With their inclusion into factory work regimes, the modern clock has regulated and routinized these women's lives. They were quickly inducted into a routine of factory time—timeliness, listening to authority, standing in lines to get food or whatever—elements that are essential for a factory worker. Moving with the clock was essential in this line of work. Clocking into work, clocking out of work, and finishing their quota on time gave them a new perspective on how time structured their lives. Their day began between 5:00 and 5:30 a.m. In the slums, workers have to make lines for a ten-minute shower in a shared bath. After that, they wait half an hour to cook their meals in a shared kitchen. Standing in line has become an everyday feature of their lived experience. The workers set out for work between 6:30 a.m. and 7:00 a.m. to reach the factory gates by 8 a.m., after which the factory gates are locked. Being late for work results in reprimands by managers and a potential loss of income. Several late arrivals would get them fired. In their new existence, timeliness equals job security.

Workers' lives were also circumscribed by overtime work at the factory. With wages so low ($67 per month at the time of my research), overtime work provided them with the additional cash necessary to cover the cost of living. Overtime work was woven into their workday; most workers did not distinguish between when the regular workday ended and the overtime work began. Women would tell their husbands, children, and neighbors, "I have to do overtime at the office [the preferred term used for factory] today." Mentioning factory work automatically indicated urgency; if she is late for work, she may face punitive action by management.

Speaking about time and work, Lovely Yesmin described their work lives as "overtime," as long hours without adequate compensation. Before the 2013 Accord and Alliance agreements to bring the industry in compliance with labor laws, workers were routinely defrauded of their overtime wages. "Theft of our overtime wages was a routine feature of work in this industry," Lovely explained. "If a worker worked for two hours, the factory would only give her one hour as overtime. What was stamped on the timecards was not entered in the official logbooks. In reality, owners were extracting excessive labor from workers at very low wages. It was easy to swindle illiterate workers who had no trade union representative in the factories." Then she said, "I have written a poem about overtime. Would you like to hear it?" When I said yes, she began to recite her poem "Overtime." In simple language, her words captured the sentiments associated with excessive overtime:

> We work from 8 a.m. to 5 p.m.
> With an hour off for lunch
> After eight hours
> All work is overtime
> We work on holidays
> That too is overtime.
> Without overtime
> We cannot eat
> We cannot pay our living cost.

Inside the factories, the assembly lines move quickly. Each worker has to finish 120 pieces per day; falling behind means being put on notice and wages getting deducted. Being late with one's work routine slows the assembly line and affects other workers with their timely progress. At work, there is constant surveillance by managers, and communication among workers is monitored. Male line supervisors walked up and down the aisle, keeping an eye on the workers. Gossiping, being slow, eating on the sly (workers often brought chutney with them to eat) were immediately noted, and workers were called out. The supervisors were strict about production lines moving without interruptions.

Many workers said that physical assaults such as slaps or pulling a woman by her hair used to be more common in the past but that these occurrences have become less frequent with the onset of regularized production operations. Management has realized that workplace disruptions cause delays in manufacturing that hurt the bottom line. In recent years they have operationalized stricter disciplinary surveillance of workers instead of physical assaults to make them work faster. Workers noted another form of punishment that they found demeaning. Workers who arrived late or were negligent at work were made to stand outside the factory gates so they were visible to passersby who mocked and hurled insults such as, "Haha, now see what fun it is to work as a garment worker." Invariably, these kinds of punishments dehumanized and infantilized the workers.

Health was another area of ongoing concern in this sector. Workers were discouraged from taking more than one toilet break during an eight-hour work cycle. Instead, they were expected to take their toilet breaks during their lunch hour and not during paid time. This resulted in workers refraining from drinking sufficient water during the day, leading to multiple forms of kidney and urinary tract diseases. The women also developed reproductive health issues from using industrial waste as sanitary napkins. They made sanitary napkins form the unwashed small pieces of clothing and balls of threads that were thrown away during the manufacturing process. The use of these industrial waste products as sanitary napkins caused many women to develop serious infections in their cervical areas. The women were unwilling to purchase sanitary napkins when they could easily collect scraps of clothing that were thrown away on the factory floor. A few NGOs provide basic hygiene and health education to workers, but they reach only a small segment of the population. One way to address this issue would be to supply sanitary napkins at a low cost to workers at the factory. If such a policy is adopted, with time, workers will get used to purchasing sanitary napkins similar to how bottled water to prevent waterborne diseases has taken on widespread acceptance in Bangladesh.

The factories that have upgraded to International Labour Organization (ILO) safety standards are called compliant factories. In these factories, workers are given masks to wear, but many do not wear them due to the heat that emanates from the industrial sewing machines. The upgraded factories have overhead fans and passage between the production lines, making the workspace spacious and airy. Most of the factories do not adhere to these standards, though. There is a lot of air pollution and chemicals from the clothing and machinery, and the poor quality of air affects workers' health, causing upper-respiratory infections. Workers also complained that their eyesight and hearing were impaired from harsh lights and the loud noise of the heavy industrial equipment. Many factories now have a nurse on duty, and a visiting doctor who attends to workers once a week. When a worker falls ill, she is first sent to the nurse's station, where she can rest for a short time. If she recovers, she returns to her post. If she is too ill, she is given a painkiller and sent home. As a result of these work conditions, female factory workers suffered from multiple work-related diseases associated with their lungs, kidneys, and reproductive organs. In their study of 360 female garment workers, Sohel Mahmud and his colleagues found that 88 percent of the

Figure 11. Workers at a health clinic run by the NGO Awaj.

workers complained of headaches, 48 percent of fatigue, 46 percent of eye problems, 33 percent of hearing problems, and 27 percent of hypertension due to the nature of the work. They also found that 69 percent of the workers suffered from depression, with fear of accident the key reason for "psychological troubles."[7] In my research, all the workers complained of chronic joint pains, headaches, and vision and auditory problems.

During their lunch break, workers gather at the factory canteen with their tin lunch boxes, which usually contains a mixture of rice and vegetables and some hot chili paste to add some zest to the otherwise mundane food. Those workers who live close to the factory go home for lunch. With the new work schedule of forty-eight hours of work per week, the workers spend eight hours at the factory plus one hour of unpaid lunch break, and another hour for travel to and from home to factory, bringing the daily workday to ten hours. If no overtime work is available, by 6 p.m. the regular workday is over and workers return home. At the end of the workday, the women shop in the markets that have developed around their living environs. Fresh produce is rarely sold in these markets. The shopkeepers capitalize on the women's lack of time and sell them day-old produce at higher prices. The frozen chicken sold there often had expired dates. In an interview, Nazma Akter, trade union leader and founder of the NGO Awaj Foundation, mentioned that "local shopkeepers sell garment workers the rotten vegetables and broiler chickens with expired dates that could not get sold in the markets frequented by middle-class people." According to her, the garment workers, despite being behind the "economic miracle of Bangladesh, are getting the worst of everything from wages to food to living conditions."[8]

WORKING MOTHERS WITHOUT DAY CARE

While factory work is essential for their livelihoods, child care was not provided to working mothers. Without adequate day-care facilities, numerous problems beset these women. Many of these women functioned as heads of households. They arranged for day care through informal networks—either a relative took care of the child while the mother was at work, or someone in the slum operated a day care. These services were not free; relatives charged money for taking care of the children. Many of the women sent their children back to their villages to be raised by relatives, but it did not end their anguish. Separation from their children is a continuous source of anxiety for these women, often hampering their work productivity. Many women said that they could not work properly because they had stayed up all night worrying about their child who is living in the village. They are haunted by questions such as "Are my children eating well? Are they getting love and care? Do they get medicine when they fall sick?" As one worker confided, "When I need to send money for my child's schooling or doctor's visits, then I often have to go without food. If I go without food, then I am too weak to do the heavy work at the factory. What is my life about?"

These days, mothers communicate with their children through cell phones, and children tell their mothers about the lack of care they receive from relatives. They cry and ask their mothers to bring them to the city. Even when women have in-laws living with them, many of them mentioned that daughters in particular are not properly cared for due to the lower value placed on female children. One woman said to me, "I had left my three-year-old with my mother-in-law. After a long day at work, I came home at 10 p.m. to find that my daughter had soiled her clothes. Nobody had cleaned her. My husband's family takes my money every month, but they are indifferent toward their grandchild. How can I continue work knowing that my daughter is neglected in this manner?" I met another young mother without day care who told me that while she was at work, her husband, who had a gambling habit, had taken their four-year-old daughter to be sold to a human trafficker. Fortunately, her neighbor realized what was happening and stopped him. As a temporary solution, her neighbor agreed to look after her child while she was at work, but the woman still felt very nervous about leaving her daughter at home while she was at the factory. When asked what she would do, she said that she would have to send her daughter to her village home, although "the separation will break both of their hearts."

The absence of day care affected women workers' overall productivity and mental health, yet very few factories offer day-care facilities. A small number of factories had implemented them only after owners faced scrutiny from labor rights groups after the 2013 Rana Plaza industrial catastrophe. These day-care facilities were recently established to showcase to Western buyers that factories were instituting the ILO's

Figure 12. Two garment workers with their children.

labor standards. I visited a couple of factories where they had day-care facilities. One factory I visited had twelve hundred workers but only fifty day-care slots. Some NGOs also operate day-care services that are independently run with funds from overseas organizations. These are all small, private initiatives undertaken by groups to cobble together a solution to an enormous problem facing factory workers, and when the funds dry up, the day-care school closes. The government does not offer day-care facilities for the children of the garment workers, although they are the social reproducers of the next generation of workers that the state depends on for its economic survival.

Lovely Yesmin takes up many of these issues in her poetry to bring attention to the plight of these working mothers. A recurrent theme in her poems is the low wages paid to workers. Her pathos reflects the workers' low wages and lack of money to pay for rent, buy food, or send money for their child. If the garment workers received a living wage, some of their suffering would be eased. Yesmin's poetic imagination captures some of these sentiments in "A Garment Worker's Cry":

Hello mother
How is my Sanji?
Has her fever come down?
Mother dear, I asked for leave
But supervisor said no
Production manager said keep working.
Mother dear, take my Sanji to a doctor
As soon as I get paid, I will send you money
Or I will take a loan.
My mind weeps
Does my Sanji call for me?
I want to bring my Sanji to Dhaka
And hold her close.
We four workers live in a small room
The cost of living is very high
I can barely pay my expenses
Allah make my daughter well.

WORKPLACE SEXUAL HARASSMENT

Since 2013, research on the garment industry in Bangladesh has been funded by international institutions interested in improving the work culture in the industry.[9] The issue of workplace harassment in this sector has gained purchase in recent years, with many researchers now studying this phenomenon.[10] Labor rights advocates working in the area informed me that since the Rana Plaza industrial catastrophe brought safety issues under intense scrutiny by Western buyers, it gave workers' rights organizations a voice in addressing workplace injustices. Labor activists and NGOs now monitor workplace sexual harassment by offering training sessions and teaching workers about their rights. Global buyers have also cautioned factory owners to clamp down on sexual harassment if they want to maintain a working relationship. As the industry has become more routinized in production processes, managers have realized that their profit margin is negatively affected when workplace disruptions occur. These factors have led to an overall decline in explicit sexual harassment in a segment of compliant factories. However, I am limited by the anecdotal evidence of talking to workers and labor rights advocates in my research area.

In the past, factory owners were indifferent to the sexual insecurities that young women workers faced when they were coerced into working overtime, often late into the night. Buses were not provided for these late shifts. One trade union leader told me: "In the 1990s, we were not savvy about these issues. Our managers would make us work late and then let us go after midnight. One day, two of us were returning home at 1 a.m. At an intersection near my residence, I said goodnight to my friend and walked home. The next day, I heard that she had been set upon by some neighborhood boys and raped. Nowadays when women work late into the night, they form groups of twenty or more to walk home together. By forming large groups, these women develop a sense of solidarity. They take over the unsafe city streets at night, an activity that middle-class women would not dare to engage in."

The older workers told me numerous stories of young women who were asked to report to the manager's room at the end of the workday. At a labor rights training meeting, a woman mentioned that these days supervisors want "smart girls." She said that her supervisor had sent her outside the factory to find some workers. When she informed him that there were three girls outside the factory gates looking for jobs, the supervisor went outside to check them out. On his return, he said that he would not take them because they are not "smart." "Smart" is a code for a beautiful woman; it does not refer to her education or skill level. When the rest of the twenty-five girls in the training session heard this, they all said "luiccha," a term used to describe a man's loose sexual morals. Another worker told the story of a young woman who was asked by her manager to wear pants with an elastic band because it was easier to pull down for sex. One worker told me that her supervisor would pick a pretty girl at work every week and ask her to wait for him by the back wall of the factory where the assault would take place. There were many anecdotes of male managers who would touch women inappropriately while they worked. Seeing their vulnerabilities, senior workers also helped younger workers by volunteering as a watchperson. An older female worker spoke of a beautiful young worker at her factory who was asked by the manager to go to his office after work. The older worker said, "I cautioned the young woman not to go to his office by herself. I told her that I would go with her after work. So, we went together and foiled his plans." These stories are too numerous to recount.

So, how did the workers evaluate sexual harassment? For most workers, sexual harassment generally meant sexual assault or rape and not inappropriate verbal comments or the touching of their bodies without consent. Workers complained that while the verbal abuse by managers ("whore/daughter of a whore," "worthless old hag," "Why is your work so slow, did you stay up all night f—ing some young man?") offended and hurt them, in general they did not view these verbal assaults as sexual harassment. In their everyday lives they hear women addressed in similar language on the streets, in neighborhoods, and in their homes, and to some degree the women have normalized this language. What became evident was that these women's understanding of what constituted sexual harassment was at variance from feminist notions of harassment, which were more broadly construed. As one labor rights advocate, Sunzida, said, "Our role as labor advocates is to make these workers realize that sexual harassment refers to unsolicited and inappropriate remarks and physical touching in the work environment. We have a lot of work to do in this area."

In speaking of workplace exploitation, workers said that in the past they were routinely physically assaulted (slapping, hitting) and that verbal assaults were common disciplinary mechanisms. Verbal assaults referred to the use of extremely derogatory language by both male and female managers to discipline them. These verbal assaults were used to shame and discipline workers in front of their co-workers on the assembly lines. Respect for one's family remained a vital structuration for these women. Female workers were offended by vulgar comments like "whore" made by supervisors, but they expressed more outrage when these comments addressed their mothers ("daughter of a whore"). However, older and younger workers responded differently to the question of what constituted sexual harassment at work. Sajeda, an older woman, echoed the sentiments expressed by many older female workers regarding vulgar language used by managers. She said, "I may have made a mistake at work, so my supervisor became angry and scolded me. But why should the manager use such language against my mother?"

I asked Sajeda, "Would it be acceptable for the manager to call you a 'whore' if you had made a mistake at work?"

Sajeda did not answer me directly. Instead, she looked away and murmured, "How can he say such words about my mother? She did not do anything."

Sajeda's answer indicated that while she felt offended by these vulgar comments aimed at disciplining workers, she did not have the lexical handle with which to articulate her pain. Gendered hierarchies in language shaped these older women's conduct, what they could say, when and how they could say it, and who would hear their pain. Not all the older workers I met had similar views. Some were courageous and spoke back to supervisors when they were insulted or saw a fellow worker humiliated. However, that was a small number of older women. I noticed that the younger women were more aware of their rights in the workplace and had developed a stronger sense of self-worth than was found in the older workers. As twenty-one-year-old Yasmin said to me, "If a supervisor speaks to me vulgarly, I will report him to the manager."

Later I met Selina, a thirty-two-year-old garment worker who was an outspoken opponent of sexual harassment. Selina had a bachelor's degree, which was unusual among workers. She knew labor laws and could argue her case with factory management and the police. Selina told us how she had the line supervisor at her factory fired over sexual harassment. In her factory, the supervisor would sexually harass a young woman. The woman asked Selina for help. A few days later, Selina saw the supervisor go to the woman and touch her and make obscene gestures. When Selina saw this, she went to him and slapped him. She called him "a son of a pig" and took him to the manager's office and explained what had occurred. After listening to her complaint, the manager fired him.

When I asked Selina how she found the courage to slap her supervisor and get him fired, she said that she found the courage by working at the factory and observing the sexual harassment faced by workers. Eventually, she decided to take on a leadership role among the workers in her factory. She said that through her work, she met different classes of people, including local politicians, whom she could call on for help to resolve work-related incidents. Local politicians recognize the organizing power of garment workers from their street demonstrations. They listen to the garment worker leaders (women like Selina); they also mediate between factory owners and workers, and when elections are held they lobby workers for votes. It is a symbiotic relation between local politicians seeking votes and factory leaders responding to harassment cases at work. Yasmin and Selina both exhibited a moral and political subjectivity that gave them the wherewithal to fight an unjust system that harassed and exploited women.

CHANGING SOCIAL AND FAMILY DYNAMICS

Migration of unmarried young women to the city has stretched and transformed the rural family organization, but familial reciprocal ties have not withered away. Modern urban survival needs have resulted in new networks of support for these women, but these reciprocal relations are now negotiated through the exchange of money; that is, kin relations are increasingly monetized. Almost every worker I met had a family member already living in the city. Initially, the women lived with relatives as they searched for work. Once they found work, they moved to a slum close to the factory where they worked. Then the normative cycle of life would begin. They would fall in love, get married, have children, get separated, remarry, become abandoned again or widowed, until they were aged out of work.

Figure 13. A narrow corridor separates the small, windowless rooms that are the workers' living quarters.

The ideal income-generating model for the rural family is to send at least one son as a migrant worker overseas and a young daughter to the garment factories. Rural families participate in the extensive microfinance programs available in Bangladesh, and the families accumulate debt that the overseas migrant son or garment worker daughter helps to pay off. In exchange, the extended family takes over some of the social reproduction duties, such as raising the children in the village. While this is a symbiotic system, it has toxic effects on these young women's lives. Women working as garment workers are seen as conduits to income for the family that makes constant demands on them for money. One woman described her situation as between a rock and a hard place (*chipar moddhyo*). However, their strong code of moral subjectivity ("I am a dutiful daughter") made them disinclined to criticize their parents, and their inability to fulfill their parents' demands caused them shame and anguish.

Work and wages offered the women a sense of agency that they had previously lacked in their rural habitations. The self as a semi-autonomous subject—this is who I am, this is what I can do—also remained an important structuration in their lives, linking them to familial obligations, especially for the older workers. For example, an older worker in my interview group raised four of her co-wife's children. She was proud of educating and marrying off her stepdaughters to men with good prospects with her hard-earned money. She was not resentful of her co-wife, who took care of her when she came as a young bride into the household, nor did she expect any monetary compensation for spending money on her stepchildren. She said, "Allah gave me the means to help them. I feel happy about it." That is, economic considerations structured their lives, but they did not fully encompass their lives. These networks of caring and being cared for are essential to the well-being of these working-class women. The women contained within them a "residue of hope" as a palimpsest, where the new and the old ways become fused, displacing and remaking new structures of being.

In this urban dynamic, associational relationships were fragile, leading to a level of anonymity that was absent in their rural homes. As workers changed factories and moved out of their slum, they no longer kept in touch with their former neighbors. Women who had walked together to work every day would lose contact once their former co-worker moved out of the slum. The typical answer to their now-absent neighbor's whereabouts was, "She left; we do not know where she went." There may have been instances where workers who were moving out had instructed their neighbors not to reveal their new location. Sometimes the women fled a domestic violence situation or wanted to escape a moneylender, and they would depart suddenly without the foreknowledge of their neighbors. Thus, a variety of motivations were at play in workers leaving a slum. This lack of interest in their former neighbors was a recurrent theme in urban lives. Life moved at a fast pace for these workers. New demands on their time soon replaced the memory of their former companions. Unlike rural relationships, these associational relationships were not durable; they were weak and expendable.

The factory women lived in the slums that have grown around the factories. These city slums have developed without proper accommodations for the sudden influx of millions of workers and their family members. The slums are filthy and have too many people living in tight spaces. Their quarters are noisy, and verbal disagreements over access to restricted shared facilities (kitchen and bathrooms) are routine occurrences. These shantytowns are often filled with noxious fumes from nearby ponds into which the factories release untreated effluents. The drains around the slums are clogged with waste, posing a health hazard to the inhabitants. In these slums, a narrow corridor in the middle separates small rooms on either side of the one-story settlements. The rooms are made from concrete or tin with corrugated tin roofs. The typical room measures ten by twelve feet and is shared by four to six single workers. Families with children also live in these single rooms, and they often sublet to a couple of workers to earn supplemental income. Sometimes, a garment worker lives in a cupboard-like space that is called a pocket-room inside the larger room. Families often rent to single male and female workers, which is a novel living arrangement. The landlord and his family (husband, wife, children) and non-kin male and female workers all share the same room for sleeping, eating, and leisure activities. Explaining this rental situation to me, one landlord said that his wife and the female garment worker slept on the bed at night, while the male worker slept with him on the floor. He added that proper decorum was always maintained in his household. He said, "The garment workers tend to work late, so we [the family] eat and go to sleep before they usually arrive. Rents are very high, so people have to adjust. What choice do we

Figure 14. A ten-by-twelve-foot bedroom shared by a garment worker's family of five plus two subletters. The pillows indicate the number of people who sleep in this tiny room. The TV is a ubiquitous feature in workers' homes, their primary source of entertainment.

have?" These are situational living arrangements that are reshaping the way women and men interact in the slums.

Family

While migration has stretched workers' physical proximity to their extended families, the life of the nuclear family has not completely dissolved. Instead, the nuclearization of the family has gradually encroached into their urban lives, disturbing prevailing kin relations. White has noted how in villages the "cultural norm of a joint family household . . . is being gradually eroded, as more separate ('nuclear') households become the norm."[11] In rural society there are usually three to four small units, based on the number of sons, that all face the family courtyard. Individual sons live with their families in these separate households. But decisions pertaining to the family, marriage, divorce, sale of land, education, and migration are all discussed by the extended family in the courtyard. The nuclearization of the family in the urban slums is more radical, because there is no shared space and the extended families do not encounter each other.

In the survey noted earlier, 59 percent of the women lived in nuclear family settings but maintained close ties with their parents and in-laws in the village. They spoke to family members on the phone and visited them during the Muslim high holidays. This is not the nuclear family of Western industrialization. Instead, rural and urban life commingled, both challenging conventional understandings of family, making women into de facto heads of households, and calibrating new social norms. Among the older women with adult sons raised in the city, I observed a new phenomenon that more closely resembled the Western nuclear family unit. The women expected that their sons would live with them and take care of their elderly parent. I found that their sons tended to marry women they had met in the city and fallen in love with, and later chose to live independently with their spouses. While they may financially support their parents, emotionally their attention diverted to their nuclear families. This disruption in familial arrangements from joint to nuclear settings had diverse consequences on the lives of the older women, which I discuss in chapters 4 and 5.

In examining this new urban nuclear household in the making, I was interested in mapping the gender dynamics around housework.

In the survey, 59 percent of women surveyed said that their husbands and children helped with housework. As noted earlier, most of these women surveyed were young and married, and many had met their spouses through romantic alliances formed in the city. Within the younger generation, especially among those couples in which both husband and wife worked in the factory, there was a shared household mechanism at play. In an interview, a young woman said, "I cook the evening meal before I leave for work in the morning; my husband warms the food and feeds our children in the evening." Her husband, who was sitting next to her, said that the income she made from working overtime at the factory enabled the family to have some additional comforts, so he was happy to do the chores when she could not manage. While the gendered expectations around women's work (she is expected to cook the meal) had not changed, the man's role had shifted. He now participated in housework by taking care of the children and feeding them. In another interview, a young unmarried male worker told me that he expected his wife to do all the chores and "wash his feet with warm water" when he came home. In all probability, the man was exhibiting a hypermasculinity in front of two female researchers asking him questions about women and factory work, questions he may have found emasculating. In the past, men were asked about jobs and money, and women were asked about reproduction, child care, and housework. Now that paradigm has shifted as women join the labor market and often earn more than their spouses.

DYNAMICS OF CLASS AND CONSUMER CULTURE

Sherry Ortner, in her analysis of class in American society, has called "ideology" its unique characteristic.[12] While class in European societies is more status-bound and rigid, the United States has always "glorified opportunity and mobility, more open to individual achievement than it really is."[13] In the United States, people do not believe that they are stuck in the class into which they were born. In contrast, Bangladeshi society is deeply hierarchical, and social mobility is limited. However, these garment workers in many ways mimicked the chemical workers in Elizabeth, New Jersey, whom Ortner writes about. These workers rejected the term "working class" and saw themselves as "middle class," in contrast to people below them on the social scale, whom they designated as "lower class."[14] Leela Fernandes and Patrick Heller have defined the middle class through the concept of "class-in-practice," that is, "a class that is defined by its politics and the everyday practices through which it reproduces its privileged position."[15] The garment workers also approximated the idea of a "class-in-practice" since they demarcated their identities through the practice of the everyday from the work life to the nonwork life.

In Bangladeshi society there are two categories of the middle class, the old and the new. The high mark of the old middle class in Bangladesh is education, civil service, nationalist politics emerging from the 1952 Language Movement and the Liberation War of 1971, and the possession of cultural symbols of arts, music, and literature. This is a salariat class. The new middle class, which emerged in the 1980s, is an aspirational class that derives its power from the market and the remittances from overseas migrant workers. According to Raka Ray and Seemin Quayum, "the middle classes practice certain methods of exclusion on the civil and the political sphere that reaffirm their supremacy while ensuring that the boundaries separating them from the lower classes remain continually drawn."[16] As more people from the lower socioeconomic ranks enter the job market and middle-class aspirations, anxieties around the loss of authority and separation between the classes heightens. Take, for example, the comment a domestic worker made to the middle-class woman who employed her: "The TVs in my slum are fancier than the one in your house." These TVs are bought with migrant workers' remittances. For the young woman, it signaled a leveling of some of the material distinctions between her and her employer, whereas for her employer it indicated the blurring of social categories that separated her from the "servant." The young woman was later fired for forgetting her place in the social order.

What was the meaning of class for these garment workers? As factory workers, they did not have the education or the social status of the professional middle class composed of teachers, bankers, lawyers, doctors, engineers, accountants, scientists, managers, and government bureaucrats. They were part of a new middle class emergent in rural families that was anchored to factory work and overseas remittances. They did not define themselves in cultural symbols; they thought of their middle-class identity in terms of money and commodities. To the garment factory workers, belonging to the middle class signaled the exit from their poverty-stricken rural backgrounds. Factory employment had moved them up the economic scale. Similarly, taking the label of middle class set them apart from the poorer people they encountered in the city. As garment workers they were not like the women who worked as day laborers, cleaners, maids, cooks, and the like. They had acquired skills. They worked in brick buildings operating complex machines that endowed them with a sense of pride and achievement when compared to their poorer rural and urban counterparts. They were the new symbol of "Made in Bangladesh" that is youthful, shiny, and hopeful. The combination of these factors gave them a sense of a new world of opportunities and their entrance into middle-class status.

One afternoon I met with twelve young women at a focused group interview. These women were between the ages of eighteen and thirty, and on average they had worked between five and ten years. We sat in a circle and talked about their work and nonwork lives. At some point, I asked the women about their class identity. I noticed that the women referred to themselves as middle class (*moddho bittyo*) and not working class (*kormojibi*). Unlike the older workers, who were mostly illiterate, the younger generation of workers had the benefit of at least a grade 8 education. Access to education had heightened their sense of self and achievement. They saw themselves as similar to the college-educated middle-class girls they encountered in the city. The combined effects of education (most of the younger women had on average a grade 8 education) and globalization had opened new ideas and pathways for these younger workers. They were moving up the economic ladder.

Aspirations around class were manifested through sentiments expressed by these women such as "I work in an office" versus "I work in a factory." Working in an office was their preferred description for the kind of work they did and the class to which they aspired. Almost all the women I met said, "My children will not become factory workers," although most of them will end up in similar jobs. Class sentiments were also expressed through their desire for education. The women invested in the education of their children so they would move up the economic ladder. While some of the older women recognized that education was not the only key to upward mobility (one also needed social contacts that they lacked), they still believed that education gave their children more options. So, they would incur debt to finance their children's college education. As for the younger women, many of them said that they plan to "marry up"—to marry a manager or a line supervisor or a migrant worker in Malaysia or the Middle East. Migrant workers are considered as desirable spouses because of their ability to earn higher wages overseas.

During our conversation, I asked what they would do should they lose their factory jobs. The women said they would find work in an office or in a retail store, both occupations signifying class mobility. When I asked them if they would consider working as domestic workers if they failed to find an office job, all of them were offended by my question. Some of them said, "We do not do that kind of work." In their worldview, they had migrated from domestic work through their factory work and they have socially distanced themselves from those lower-class people who work as household help. In reality, however, the retail and hospitality industry in Dhaka cannot accommodate the number of unemployed factory workers seeking employment, and many of them end up as domestic workers once they are laid off.

Wages were also constitutive of how the older and younger generation of workers constructed their classed possibilities. Longtime workers had entered at very low wages. Between 1994 to 2006, wages were held at $11 per month. Many of them exited soon after wages were raised to $67 per month in 2013. The younger workers I met entered the job market either at $22 a month in 2006 or $30 a month in 2010. Monthly wages were raised to $67 in 2013 and to $90 in 2018, so within a shorter time their earnings had gone up considerably. The rise in income from practically zero in the village to $30 to $67 to $90 in 2018 gave these young women a sense of upward mobility. A factory owner who spoke to me about his young workers said, "The workers nowadays desire Samsung cell phones, flashy clothes, and a more improved lifestyle. Sometimes, I cannot visually distinguish between a middle-class college woman and a female factory worker."

For the young workers, a middle-class identity was also facilitated through the fragmentation in their work life. Factories readily fired workers if they failed to show up for work due to illness or a sick child. The younger women also left factories when they found a new job at another factory at a slightly higher pay. These horizontal moves made the younger women feel that they were learning new skills (moving from stitching zippers to ironing, for example) and becoming more upwardly mobile. If the younger workers had entered middle-class status, the older workers had a more complex relationship to class. They saw themselves as part of the lower classes where scarcity and poverty dictated their life outcomes. Even as factory workers, the older workers could barely cover their room and board in the city. Many of the older workers said that if they lost their factory jobs they would first look for work in another factory. If they failed to find one, they would work as a domestic worker.

These older women did not have a substantial arc of change in their class identity, whereas the younger women did. For the older women, education for their children was the pathway to class mobility. They wanted to educate them beyond high school so their sons and daughters could achieve middle-class status as teachers, nurses, technicians, managers, and IT specialists. With neoliberal development, the number of private universities and technical schools has grown exponentially in Bangladesh. It has led to a democratization of education that has enabled children of the working class to attend college and gain new ideas of self, increased social knowledge, and income potential. Globalization and overseas work opportunities have also broadened these younger workers' horizons in ways that were not available to older workers. Nowadays, factory women increasingly want to go overseas for work. Many Chinese and Indian industrialists have opened garment factories on the island of Mauritius in the Indian Ocean, and they hire workers from Bangladesh to work there.

One day I met Maleka, a garment factory worker in her late twenties. Her husband operated a small dry goods store. They had a ten-year-old son and a twelve-year-old daughter. In comparison to most workers, they were comfortably off. Maleka had received land from her father, who was a well-to-do farmer, and she and her husband had built a small two-bedroom brick house. The house had electricity, piped water, and a flush toilet. One room was rented, giving them additional income. When I met them, husband and wife had constant arguments over Maleka's work. She wanted to go to Mauritius to work in a garment factory. Her cousin was working there and made three times what one could earn in a factory in Bangladesh. Maleka was an ambitious woman, but her aspirations far exceeded what her husband expected of a dutiful wife. One day, he hit her. On that day, I met Maleka and found her lying on her bed with a bandage on her head. She said that she was planning to go away to her father's house.

Later that day I met her husband at his shop. He was a short-statured man and soft spoken. In my opinion, he loved his wife but could not control her. Maleka was a strong-willed woman. When I asked him if he had hit his wife, he was embarrassed and admitted to hitting her. He said, "I was so angry with her, I saw red. So, I hit her. That was very wrong of me." Then he continued, "When I was struggling to build my business, I allowed my wife to work in a factory. Now, my income from my shop is stable and I can provide for my family." This was said with a lot of pride. He continued:

> We own our house. It is not fancy but it is our own. I want my wife to leave her factory job and focus on raising the kids. City life is dangerous for children as they grow into their teenage years. In the city, you have drugs, gambling, and human trafficking. A mother needs to be at home watching over her children's education and whereabouts. My wife is at the factory all day, and I am at my shop. My mother who used to watch over the children is now very ill and bedridden. My children are growing up on their own. My wife not only wants to work, but she also wants to go overseas for a couple years. How is that right?

I asked her husband, "If you had the option to go and work overseas and leave your wife and children behind, would you do it?"

He replied, "I would not go, because we are doing well financially. However, it is the duty of men to take care of their families financially. Those men who cannot provide for their families should go overseas. But a woman's job is to raise the children. If women also start leaving for overseas, then who will take care of the family?"

A couple of weeks later, I heard that husband and wife had reconciled. Maleka's father had intervened and forced her to give up her plans. Maleka's desire to go overseas was not only about earning more money, but seeing the wider world of opportunities. This world came into her house every day via TV shows and gossip she heard in the neighborhood about other women who had gone overseas. It appeared grand and promising. For the first time in her life, she felt that this world was within her grasp. In Maleka's case, her family intervened to crush her desires because of what they saw as her duties as wife and mother. At the end of this chapter I discuss Rabeya, whose family actively assisted in her travel to Jordan for work. Families carefully calculate the social costs of work, asking how much she can earn and what would happen to their reputation, before allowing their daughters to go overseas.

Consumer Culture

According to World Bank data, the per capita income of Bangladesh went from $306 in 1990 to $1,698 in 2018, which was largely a consequence of the garment industry.[17] While the free-market economy has ushered in a tsunami of changes around the aspirations of middle-classness for its large public, these sentimental structures are "difficult . . . to narrate, for all these elements are intertwined, mutually constitutive, permeable and dynamically in flux."[18] In recent years, globalization and the population's increased purchasing power have led to the introduction of lower-end shopping malls, restaurants, and beauty parlors that cater to garment workers. A major change in the lives of these working-class women is the presence of consumer culture, from shops to restaurants to day outings. The young workers are growing up in an era of rampant consumerism, television advertisements selling commodities, the sparkling new malls in the city, restaurants and shops, all of which beckon to the consumer. They have more disposable income compared to the older workers and can participate in a consumer culture that feeds their desires.

On Friday evenings (the Muslim sabbath and the weekly day off for the workers), consumer culture awakens. In my research area, the main street transformed into a market with food stalls and temporary shops selling a battery of consumer goods, from clothes, jewelry, household pots and pans, children's toys, and all sorts of cheaply manufactured Chinese bric-a-brac. In the evenings, the young women came out in hordes. Dressed to the nines, they walked the streets, flirted with the neighborhood men, and shopped at the marketplace. The young women haggled with shop owners. They bought inexpensive items—earrings, cosmetics, hair clips, clothes. One could see them looking at the shop owner's mirror to check out a pair of earrings. Young women sat with their boyfriends holding hands and eating snacks at the various food stalls. Mothers with children also walked the neighborhood malls, purchasing toys, clothes, and chocolates for their kids. This is one of the rare instances of euphoric happiness among the workers that I noticed. It was their day off, and they were out to have some fun after a long week of grueling work.

Compared to the new generation of workers, the older, aged-out workers lacked the means to participate in consumer culture. These older workers had adult children whose education they had to pay for, whereas the younger workers were mostly single or had small children. The meager wages of older workers went toward room and board, and what they could save went toward their children's education. These older women ate very simple meals and seldom bought clothes or trinkets for themselves. They forsook simple comforts like a basic platform bed (*chowki*). Instead, they slept on the hard floor on a thin mattress. All the accoutrements of a modern lifestyle that are increasingly available to the industrial working class, such as a TV or a refrigerator, were absent in their lives.

A key source of entertainment for the young workers was the Indian serial dramas broadcast on TV, and they followed the Bollywood fashion industry closely. Moreover, given their exposure to TV, where they watched middle-class women in serials, they were exposed to ideas of the good life through advertisements that target middle-class lifestyles. In fact, at the time of my research there was not a single TV serial about the life of a garment worker, although millions of women worked in the garment industry. Some of the younger women I met bought a new set of *shalwar kameez* every month. Trade union leader Nazma Akter pointed out that a majority of these young women do not save; after sending money home to their parents, they spend most of their money on consumer goods or buying a new dress every month. She said, "They earn taka 6,000 a month, and buy a dress for taka 3,000. Then they go into debt trying to pay for their living expenses. I try to teach them through my organization about the importance of savings. I tell them my life story of sacrifice. I started as a garment worker. Now I am a successful trade union leader. I can buy two hundred dresses if I want. But I still don't. Thrift is key to success."

The presence of garment workers with disposable income has led to a rise in beauty parlors in Dhaka. Younger garment workers often go to beauty parlors to shape their eyebrows, which is one of the most affordable services available. They put on colorful nail polish and bright lipstick. Sometimes they even get their hair cut and have facials at these beauty salons. The visible changes in the lives of these working-class women have not gone unnoticed by the clergy, who continue to speak against women straying from Islam through factory work. One such cleric is Sheikh Abdur Razzak Bin Yousuf, who has a huge following on YouTube for his sermons. In a sermon titled "How Will Women Dress?" he tells the male congregation that women must not go to beauty parlors, put on nail polish, or shape their eyebrows.[19] Instead, he asks women to use henna on their hair, nails, and lips. Here he also offers an indigenous critique of consumerism—that is, he instructs his congregation to reject commercially produced goods and find their equivalents in indigenous commodities, such as replacing nail polish with henna that is locally available and inexpensive. He tells his adherents to remember that the Prophet Muhammad applied henna on his hair, and that therefore henna is sunna—a practice of the Prophet that constitutes a model for all Muslims.

On initial examination, these comments and the cleric's manner of addressing women are misogynistic and vulgar. However, when we locate his comments within the beauty regimes of young garment workers, more complex interpretations emerge. From the perspective of the clergy, these women's life choices make it very difficult for their congregation, the madrassa-educated men, to support these desires in their wives. Madrassa-educated men usually get jobs teaching the Quran to young people as private tutors where the pay is nominal. Many of them live in the slums where garment workers live. A Quran tutor's wife now witnesses a lower-status woman, a garment worker, looking smarter than her and demands money for visits to beauty parlors, cosmetics, shampoo, new clothes. How can a teacher afford these small luxuries? What we are witnessing is the fast incursion of a new world into the private sphere that is changing social dynamics, particularly in areas that affect gender roles. This new world is also indicative of men's loss of control over women, creating anxieties that finds expression in toxic masculinity and misogynistic behavior. These are the unexpected contours of Appadurai's modernity at large and Freeman's aspirations that are conjured, released, and brutally suppressed and are "critical dimensions of subjective meaning making."[20]

Entrepreneurship

In her work on Barbadian workers, Freeman notes that neoliberal sentiments have spawned a whole industry of spas, gyms, New Age and alternative churches, and therapeutic massage parlors—all of which "signal radically new domains of experience for this Caribbean island."[21] The Barbadian workers who had entered the lower tiers of middle-class society felt that their increased income could usher in new lifestyles. Freeman remarks that these sentiments structure ways of being that are not solely tied to income generation; higher income creates new imaginaries about oneself and one's gendered and classed possibilities. She concluded that entrepreneurship came to symbolize "a mode of labor and a way of life" for her Barbadian interlocutors.[22] In Sri Lanka, Sandya Hewamanne has examined how former factory workers who returned to their villages transferred skills learned from factory work in Free Trade Zones to entrepreneurial activities. She contends that "their experience at the FTZ, which generates savings (besides allowing them to develop a set of skills, connections and know-how), and their ability to manipulate this monetary capital by combining it with varied forms of capital available locally are what makes most former workers economically and socially successful within village contexts."[23]

Neither Freeman's notion of entrepreneurship as a new structure of being nor Hewamanne's study of former workers as successful entrepreneurs in village society was applicable to the Bangladeshi workers. Garment workers did not aspire for entrepreneurial activities that they saw as risky with uncertain payoffs. Instead, they opted for the security of guaranteed monthly wages. Unlike their Sri Lankan counterparts, they could not save due to their low wages and the high cost of living. However, there were a few women who took on entrepreneurial risks to increase their economic opportunities. In the early phase of the garment industry, ancillary economic options were few. In the post-2010 environment when growth spiked, many new businesses that feed into the garment industry started up, providing some opportunities to workers. However, starting a business required capital and family support that many workers lacked.

I met few women who were able to create small businesses from the capital or skills from factory work. One young woman I met had left factory work and started a small tailoring shop that her uncle helped manage in the male-dominated local market. She employed two young men as her assistants. I met an older, aged-out female worker who started providing cooked meals to young male workers in the evenings to supplement her income. Initially, her business was going well. Six months later I returned to her house and found her crying. Her husband, who had earlier abandoned her, had returned and broken up her meal service business. She said that he did not want unmarried men coming into their house. A female worker in her thirties raised capital through family members and opened a tailoring shop that her husband managed while she worked at a factory as a sewing operator. In the evenings, she would also work in the shop. This was one of the rare successful independent businesses that I saw. Her tailoring shop allowed her to move out of the slum into an eight-story apartment building where she lived with her husband, her children, and her mother, sister, and brother. The

Figure 15.
An entrepreneurial garment worker in front of her tailoring shop.

apartment was modern: it had two bedrooms, tiled floors, decorative wooden doors, plumbing, refrigerator, a TV, and a kitchen with piped gas. Her ability to be successful was due to a cohesive family unit that planned, saved, and worked together to provide for their future.

The ability to run a successful small business depended on three critical factors: support from family members who saw it as joint income; some seed capital that the person had accumulated or received from family; and knowledge of how markets operated locally, that is, how many shops the local neighborhood could sustain. Successful individual enterprises were rare; those that succeeded were based on collective effort. This point brings me to the final section of this chapter—the case studies of two young workers: Happy, who worked as a recruiter for an outsourcing outfit that took overflow work from factories; and Rabeya, who went to Jordan in search of a better life. Their life stories illuminate many of the social strands that I have outlined in this chapter and indicate the paths some young women are taking in their encounters with globalization.

Happy: A Sub-subcontractor's Story

Under subcontracting, a parent company outsources all or part of an order to a subcontractor. All garment factories have at least one subcontractor who performs various specialized tasks for the parent firm. Subcontracting is conducted informally, without any written contract, making it difficult to track the labor conditions in these off-site places. Garment factories use subcontractors for core production and specialized activities such as printing, washing, and embroidery. The world of subcontracting is a gray area that often uses child labor under hazardous work conditions that violate labor codes. Factories use subcontractors to meet deadlines, reduce costs, and speed up production. Subcontracting displaces production risks and insecurities to workers further down the supply line. In these unregulated and shady environments, subcontracting also weakens workers' rights and ability to join trade unions.[24] I interviewed a total of seven men and women working in the subcontracting industry. Subcontracting is akin to a gig economy; many said that they find the hours flexible and earn more money working for a shorter time. But the work is irregular, and unlike factory work, there is no guaranteed monthly income for workers. During my meetings with workers, I met Happy, a twenty-eight-year-old garment worker who worked for a male subcontractor to recruit workers for his subcontracting business.

Happy grew up in Dhaka. When she was twelve years old, her father was involved in a traffic accident and went to prison. After that incident, Happy, who only had a grade 5 education, joined the garment factory to financially assist her family. She began as a helper at a rate of taka 600 a month in 2002. After working for five years, at age seventeen, she became a sewing operator. She married a construction worker, but after two years of marriage and the birth of two daughters, her marriage dissolved due to extreme abuse from her husband, who would burn her body with cigarettes.

The dissolution of her marriage affected her work at the factory; that is, her private live and her work life merged, creating chaos. In the space of two years she lost four jobs. Finally, at her fifth factory job, she met Dulal, a subcontractor. He worked for factories supplying clothes to overseas markets as well as the domestic market, making his income less dependent on the volatility of global market forces. Dulal was a former garment worker himself. He had saved money and started a small factory inside a flat with fifteen plain-stitch sewing machines and accessories to complete simple jobs such as stitching zippers and sewing pockets. Workers at his factory worked at a range of work activities that spanned from a single day to two weeks per job order. At Dulal's factory, some workers are full-time, others part-time. These part-time workers were garment workers who wanted to make additional money. They would come in the evening after their day shift and work part of the night.

Within a short time, Happy became Dulal's primary supplier of workers. During the day she worked at her regular factory job until 5 p.m., and in the evening she worked at his factory until 11 p.m. Soon after joining his operation, she got the responsibility of finding short-term, skilled workers. Happy made an additional three to four thousand taka per month by working for him, raising her monthly income to taka 10,000. Happy said, "In the subcontracting line of work, there are many opportunities. You can earn more money. But uncertainty is high in subcontracting work. Sometimes there is no work at Dulal's factory." Then she paused and added, "If I didn't have a regular garment factory job, where would I get money at the end of the month to pay my bills?"

In response to my question of whether she ever wanted to become a subcontractor herself instead of being a supplier to a subcontractor, she replied, "We humans have many dreams, but how can I fulfill my dreams if I don't have capital?"

When I asked what she thought would happen to her when she was around forty-five years old and the factory would no longer employ her, she laughed and said, "I don't know. Allah will look after me. I have two daughters. Hopefully, I can educate them well, and they will get good jobs, but not at a garment factory, no, never. They will look after me, and if they don't, I will live alone."

I asked her, "What are the changes that you have seen in your life from working in a factory?"

Happy said, "If by change you mean whether I have been able to save money, then there is no change in my life. I have to pay for my elderly parents' health-care needs. Sometimes my mother falls sick and needs hospitalization, and half of my salary goes toward her medical expenses. I have to pay for my daughters' education. People say that happiness and sadness are like the wind flowing through peoples' lives. Sometimes you have good news, at other times you have bad news. So far in my life, I have only had bad news. However, there is one change that has occurred to me. In the past, I didn't understand much, but now I do. I now know how not to trust everybody in the city. You could say I have become wiser or perhaps more cynical about life in this unhappy city."

Rabeya's Life in Jordan

In contrast to Happy, Rabeya's story takes us to a garment factory in Jordan. On October 29, 2017, I met with Rabeya, a twenty-nine-year-old garment worker who had returned to Dhaka after working in Jordan. She was divorced and had a grade 9 education. Rabeya's story is a window into the decision processes that structure these younger women's life trajectories as they seek their fortunes overseas. Rabeya was the daughter of a poor rickshaw puller. Her family consisted of her parents, one brother, and one sister. Her father's inability to sustain five people on his meager earnings made Rabeya join a garment factory at the age of eighteen. Rabeya was a quick learner, and within a few months she became a sewing operator. After working at the factory for seven years, Rabeya married her cousin. Within a few days of marriage, her husband started to demand money from her father, but her poor father did not have money to give him. In anger, her husband would physically beat her. Finally, unable to take the beatings any longer, she spoke to her parents. They suggested that she divorce her husband. So, Rabeya divorced her husband, returned to her family, and gave her parents control over her income. Rabeya's moral subjectivity as a dutiful daughter was pronounced, and she would fulfill her parents' demands before meeting her own.

Rabeya had a female cousin who found a job at a garment factory in Mauritius through the government agency known as Bangladesh Overseas Employment and Services Limited. In three years, her cousin had earned a lot of money. Rabeya wanted to seek her fortune overseas as well. Her parents agreed to her going overseas because it meant more money for the family. Through the German Technical Training Center in Dhaka, she was recruited on a three-year contract to work in a garment factory owned by the Chinese in Jordan.

Rabeya had a very positive attitude toward her work life in Jordan. She went with a group of fifty female workers. In Jordan, factory management provided meals and housing to all its workers, which allowed them to save money. The same compound housed the factory and the workers' living quarters. Once they arrived, they were taken to a five-story building for housing. The first two floors were for male workers, and the rest were for female workers. In each room, four bunk beds housed eight workers who had to share one bathroom. Upon arrival, they first rested in their designated rooms. The Chinese hired several Bangladeshi managers to work as translators with the workers. Later, they went to the factory where the work procedures were explained. The rules stated that men could come to women's rooms, but women could not go to the men's rooms. "Men and women found ways to amuse themselves," she added, smiling mischievously.

After two days of training, the women started work at the factory. Rabeya soon learned that four workers from their team had been disqualified on medical grounds and sent back to Bangladesh. Realizing that they too could be sent home at any time, the workers became anxious. They met with the Bangladesh country representative at the factory, but he assured them that they had all passed the medical exam. The factory manager was a Chinese woman. She did not verbally or physically abuse them, a typical management pattern in Bangladeshi factories; instead, she threatened them with deportation if they failed to work fast.

Rabeya was hired as a line supervisor at taka 17,000 per month, which was almost a threefold increase over her monthly wages in Bangladesh. As line supervisor, her job was to ensure that by 4 p.m. the production goals for the day were met. For overtime she was paid taka 100 per hour. Sometimes workers were taken from their factory to work in other factories. Apart from the Chinese factory manager's threats of deportation, Rabeya did not find the factory environment hostile. The workday went from 8 a.m. to 4 p.m., for a total of eight hours. At the end of the workday they could work an additional hour overtime. Other than that, all workers left after they finished their target and returned to their dormitory. She also mentioned that unlike factories in Bangladesh, supervisors did not walk up and down the lines harassing workers. Supervisors in Jordan had a specific spot where they would sit, and if they saw any activity out of the ordinary, they would speak to that particular worker. Workers could talk to workers next to them and use the restroom as often as needed. Each line had a separate area for drinking water. The factory also provided breakfast, a tea break, and a late-afternoon snack. From her perspective, management had thought about the worker's nutritional needs and caloric intake. The factory prepared decent food for their meals.

In comparing her experiences between Bangladesh and Jordan, Rabeya described the difference as "significant." For example, the level of industrial equipment noise was low in Jordan, and managers did not speak loudly or offensively to the workers. She mentioned that supervisors in Bangladesh were very abusive to workers because factory owners tell them to discipline workers through harsh language. The assembly lines were also different in these two countries. In Bangladesh, the smaller assembly lines have fifty to sixty workers and the longer lines have seventy to eighty workers. In Jordan, the lines were twenty-five to thirty workers. Rabeya recalled the Jordanian work environment as pleasant; there were not too many workers packed into small spaces. At the end of each line, there were fans that kept the room cool. Rabeya also added that in Bangladesh, the hourly target was about 120 pieces per worker, whereas in Jordan the target was 60 pieces.

In the first seven months, the factory sent seven workers back to Bangladesh. Rabeya said they would hear the name of a worker being announced over the intercom during work. The worker would have to leave her station and go to the manager's office. From there, the worker was taken to the dormitory to get her clothes and then bused to the airport. As a result of these actions, the workers lived in a state of fear. At any time, they could be called and deported. These kinds of tactics were deployed to discipline workers to work very hard. After a significant number of workers were deported, some workers started to speak out. One day, all the workers decided to stop work. They got up from their stations and stood next to their machines. This led to an argument with the Chinese factory manager. During this work interruption, someone informed the Jordanian police about worker unrest at the factory, and police came and surrounded the building. After listening to the complaints, they took the manager to jail and the factory was closed. Within a month and a half, all the workers were sent home. Rabeya was paid for twelve months of work, although she had worked for only seven months. After she returned from Jordan as an experienced worker, she joined a factory at taka 7,000 a month, which was low compared to her wages in Jordan. As for future plans, Rabeya was planning to go overseas again, this time to Mauritius.

CONCLUSION

This chapter introduced the changing landscape of factory work and urban life for garment workers in three broad categories—family life, factory work, and class aspirations. Compared to the older workers, the younger workers were more exposed to new ideas, lifestyles, and consumer goods. They had higher education levels and operated in an environment where trade unions were more active, inculcating in them a durable sense of their rights as workers. They also exhibited stronger economic and aspirational subjectivities due to the higher wages they earned compared to the older women, who viewed their world as extremely limited. However, one's ability to be a more independent subject is contingent on multiple factors. Factory work in and of itself (women learning to live on their own, forming new relationships in a city, working in a factory, walking the city, meeting other workers, sharing stories and experiences, and so forth) provides a space for greater social awareness and confidence among the women, but that can get foreclosed by the precarious conditions of the global supply chain of production and the social constraints that they face. The next chapter introduces the emergent geography of workers' experiences with romance, marriage, and sexuality.

4

CHANGING NORMS OF ROMANCE, MARRIAGE, AND SEXUALITY

WHILE THOUSANDS OF RESEARCH PAPERS, policy documents, and news reports are written about these women's public lives as industrial garment workers, scant literature is available about their private lives of affection, desires, love, care, and happiness. This chapter addresses one of the key questions that shaped my research: What are these women's nonwork or private lives like? That is, how do both younger and older women experience the intimate sphere of love, marriage, and romance? To ethnographically study their private lives, I discuss the following themes—romantic love, sexuality, changing marriage and divorce norms, causes of marital discords and abandonments, family courts, and older female workers' and males' attitudes toward female sexual autonomy. The chapter ends with two case studies: one of a garment worker couple, Kajol and Babul, who found love and mutual respect in this dystopic world, and the other of an older woman, Moni, whose affective desires were brutally crushed by men and a society that saw her as a transgressor.

Arjun Appadurai writes about globalization as the flow of people, goods, and ideas across national borders, creating "scapes"—shifting landscapes where movements create mobile belongings.[1] Following Appadurai, many scholars have examined a variety of "marriage-scapes" and "sex-scapes" across national borders and among different occupations and social classes.[2] The marriage-scape in the context of Bangladeshi garment workers is patriarchal, monetized, and hierarchical. Unlike Denise Brennan's study of Dominican women who perform love in order to get money, gifts, and potential marriage offers from men, the Bangladeshi garment worker gives her wages to the man in exchange for an intimacy and sexual security that is often short-lived.[3]

In speaking of the commodification of intimate relations, Nicole Constable points "to the ways in which intimacy or intimate relations can be treated, understood, or thought of as if they have entered the market: are bought or sold; packaged and advertised; fetishized, commercialized, consumed or assigned values and prices, and linked in many cases to transnational mobility and migration, echoing a global flow of goods."[4] While commodification as a system of "assigning market value to goods and services" that were previously outside a market economy increasingly subsumes the care economy as it gets monetized through migration, I argue that the interiority of these women's feelings is irreducible to commodification.[5] I evaluate the garment worker's longing for intimacy—touch, embrace, arousal, gifts, care, and conversation—as residing outside the reach of the market. It is a deeply held private place of emotional sustenance. The roman-scape of the Bangladeshi garment worker is nestled in emotive urges released by migration and the profusion of new models of intimacy available in a media-saturated world.

To comprehend these erotic feelings released by the forces of globalization in garment women's lives, I turn to Carla Freeman's exemplary article "Feeling Neoliberal," which takes the feminist anthropology conversation beyond the theoretical parameters of affect theory, which have primarily shaped the discussion around optimism and its brutal suppression. Freeman examines neoliberalism as the crucible where "feelings of intimacy, tenderness, happiness, and hope" converge and disrupt the prevailing social order.[6] She argues that in the process of disruption, neoliberalism also creates possibilities of healing and happiness that remain invisible to cynical reason. She moves the discussion of neoliberal affect theory to highlight through "ethnographic specificity that ambivalence and hope are neither generic nor singularly gloomy signposts of neoliberal 'aspirational normativity' and that their significance transcends mere 'projection of sustaining but unworkable fantasy.'"[7] In this respect, ethnography can be productive in analyzing minute shifts in social life by attending to these tiny sparks that animate emotions and examining how these sparks endure despite capitalism's crushing weight. In this chapter I illustrate through ethnography and case studies the cultural nuances of garment workers' struggle to craft meaningful lives through romantic love despite diminished possibilities.

The rapid spread of global capitalism has begun to dislodge the normative family and gender roles in Bangladeshi society. As more women work outside the home as factory workers, families have to adapt to changed expectations around women's conventional roles in society. As noted in previous chapters, many of these garment workers were abandoned by their husbands. As heads of household, these women have displaced male authority as the primary locus of power in the family. This reordering of gender roles introduces heightened antagonisms between the sexes and invents new social arrangements around family and the care economy. The burden of these social transformations is primarily borne by women who work outside the home.

The women and men I studied are heterosexual and reproduce the heteronormative patriarchal family, in which the lines between feminine and masculine duties and roles are clearly demarcated. In rural society, the man is the head of household and the family is organized as an extended family with rules of reciprocity regulating the behavior of its members. What I outline next are the prevailing norms of family life in Bangladesh, and it should be noted that these norms are being transformed under the pressures of global dislocations as family members migrate. In families, older members have higher status than younger members, and within that classification, men have higher status than women. With status comes responsibilities—the man as the head of household is the provider, the woman the nurturer. All members of the family are expected to respect the eldest living male and accept his word on marriage, inheritance, work, education, and so on. Women's roles are largely situated within the household, and women's mobility is strictly regulated by older members. In public, women are expected to be unobtrusive and maintain Muslim female decorum by covering their bodies properly, walking in small steps, and keeping their voices low. However, Bangladeshi women have not always accepted these gender rules silently; they have trespassed social conventions, often at great personal cost, as some of the case studies showed.

Births, marriages, divorces, separations, sexual violence, burials—these are all matters of community involvement. Families arrange the marriages of their young daughters and sons, and weddings are important village events. In these marital engagements, the bride's family inquire about the groom's family's social standing and the groom's income potential. Women are judged for their appearance, domestic skills, and character. In Bangladesh, Muslims observe both the dower (*mahr*), which is mandatory for all Muslim men, and the dowry, borrowed from Hindu religious practice. At the time of marriage, a Muslim man is expected to pay his wife the dower, an amount agreed upon by both families. However, the man and/or his family delays the payment of the dower by citing various excuses, and in most instances it is never paid to the wife. In many instances, the wife is forced to forgive the man the payment of dower. It is the exchange of the dowry (a Hindu custom)—the transfer of cash, gold, and physical resources from the bride's family to the groom's family—that has become the norm in Muslim marriages.[8] These dowry demands far exceed a family's ability to pay, resulting in spousal abuse, marital discord, and abandonment.

Divorces and separations are considered family affairs where the older members of the family determine the outcome. If the two parties cannot come to an amicable resolution, a village *shalish* (public adjudication) is held, and the community participates in the process. Nowadays, with the advent of courts in small towns, families often take these matters to be adjudicated by a presiding judge instead of the village *shalish*. During the peak of microcredit in the 1990s and early 2000s, NGOs, especially BRAC, taught rural women how to properly register marriages and divorces in order to instill in them their marital rights. These NGOs taught women and men that verbal divorce, the customary practice of a man saying "I divorce you" three times, was not legal according to the Muslim Family Laws Ordinance of 1961. A divorce had to go through proper procedures and could not be initiated arbitrarily by the husband.[9] Through the work of BRAC and other NGOs, general knowledge about the registration of marriages spread in rural areas. What is occurring, then, is a gradual displacement of decision making from family and community to the sphere of the courts, and a new rights-oriented legal subjectivity has emerged that is more pronounced among younger women.

ROMANTIC LOVE

One day, I was discussing the concept of romantic love with Lovely Yesmin. Lovely and I spoke about the upsurge in popularity of Valentine's Day among young garment workers. In Bangladesh it is called The Day of Love (Bhalobashar Din) and was popularized with globalization in the 1990s. Valentine's Day has introduced cultural idioms around love that are now mediated by the exchange of flowers, chocolates, and romantic cards. Men and women exchange trite images and memes on their cell phones such as "You are like a red rose" or a few melodies from a popular Bollywood love song. Speaking on this occasion, Lovely said, "On Valentine's Day garment workers come out in droves. We wear nice clothes, buy flowers, and chocolates. We hold hands and walk around town. Our boyfriends give us flowers, we give them flowers. Our demand for flowers is so great that the flower vendors cannot keep up with us." In our conversations, Lovely always underscored the ways garment workers were pioneering cultural forms and challenging society's tight grip on female sexuality. For her, these women were bold; they overcame countless impediments every day and still found pleasure in life. In our conversations, she referred to garment workers as the "real feminists."

In her earlier poetic works, written in the 1990s, Lovely wrote about the pathos and passions of the lives of garment workers. In her later works she is more political, which is a result of her ongoing work as a trade union leader. She uses her political imaginary not only in her activism for workers' rights, as the poem "I Am a Machine Operator" in the introduction shows, but as a radical critique of the vectors of capitalism—the state, factory owners, and global buyers. Written in plain language, her poetry holds a mirror to the consumers about their complicity in the oppression of workers. It was her love poetry, though, that became a window into the lives of garment workers and their passions and longings. This love is exhilarating and sometimes, as the case studies show, traumatizing.

There is an oversaturation of Indian popular culture in Bangladesh, and Lovely's poetic imagination is mediated by the cultural flows of Bollywood and Indian TV serials. Garment workers often spend their weekly day off watching a Bollywood movie or a serial drama on TV. These days children can speak fluently in Hindi, which they have absorbed from watching Indian TV shows. That is, a whole generation is growing up on a diet of Indian media culture, and their cultural references are drawn from these images. In her poem, Lovely speaks of a love that is globalized à la Appadurai, where imagination and affects are mediated by migration and media.[10] In writing her paean to love, "Krishno, the Lover," Lovely interchangeably uses three historical characters representing model lovers to speak of a woman's intense longing for romantic love—Krishno, the lover in Hindu mythology; Rasputin, the reputed lover of Empress Alexandra; and Sanjay, a Bollywood star famous for his starring roles as the ideal lover. It is a bizarre collage; one could call it a postmodern collage, but what it indicates is her exposure to global flows of ideas in the 1990s (the poem was written in 1994) when her world was suddenly inundated by new ideas and images. The woman that she writes about is an ordinary woman, a garment worker whose world is not full of shiny clothes and glittering objects.

> Krishno, the Lover
>
> Whether you are burned by sun
> Or soaked by rain
> You are my dark one.
> I have no words to describe
> How your beauty dazzles me
> How that blazer becomes you.
> Your hair outshines that of Bollywood star Sanjay
> Your eyes become Rasputin
> Your lips pull me in like a magnet
> When I touch you,
> I am maddened by the fragrance of jasmine
> There is no limit to my desire
> I want all of you
> Against the empty pages of the past
> Let life begin afresh.

After reading "Krishno," I asked Lovely what led her to write the poem. Lovely did not answer me directly. Instead, she replied, "We also have human emotions." Her wide eyes looked directly into my face, posing a question that made me face my limits: a working-class woman has to explain her emotions to the researcher, whereas a middle-class woman can dwell comfortably in her desire.

Conversations with Lovely opened a gateway to the passions and frailties that inform the lives of garment workers. Her poetry helped me see the garment worker as a multidimensional subject, one who was not only a worker who fought for her rights but also a woman who struggled with her desires and the emptiness that engulfed her life. This world of love and desire is trapped in the inescapable trauma of Berlant's cruel optimism that engulfed these women's feelings, "the affective attachment to what we call 'the good life,' which is for so many a bad life that wears out the subjects who nonetheless, and at the same time, find their conditions of possibility within it."[11] These women, living halfway across the world from the lonely working-class women in Buenos Aires who dance the tango with strangers that Julie Taylor writes about in *Paper Tangos,* resembled similar awakenings in their bodies.[12] As Taylor, notes, "While tango lyrics speak to the confusion and isolation of former lovers, tango bodies are thrown back into a lover's embrace that paradoxically can establish the most intimate of links or none at all."[13] The rhythm of the tango makes lonely women forget the emptiness of their lives as they are transported to a zone of forgetfulness through the dancer's embrace. These zones of forgetfulness are essential to being human in a world that refuses to recognize marginal subjects as fully humans capable of loving. As I began to explore female workers' stories about love, this love took many forms and countless invisible shapes, and innumerable feelings remained unspoken. It was between the said and the unsaid that love resided. Age and gender also intersected in how ideas around love were communicated to external observers. Older women were shy about their love lives and used more coded language. The younger women were more forthcoming about their love affairs; they inhabited a world that was cosmopolitan about explicit expressions of love and freed them to give expression to their erotic feelings.

An extreme position on the love spectrum was Selina, a thirty-two-year-old woman. She had met her husband at her uncle's subcontracting garment factory, where she was a sewing operator and he was a line supervisor. When she became pregnant after five months of marriage, he left her and married his niece. Later, Selina's family found out that he had deceived multiple women into marrying him and then abandoned all of them. Her husband was also physically abusive. In our meeting, Selina said, "I love my husband with tremendous passion. This love cannot be compared to any other love. I made him return to me, but he again left me." When I asked Selina why she desired a man who had betrayed her so many times, she replied, "I love my husband in a primordial way." Primordial love for Selina had an element of violence and unpredictability in it. She suffered from his actions, but she forgave him because he was her lover; he was her Krishno, the one she desired the most. My research captures part of this spectrum of desire that enfolds the women in a bewitching array of betrayals.

I interviewed both younger and older workers about their relationship with their partners and how they experienced romance and love in the city. Some of the women I interviewed mentioned that their husbands did not hold them in an "embrace" at night. Then there were those who said, "If my husband does not hold me, I cannot fall asleep. When two people hold each other, there is a connection and pleasure between them." Some of the women said, "I never get enjoyment from my husband." Others said that their husbands did not sleep properly with them. This was the coded language in which they expressed their sexual needs in a culture that has not provided women with explicit language with which to speak about sexual desire. It is what Freeman has termed "the relationship between states of feeling and the language with which we give expression to such states."[14] Freeman probes how neoliberal sentiments have also spawned "a growing desire to feel in new ways and the availability of a new lexicon of feeling."[15] In other words, how are language and feelings "circumscribed by other cultural modes of expression?"[16]

When I asked Tithi, my research assistant, and Sahanaj, a long-term labor rights organizer, to explain the coded language of sexuality used by the women, Sahanaj said, "She is saying that he does not do the sex act properly. As soon as he is satisfied, he moves over. He does not wait to give her pleasure." Tithi added: "The woman works long hours in the factory and gets such low wages that do not adequately cover her living expenses—rent, food, clothes. At work, she often has line supervisors who speak harshly when her work slows down. At the end of the eight-to-ten-hour shift, she comes home to her husband and they have arguments over money. And at night, she does not get any sexual pleasure. She is mentally, physically, and sexually impoverished." It is important to note here that middle-class women face a similar predicament, but they are not the focus of my study. The discourse of sexuality to a great extent in research papers is in terms of sexually transmitted diseases and the importance of educating the public about safe sex. Such discursive practices fail to see these working-class women inhabiting the world of affects. One author who wrote candidly about female sexuality is exiled feminist author Taslima Nasrin, but she wrote about the Bangladeshi middle-class woman.[17]

A woman in her twenties with two daughters explained this impoverished sexuality experienced by many married workers in the following terms: "I am a mother, a worker, and a wife. In the course of a day, I have to fulfill all three roles. After the birth of my children, I had to continue to work. At the end of the day, I have to take care of my children, then my husband. My husband does not understand my work burden. He expects me to satisfy him. That is why after the birth of children, many husbands leave their garment-worker wives and seek pleasure elsewhere." A woman in her late thirties spoke about the love of her elderly parents-in-law in different terms. She said with sadness, "They take care of each other, they sleep together. When one of them bathed, the other person cooked. They are old but happy together. My husband and I do not share a similar relationship."

The fact that these factory women spoke so frankly about their desire and their sexual needs underscored an elemental aspect of their lives: their need for their love to be heard and accounted for. Many of the women said that my research assistant and I were the first people who had asked them about their love lives, and the only people with whom they had shared their intimate stories. While their stories were mostly poignant, they also yielded a freeing space for the women. A woman's sexual urges no longer had to remain hidden; they were an essential part of her being human. As Lovely wrote in "Krishno, the Lover," "Against the empty pages of the past / Let life begin afresh."

SEXUALITY

Although premarital sex was common in this demographic, it remained a social taboo, and people were reluctant to talk about it openly. In conversations, many cloaked comments would come up. I was also hesitant to raise a topic that my interlocutors were not comfortable acknowledging.

Women would often remark, "Yes, it happens, but I don't do such things." Premarital sex posed a radical challenge to existing sexual norms regarding whom one can sleep with and under what circumstances, and these newly arrived migrants were testing those rules. As noted in previous chapters, these women either lived in a nuclear family setting or rented a room with several other unmarried young women. In some rare instances, men and women lived together without being married, but they hid this fact from neighbors. Since this is such a radical dynamic in a predominantly conservative Muslim society, it deserves some comment. Some of these arrangements were for social reasons. Landlords tend to rent to married couples, so male and female friends sometimes made these tactical decisions to get affordable housing. There were instances where a friendship followed by cohabitation led to a romantic relationship and marriage. Also, young women found it safer to live with a male partner because of the social protection it offered.

One young garment worker who spoke candidly about premarital sexual relations was Jamila, a twenty-year-old woman. At age fourteen, Jamila came to the city and joined the garment industry. There she met a male garment worker with whom she developed a romantic relationship. They have maintained a relationship for four years. Jamila said: "My boyfriend and I live together. I am not ready to get married. I want to work and save money. I also have physical needs. Living together helps us cut down on our expenses. It also offers me physical protection; a young woman on her own in the city faces insecurity. Nobody in the slum knows about our living arrangement. If asked, we say that we are married. Both of us are trying to go overseas to work. I may go to Mauritius to work."

Jamila's horizon of possibilities has expanded; marriage and children are no longer the sole stepping-stone to a secure and fulfilling life. For her it was Mauritius, where the wages of a garment worker are triple that of a worker in Bangladesh. Traveling to Mauritius was also part of a global dream to see the world, as Rabeya's voyage to Jordan revealed in chapter 3. Jamila's economic subjectivity as a wage-earning worker and her aspirational subjectivity as a sexually active person were both well developed. With a view toward increasing her income, Jamila was making calculated choices about her future, from choosing her partner to delaying marriage and children. She did all this in the hope of a life of experience and opportunities, but she did not sacrifice her sexual needs. In this new world of global movements, migrants like Jamila seek money and adventure, but it is a precarious world, as Rabeya's experience showed.

The outcomes of these new living arrangements are often unexpected and sometimes detrimental to women's reproductive health. The fact that the young women were choosing to delay marriage was a result of urban living and wage labor. Studies show that garment workers are at high risk of contracting sexually transmitted infections (STIs) and human immunodeficiency virus (HIV) because of lack of a knowledge about safe sex or because they do not want to reveal their intimate sexual lives to others.[18] Sexuality remains a hidden discourse because it is not a socially sanctioned topic. In meetings with maternity health workers I was informed that increased sexual relations between young women and men who are not knowledgeable about safe sex has led to a rise in STIs and abortions (called "menstrual regulation" to bypass barriers to funding from countries that ban abortions). Many young women also suffer from prolapsed uteruses, and leukorrhea is common among the garment workers, often caused by STIs. Many of these health issues remain untreated, posing increased health hazards.

"Abortion is illegal in Bangladesh except to save a woman's life. Menstrual regulations are allowed. Menstrual regulation is when someone has a procedure or takes medicines when they have not had a period for 10–12 weeks. There are clinics in Bangladesh that do menstrual regulation safely, but many people try menstrual regulation outside of clinics, which sometimes causes health problems."[19] Unlike neighboring India, sex-selective abortions are rare in Bangladesh. In Bangladesh, abortion is not an unspeakable act; it is not shrouded in shame and stigma as in the United States. Its widespread acceptance is a result of the family planning programs implemented by the government in the 1970s that successfully brought the birth rate down from 6 children to 2.2 children per woman by the early 2000s.

Among married couples, abortions occur based on whether they can financially afford to have a child. Married women, including middle-class women, speak frankly about having an abortion on the grounds of an "unwanted pregnancy." For these married women, pregnancy is an issue of appropriate timing and finances, not a cause of moral objection.

When a pregnant woman realizes that she is not ready for a child, the couple decides that their current child has to grow up before they can have another child. Then the woman may seek an abortion. Unmarried women have abortions because it is socially unacceptable to have a child outside of wedlock. Although a number of reproductive health clinics that offer abortion services were operating in my research area, most women chose the lower-cost option of the local midwife, although this often led to complications. In almost every slum, at least one back-alley abortion clinic was in operation.

The morning-after pill (euphemistically referred to an "iron pill" by the garment workers) is readily available at the local pharmacies and is widely in use. In Bangladesh, prescriptions are not required for birth control medication, and local pharmacists not only dispense the medicine but also act as the morality police regulating women's sexual choices. Female workers told me that when a woman goes to a pharmacy for reproductive health reasons, the male pharmacist usually asks her if she is married. If she says her husband has left her, his response is, "Your headaches and pains will not go away with medicine. You have to marry again." Some of the younger women who exercised more sexual autonomy told me that they scoff at the pharmacist for his comments. We say to him, "Brother, keep your comments to yourself and give me my medicine."

During my research I met Runa, an unmarried woman who took an abortion pill to terminate her pregnancy. When that failed she went to a clinic for a late-term abortion, but the procedure led to excessive bleeding. Finally, she was forced to leave the city and return to a provincial town next to her village, where she could recover under the care of a gynecologist. She later returned to work, but she never fully recovered her health. The winds of change over sexuality had arrived at these women's doorstep, and patriarchy did not altogether dictate the rules. Now women were able to enjoy sex outside of marriage, but their sexual lives remained vulnerable because male attitudes toward women who had sex before marriage had not changed significantly. Most men saw these women as morally corrupt and unfit to be wives. Compared to the older generation, though, the younger generation of workers were less constrained by these patriarchal views, freeing them to enjoy their sexual desires.

MARRIAGE AND DIVORCE

Marriage as a normative heterosexual arrangement continues to regulate social life in Bangladesh, and spinsterhood is considered a socially inappropriate choice. An unmarried woman is deemed an enigma, a sexual loose cannon or a madwoman, as someone who does not fit into existing categories of womanhood in a society that is organized around marriage and motherhood. One area of increased autonomy for women was their ability to choose their husbands, a choice they had lacked in the villages. Many women now meet their husbands at work and contract love marriages as opposed to arranged marriages. However, these romantic alliances have not increased marital security for women. In many instances, these marriages break down after the birth of a child, especially if the child is a daughter, due to the lower social value placed on female children. Nevertheless, one of the positive outcomes of these romantic alliances is the absence of dowry demands by the groom. Men who marry women for love do not seek dowries from the wife's family. In these circumstances, a wife who works at a factory ensures a steady income for the couple, and her earnings stand in for the dowry. The families of these women are eager to avoid paying for dowries and agree to these romantic alliances, and consequently they do not vigorously vet the character of the potential groom.

In Muslim families, marriage between first cousins is common, and rural marriages usually occur among close kin to reduce property disputes and fragmentation of the family unit. So, the families are familiar with the prospective groom and bride. With increased migration, though, that relationship is being challenged. Factory women now meet men from different regions of the country, widening their choice of potential partners. These mate choices decrease a family's ability to carefully scrutinize these men's character prior to the marriage. As a result, most of these romantic alliances fail. After marriage, many women find out that the man they married misrepresented himself. She discovers that he already has a wife in the village, is a gambler, does not have a job, is physically abusive, or demands that she hand over her money. In such cases, the younger women tend to initiate a divorce. Due to their education and higher income potential compared to the older women, the younger women refuse to accept husbands whose behavior they do not condone. Had they remained in the village, these women would be subordinated to the wishes of their family, and older male relatives would mediate marriages and divorces on their behalf, although that social structure is also undergoing changes as globalization enters village life. While a woman's ability to make independent decisions about her sexual and marital life is a significant social change, it has come at a social cost to these women.

Due to the higher social status given to married women in Bangladeshi society, the older women were not initially forthcoming about their marital status. Although many of their husbands had taken a second wife and were absent from their lives for long periods, the women retained the idea of being married. A married woman had social status and security, whereas a single woman did not. Divorce was rare, and separation (*chara-chari*) was common, because men tend to abandon their wives instead of divorcing them so they will not be required to provide alimony. While society grudgingly accepts a woman leaving an abusive husband, it is less willing to accept that same woman if she remains unmarried. I met only a few garment workers who had remained single. Several of them said that the idea did not appeal to them (*bhalo lage na*). One woman claimed that she did not marry because she wanted to take care of her sick mother. She was a deeply religious woman who always wore the burqa in public. People in her neighborhood saw her as a pious and dutiful daughter who sacrificed for her ill mother. They considered her an ideal daughter who spent her free time at the local women's Quran reading circle learning about Islamic womanhood. Due to her piety, her community did not question her choice.

Similar to the attitudinal changes around women's work in the factory, there is a change in the acceptance of divorce within the middle and working classes. Divorce no longer has the social stigma it did twenty years ago, and rates of divorce are on the rise. My ethnographic observation regarding an increase in divorce rates is restricted to urban Dhaka and does not refer to other regional areas. Nowadays, in many middle-class families, marriages break down within six months after the wedding. Attitudes toward a middle-class woman's divorce are linked to an increased sense of her individual autonomy. These days, women get an education, have jobs, and can provide for themselves—they do not become a burden on the family's resources. Women's rights groups have mainstreamed ideas around spousal abuse and helped to pass the Prevention of Women and Child Repression Act 2000, which has offered women some protections from abusive spouses and provided access to child custody that were not readily available to women in the past.[20] Explaining this spike in divorce rate within the middle class, and overall societal attitudes toward divorced women, social historian Ahmed Kamal said:

> Acceptance of divorce is not widespread, but it is an improvement over social attitudes that blamed and ostracized women in the past. In this respect, NGOs have played a critical role in raising society's consciousness about spousal abuse. Laws that prohibit violence against women have been passed, and families nowadays take advantage of these laws. An equally important factor for this change is the fall in the birth rate. In an earlier generation, families were large with ten to thirteen children. With so many children, parents' emotional investment gets stretched thin. Financially, many families could not afford to take in a daughter who wanted to leave an abusive relationship or was unhappy in her marriage. It is not that the parents did not care, they did, but they had to navigate a difficult terrain and respect many social rules. Nowadays, families are smaller with two to three children, freeing parents to emotionally invest more in the welfare of their daughters and sons.[21]

Another novel trend is that rural families increasingly support their daughters if they want to separate from abusive husbands, but the reasons for this are somewhat different. What came through in the interviews was how wages have made these working-class women into conduits to capital for their families. A woman's income was an economic lifeline for her family in the village. For medical emergencies, to fix a leaking roof, or to have money for sending a son overseas to work, families made claims on their daughters' incomes. A marital separation meant that the family, not the spouse, could make full claim on her income. Here the woman's morality converged with her duties as a daughter. The daughter as a pious and moral subject took care of these familial demands. In this instance the economic subjectivity as worker, the aspirational subjectivity as a desiring person, and the moral subjectivity of a dutiful daughter coalesced around the family's survival needs, with the moral subjectivity eclipsing the others.

MARITAL DISCORD AND ABANDONMENT

The life history of a working-class woman is complicated by many factors. The woman may have left the village because of her oppression by a man (usually her husband), to feed her malnourished body, or to help her family meet their financial ends. Many women separate from their husbands in the village and then come to the city to work. Women often say they are married or unmarried based on situational specificities, that is, in order to increase their social security in the urban jungle of Dhaka. Many women find that if they say they are married and have a child, men will not financially and socially support them as willingly as they might support an unmarried woman, since if a woman has a husband, it is his responsibility to provide for her. In the factory work culture, women often find that their supervisors prefer unmarried women for potential romantic relationships. Thus, some women try to present themselves as unmarried to take advantage of such opportunities, for it may result in a hypergamous marriage or a better work routine at the factory. Unlike her life in the village, where the community participates in her life cycle, in the city a woman's private life—whether she was married in the village, whether she had left her children with her parents—is not a matter of public knowledge. Thus, life in the city also symbolizes the privatization of life.

Despite these changing attitudes, very few garment workers marry without their parents' consent and blessing. Elopement is uncommon among these workers, and only those women who face social obstacles will elope. The conventions of marriage are still observed, but since the married couple now live in the city, the family does not interfere in their lives on a regular basis. In most cases, the couple becomes nuclearized and their familial ties are weakened but not broken, as they stay in touch with their relatives in rural society, whom they depend on in times of need. Women living in a nuclear family setting have greater autonomy from their in-laws, but they also lack the familial support of an older family member who could offer advice in times of a crisis. This forces many women to rely on their limited resources, knowledge, and social skills to handle challenges that often push them into vulnerable situations.

The following stories illustrate some of the predicaments that young women face in the city when they try to harness resources for their well-being. A young garment worker told me that she had met a man at her factory who claimed to be from the garment manufacturers' apex organization, the BGMEA. He came wearing a suit to the factory. In her words, he displayed "authority and power," and the managers at her factory were obsequious in front of him. When he met her, he chatted with her for a while, and then told her that she could call him if she needed help. He did not give her a business card; instead he gave her his cell number written on a piece of paper. A few months later, her factory suddenly closed down. Before shutting the factory, management took away their identity cards, making it difficult for them to go to labor court to recover their past-due wages. It was then that she called the man, thinking he could help recover her wages. He asked her to come to Gazipur, an industrial belt of Dhaka. The head office of BGMEA is located in Dhaka, not Gazipur. Had she known that fact she would have realized that something was wrong. If she had lived with her family, her father or a sibling would have accompanied her on the trip. If she possessed more social knowledge, she would have questioned why he did not give her his business card. Lacking these social safety nets and knowledge, she went by bus to Gazipur, where the man met her at the bus station and took her to an empty office where he tried to rape her. She said that she escaped after fighting back. In the absence of familial structures of support, young women who live independently often become victims of sexual assault.

As mentioned earlier, it was uncommon to find Hindu women workers in the garment industry, and even less common to find marriages between Hindu women and Muslim men, but they do occur, although those statistics are not available. Shikha, a twenty-two-year-old Hindu garment worker, had married (against her family's wishes) a Muslim man she had met at work. Soon after their marriage, she found out that he had been married twice before, a fact that he had hidden from her. After she had a child with him, he abandoned her for another woman. With a seven-month-old baby to care for, she could not return to work. It was at this time that her mother began to help her and convinced her father to take her back. Shikha now lives with her parents and has returned to work at the factory. However, she has remained Muslim. Her marriage to a Muslim man had social consequences for her parents. They could no longer visit their village because their daughter was now an outcast in their Hindu community. Shikha could return to her Hindu faith through a process known as purification (*prayeshchitra*), but she said that she would not do that. When asked to explain her decision, she replied, "For a Muslim woman the social sanctions against remarriage are not as severe as those for Hindu women. It would be difficult for me to find a Hindu man who would marry a divorced woman. Remarriage of divorced women and widows is allowed in Islam. Also, my Muslim daughter will not be accepted by my former Hindu community. So, why should I convert back to Hinduism, since it will not offer me social protection?"

Among the older women I met, the majority were married but had been abandoned by their spouses. Many of these women later married men they met in the city. So, the second marriage was in most instances a romantic alliance. Their second marriages were equally unstable. The men they married tended to abuse them and forcibly take away their money. There was a familiar pattern to these marriages. The husbands saw these women as money-making machines. On days the women got paid, many of their absent husbands would show up outside the factory gates or in their homes, proclaiming their undying love. For the next two days they would remain with them, eating well and enjoying sexual gratification, and then they would demand money. If the woman refused, it would lead to physical and verbal assaults. Then these men would disappear from their lives for a couple of months and resurface again.

I found that disputes over money were the primary cause of marital discord. When a woman works in the garment industry, a man thinks that if he marries her, she will earn a guaranteed monthly wage. The man views the woman as his property and not as an independent subject. As one garment worker said, "The man thinks, I let my wife work. She belongs to me, so the money belongs to me." However, factory work has made the woman view herself as a person with relative autonomy, and this comes into conflict with the idea of being someone's property. On the day they get their wages, about 70 percent of the women argue with their husbands over money. These days some women have become prudent about their money through training workshops offered by labor groups. They have opened bank accounts in their own names. But the husband soon finds out about the bank account and demands that if

Changing Norms of Romance, Marriage, and Sexuality 141

Figure 16. A meeting to resolve a marital dispute at the NGO Kormojibi Nari.

she opens an account, it must be in his name or a joint account. I found that the majority of married women who lived with their spouses would hand over the money to their husbands after verbal arguments and physical assaults.

One day, Tithi, Sahanaj, and I were at a focus group meeting with several young workers who were all unmarried. During our discussion, the topic of spousal abuse came up. One of the more outspoken younger workers said, "If my husband beats me, I will not stay with him. I earn, why should I stay? I will take him to family court and ask for my alimony." The other women nodded and laughed when they heard her speak.

After the workers had left, Sahanaj said:

> Younger women are now more aware of their rights. This is a new behavior that the men are not accustomed to. The men are used to beating outspoken women. If we could train women properly of how things work in the city, these women would not get easily

trapped into precarious situations. When a young woman joins a factory, her manager tests her reaction by putting his hand on her body. If she does not respond, he assumes that she is available to him sexually. But the woman does not respond because she does not know that she can speak back to male authority and that there are laws that protect her. In the factories, the ratio of women to men is 80 percent female to 20 percent male. Thus, a man can conceivably have an affair with two to three women. Outside the factories, you will see men and women sitting together at a tea shop, holding hands and chatting. I have met many foolish women who were lured into sexual relations that did not end well for them.

Both Tithi and I disagreed with Sahanaj. We felt that the women also desired attention and amorous relations from their male companions, and they sometimes went into these relationships knowing that they would not last. After it ended, they would have to endure a lot of suffering. But they desired that momentary pleasure to keep on living. They were trapped in Berlant's cruel optimism. It was part of the arc of their emotional existence.

FAMILY COURTS AND MARRIAGE REGISTRATION

In Bangladesh, the family court is active in pursuing cases of abandonment and tends to settle them expeditiously. Most marriages are not officially registered, and because the courts do not recognize unofficial marriage agreements, it can be difficult for these women to get any alimony. The older workers tend not to have proper marriage documents, which prevents them from getting financial compensation through the courts. Many workers, especially the younger workers, now seek the help of legal aid NGOs when issues around spousal abuse and abandonment come up. The NGOs assist them with their petitions to the family court in the city. In negotiating these matters, the factory worker is comparatively advantaged over her rural counterpart.

I once witnessed a negotiated marriage separation under the umbrella term alternative dispute resolution (ADR) organized by an NGO in a village. An ADR is an extralegal adjudication that bypasses the courts and settles disputes over land, marriages, child support, and so forth informally with support from family members and village-level elected officials called union council chairmen. ADRs offer women swift relief from unpleasant situations, but the monetary compensation is much lower than what they would get from a court settlement. These decisions are socially but not legally binding on the litigants. In this instance, a young woman in her early twenties wanted a divorce from her husband. At this meeting, the woman's family, the husband's family, the NGO representative who was negotiating the divorce on behalf of the woman, the chairman who acted as the judge, and some spectators, including me, were all gathered in the courtyard. The chairman decreed in favor of the divorce and asked the man's family to pay the woman her alimony. As we were all leaving, someone raised the objection that the couple had a small child, and no one had taken the child's welfare into consideration. This man asked, "Who will take care of this child?" The chairman said that the mother should take care of the child. The woman said that she could not take the child. The money she received would not cover her expenses; how could she be expected to support the child? At this point, more money was demanded of the father. The man's family said that they had brought the agreed-upon amount and would not agree to a higher amount so late in the process. Finally, the negotiations broke off and all parties walked off.

Poor people see the courts as a formidable force. People tend to be afraid of the courts, and when notices are sent to show up in court, they heed those instructions. Often in front of the judge in family court, the husband agrees to pay a small sum of alimony money to his wife up front and promises to pay the remainder later. He usually fails to pay the rest of the alimony. So, the woman has to take him to court again, which is time consuming and takes an emotional toll on her mental health. Labor rights NGOs have introduced many workers to the courts, and they also provide workers with lawyers who help with their cases. Through this mechanism, younger workers have become more familiar with the judicial process, which gives them rights that older workers could not access in their youth. Despite these changes, the knowledge of marriage registration remains spotty among women workers. Among the younger generation of female workers, marriages increasingly occurred through the office of the *qazi*, the government officer in charge of registering marriages and divorces. The *qazi* registers the marriage and gives the woman a receipt with a number that is her proof that the marriage is legal. If the marriage breaks down, this document gives women access to alimony and the custody of their children.

A labor rights advocate who had long-term experience with younger garment workers had a different interpretation of how marriage registrations worked in the city. She mentioned that in her area the local *qazi* had opened his own shop in the market to offer false documents for marriage and divorce in exchange for a small sum of money. According to her, this particular *qazi* had realized that marriages/divorces were on the upswing among garment workers. So, he offered them false marriage documents (unbeknownst to the women) that did not have a registration number. When a marriage is legally registered, it is difficult for a man to simply walk away from his marriage without any financial responsibilities. He is expected to fulfill the terms of the marriage contract (*kabin nama*) and pay for the maintenance of his wife and children. From the *qazi*'s perspective, issuing false marriage documents at a low price made it easy for the couple who are madly in love, who may be facing a sudden pregnancy or in need of housing, or some other social or economic exigency, to marry without official delay. When they want to get divorced, and that occurred frequently, it was just as easy for the *qazi* to issue the divorce, because the marriage was never registered with the state in the first place.

It would require more research to establish whether this was a widespread phenomenon or simply the cunning of the *qazi* in that particular area that the rights advocate had encountered. Suffice to say that different groups were strategically maneuvering to take advantage of these social dynamics that were on the upsurge, with millions of workers entering the labor market and making new lives in the city. Despite all these radical shifts, I found that the Bangladeshi woman remained anchored to her family, kinship, and rural origins, but those anchors were shifting and accommodating the new forces at play.

OLDER WORKERS' ATTITUDES TOWARD YOUNGER WORKERS' SEXUAL CHOICES

In my conversations I found that the older workers did not necessarily endorse the life choices of younger workers. One found scathing critiques of younger workers by older workers. Sajeda is a forty-five-year-old former garment worker with a young daughter. Explaining why she did not want her daughter to work in the garment industry, she offered a derisive critique of younger workers. She said that young women these days are explicit about their sexual feelings. They will go and sit next to a married man and entice him into a relationship. Sajeda added that these younger women "make love in an unrestricted way; they do not care whether someone is married, has children, whether the love affair will break a home . . . these women are simply focused on their amorous desires." When I asked her if she had spoken to the younger women about their attitude, she said, "I have tried to get them to change their behavior but I have failed. I said to these young women, 'You are good looking. You can have a good marriage. You have parents, they can find a suitable match for you. Why are you with a man who already has a wife?' But these days, young girls ignore such advice. They say, 'I have fallen in love, that's why. Don't say any more to me, auntie.'"

Sajeda blamed women and men equally for these affairs. She mentioned that the widespread use of cell phones was the leading cause of these illicit relations. She said that men and women use cell phones to form relationships outside of the surveillance of family and community. In her opinion, they form amorous relations by exchanging pictures and videos; they do not always have to be physically present to carry on an affair. It should be noted here that the rise of cell phone use has not only created greater communication among people but has also given rise to online dating, extramarital affairs, sex, and marriage proposals among all classes of people, including working-class men and women. Almost all the garment workers have cell phones, and many of them, young and old, use their cell phones to seek potential marriage partners and boyfriends by exchanging Bollywood love songs, often sending stock internet pictures with messages like "I Love You," "Without You My Life Is Over," and similar trite missives. Some of them use FaceTime to talk with their online boyfriends, many of whom are overseas migrant workers in Malaysia and Dubai who are also very lonely and socially isolated in their work camps and seek girlfriends in Bangladesh. These male workers have an erotic break in the midst of their grueling work life, but most of these men do not intend to marry the women with whom they have online dating conversations, because they consider them to be morally loose and unfit as wives.

Sajeda added that having multiple marriages is profitable from a man's perspective. The more marriages he has, the more fun he can have. She mentioned that her husband had two wives (she and her co-wife) to attend to his physical needs, and he also lived off their wages. After seeing these relationships occur multiple times at the factory, she said that she was afraid to put her daughter to work in a garment factory. When asked if she had seen such relationships in the village, Sajeda said no but added that if one searched one could find one or two similar relations that are initiated by women in the village, versus the profusion of female-initiated relationships in the city. The fact that more young women are initiating relationships can be evaluated as a form of sexual empowerment, but it is not the kind of empowerment envisioned by the labor rights activists I spoke with.

One day, I was sitting in the labor rights office when a woman in her twenties named Yasmin came in. She stated her case to the rights advocate, Farida. Yasmin was married to a man who already had a wife and a child. He had left the first wife but had not officially divorced her. Yasmin was his second wife, and she wanted him to leave his other wife. When he refused, she came to the labor rights organization to file a case against him. Farida asked Yasmin for more details about the marriage. Upon some cross-examination, Yasmin revealed that she was aware at the time of her marriage that the man was married. Farida felt uneasy about this case. She told Yasmin that their organization did not teach female workers to break up the home of another woman.

She asked Yasmin, "Did you find out if she had really left him before you married and moved in with him?" Yasmin said no, she did not.

Farida told Yasmin, "We at our labor rights office teach you well. You should have gone to his house to find out about his marital life before you married him. My advice is this, either you leave this man or you stay with him under the circumstances that he wants. I will not be able to file a case on your behalf."

A few days later, Yasmin returned to the labor rights office. Her situation had become a bit more complicated. When the first wife found out that the husband was living with another woman (Yasmin), the first wife filed a case against him for alimony and violence against her under the Prevention of Women and Child Repression Act 2000. In order to have his first wife drop the case against him, he had tried to convince her that he had left Yasmin, but the man's first wife asked for proof of his divorce from Yasmin. The man explained to Yasmin that they would go through a fake divorce to satisfy his first wife. He asked Yasmin to sign the divorce papers, saying, "This is a fake divorce paper. I will just show this to my first wife. You do not have to worry; this is just to make her withdraw the case against me. After I show her the divorce papers, I will stay with her for a few days. Then I will come over to you."

Farida said to Yasmin, "Divorce cannot be fake. Once you sign the divorce papers, you will become divorced. This man is playing games with you. Once he has settled his differences with his first wife, he will come back to you, yes, but you will no longer be legally married to him, and should any misfortune occur, you will not get any alimony from the courts. Then the man will want to continue to profit from his two wives."

Later that day, Sahanaj, Tithi, and I discussed the case of Yasmin. Sahanaj gave an expanded explanation of why these issues crop up among garment workers.

> A village girl comes to the city with limited social knowledge and skills. In the factory, if she cannot fill her production target, she has to hear abusive language from her production manager. She goes home and has to face demands from others who rely on her income, her child, her parents, her siblings. She is caught in a vortex of obligations. In such situations, when a man comes into her life, she feels she can forget all her problems for a few days and does not tell him that she already has a child. She begins to swim in a sea of hope. She is married but abandoned and hides that fact from the man she meets. From the man's perspective this unmarried woman has no familial obligations but he has responsibilities that he needs to meet as the breadwinner. If he can make her his wife, then he will be able to manage his fiscal responsibilities better. Thinking of this, the man marries her. Then they fall into a more complex trap since both have hidden their previous marriages, wives, children, and familial obligations.

I asked Sahanaj, "What do the men say about the behaviors of their wives?" Sahanaj replied, "The man blames the woman. He says that she had a previous marriage; she had children but did not inform him. Then he complains about how she treats his parents. The man says that she sends all her money home; she does not take care of him or his parents. And the woman says the contrary. When her parents come to visit, he does not behave well, he does not buy good food. Each party blames the other, and eventually they break up."

MALE ATTITUDES TOWARD FEMALE WORKERS

During the research, I documented numerous cases of marital violence suffered by these women. Violence as an everyday occurrence was normalized in these women's lives. Making sense of such high levels of violence was an essential part of understanding these women more intimately. While there are multiple reasons for violence against women, particularly their financial autonomy from factory wages, her body plays a vital role in sexual violence. For men, the female body is the primary site of pleasure and pain and the women pay the price for the sexual demands of the men. Misogynistic attitudes toward women are commonplace in multiple cultural forms, from proverbs to literature to movies to government documents. In this respect, several Bengali proverbs that are commonly used by men offer an expression of male aggression and disrespect toward women in Bangladesh:

> Drums and women must always be beaten.
> (ঢোল আর মেয়েলখ সব সময়ই বারির উপর রাখতে হয়)
> Given attention, monkeys and women become disobedient.
> (বান্দর আর মেয়েলখ বেশী লাই দিলে মাথাই ওঠে)
> Women are the sticks that light the fires of hell.
> (মেয়েলক হচ্ছে জাহান্নামের খড়ি)
> Bitch only thinks of her vagina, i.e., her sexual pleasure.
> (মাগী তার বধা ছাড়া কিছু বোঝে না)

One day I sat down with Zahid, my male research assistant, to discuss reasons for male sexual violence that had come through numerous times in the case studies of both older and younger female workers. He said:

> For sexual pleasure and fantasy, these men tend to watch Bollywood movies where they see female stars who are beautiful, lively, sexually inviting with perfect physiques (breasts and thighs). The

man gets seduced by her beauty on the digital screen. These men have little money and cannot frequent brothels to satisfy their sexual urges. If they go to the brothels, they have what is called "one-shot" (the man can only come once during intercourse), which costs between taka 250–300. The duration of the sex act cannot exceed fifteen minutes without paying additional money. So, the man comes home to his wife to seek pleasure. The garment worker does hard, physical labor. After a long day at work, she finally comes home tired and too exhausted to have sex. In bed, her body disappoints him, her breasts and thighs sag. She does not resemble the Bollywood star Moon Moon Sen.[22] It makes the man feel impotent for the lack of sexual fantasy he has conjured in his head, and he takes out his anger by physically assaulting the woman.

A few weeks later, I met with twenty men who were between the ages of twenty-five and fifty in a series of extended meetings. These men were the adult sons and husbands of garment workers. I found that these men expected their wives to do multiple functions—work, housework, and childrearing—and also provide them with sexual satisfaction. While there was a substantial change in how older and younger women thought about their roles as wives, there was little change in how older and younger men evaluated their roles as husbands. Younger men who grew up in the city with their working mothers were more amenable to shared housework as, the survey in chapter 2 showed. Men who grew up in the village and did not see their fathers helping their mothers with housework tended to be opposed to doing "women's work." None of these men would admit to physically assaulting their wives.

An older male worker, Babul (whose story is discussed at the end of this chapter), explained that "education is a key factor in how men behave toward their wives." According to him, among those men who have an education beyond high school, one would find a higher percentage willing to share housework. This is because an educated man understands the importance of a working wife who brings home a guaranteed income every month that helps the family to live better and achieve some of their goals. Babul said that within his cohort of male workers in their late forties and early fifties, only 5 percent shared household chores. These men had all grown up in the village and had arrived in

Figure 17. Two male garment workers who were interviewed regarding their attitudes toward women working in the factory.

the city as adults. Speaking of his sons, Babul added that they grew up watching him help their mother with housework. Thus, education, age, parenting, and one's place of socialization—city versus village—all intersected in the attitudes toward sharing parenting and housework.

Almost all the unmarried adult sons of garment workers said that they would not marry women who worked in the garment industry. This was unexpected, since it indicated that they resented their mothers for working in the factory instead of staying at home to take care of them. The reason for their disdain of factory women was that these women wanted to marry up, such as a factory manager or a supervisor. Several of them said that factory work made women into "immoral" women. When it was pointed out that their own mothers were factory women, the men immediately retracted their statement and said that their mothers worked because they had children to raise. One of them said, "They did not work for commodities. These days you meet young women who work in factories because they want consumer goods. They do not have children. They are young and single with many demands, many boyfriends."

As globalization has increased the experiential domains for women, men have developed heightened anxieties toward women engaging in sex outside of marriage, having boyfriends, exercising their autonomy over their income, and telling their spouses "This is my money." Men showed their anxieties toward women's increased autonomy by saying, "I will not marry a garment worker; I will marry a village girl." They claimed that girls raised in villages were dutiful women, whereas factory women had multiple affairs and their fidelity could not be trusted. One young man, the son of a garment worker, said, "A man will have one girlfriend whereas garment girls have two to three boyfriends simultaneously. They try to get gifts from everyone; they try to see who will give them the best life. These women cannot be faithful."

Another young man, also the son of a garment worker, said that he had a former girlfriend who worked in a factory. One day he took her cell phone and found pictures of many men, some of them working in Malaysia and the Middle East. He said, "I asked her, why do you have pictures of so many men on your phone? And she replied that it is her business. She did not feel any shame for what she was doing. After that, I left her." For a garment worker, marrying an overseas migrant worker is considered a prosperous match, since his income is much higher there than in Bangladesh. In this instance, the woman is increasing her number of potential mates. It is a sexual game that has been played by men for many years against their spouses. But with women gaining financial independence, men have lost their traditional dominant roles over their spouses. This, in turn, has turned into an intense form of gender envy among men of this social class.

Expanding on the anxieties released by the modernist project on Bangladeshi men, political scientist Ahrar Ahmed said:

> The rapid changes brought by capitalist forces have also undermined people's moorings. For men, women's public roles brought on by poverty, ecological disasters, and capitalism create anxieties about masculinity. A man is unable to provide for himself and his family. Thus, capitalism also threatens masculinity and becomes infused with heightened sexual insecurities. The man says, "I have to keep control over women by keeping them in purdah [seclusion]."

Thus, our intellect and psychology have not kept pace with the speed of change under capitalism—travel, social media, migration—everything moves faster than our psychological abilities to make sense of this rapidly transforming world, and our new places in it. Our intellect and psychology are at a disjuncture with the modern world.[23]

These men experience to some degree what Pierre Bourdieu wrote about in *The Bachelor's Ball: The Crisis of Peasant Society in Bearn,* where the young women had left the men behind.[24] Bourdieu's middle-aged man in peasant society, a solitary figure at the local ball, is no longer found desirable by modern women who have left the village for the city. These peasant men are tied to the masculine roles of a society that has been broken by the force of globalization. Similarly, women in Bangladesh are leaving rural men behind, and that is not how the men expect society to work. The women now get factory jobs that pay more than the men can earn as day laborers and vendors. Socially, women are preferred for jobs in factories, shopping malls, and offices. Women work as cashiers, waiters in upscale restaurants, receptionists, store clerks, assistant managers—jobs that previously went to men of the same social class. The men who could not go overseas as migrant workers now feel like Bourdieu's trapped peasant men of Bearn who are alone at the ball, unable to find a woman because they cannot provide for a family. The social rules they grew up with are no longer relevant, and they have been trapped in a vise. The Bangladeshi working-class men's stories are equally poignant. They, too, are the castoffs of capital who need their story to be told someday. That said, there are a few dim lights of hope in this dystopian world of failed love and broken marriages, as the following case study illustrates.

A LOVE STORY: BABUL AND KAJOL

When I first met Kajol (thirty-five years old) and Babul (forty-one), I was a little late for my meeting. This meeting, like most of these meetings, was scheduled after their workday ended, usually around 7 p.m. when the workers were tired after a long day at work. When I walked into the office, I saw a couple waiting for me. Their faces had a joyfulness that I had rarely seen among the workers I met. Babul looked at Kajol, then turned to me and said, "We have heard that you want to talk to married couples in the garment industry. We are here to tell you our story."

Unlike most of the other garment workers, Kajol's life in the city took on a meaningful turn after she married Babul, a man she met in the city. They fell in love and shared an intense longing for each other. This relationship, unlike most I documented, became a loving and caring relationship. Yet their journey was full of unpredictability in its early days. When Kajol arrived in Dhaka, she lived with her sister and brother-in-law. In the evening, everyone would go to the house of the landlord to watch television. Some evenings, a young man named Babul would join them. That is how Kajol and Babul met and fell in love. After meeting Babul, Kajol returned to her family in the village for a year. During this time, they corresponded by mail. Kajol said that she had to hide her love affair from her father, so Babul disguised his name as Babli (a female name). But Kajol laughed and said that her father realized this deception. One day, he inquired, "Who is this Babli who writes to you every day?" But he allowed the letter-writing romance to

Figure 18. Babul (*center*) and Kajol (*left*) speaking with Tithi.

continue. Babul said that he composed love poems in his letters. When I asked them to tell me about these poems, Babul immediately recited one from memory.

> Dearly beloved,
> The night is quiet
> The sky is lit with heavenly lights
> Everyone is asleep in their own rooms
> But beloved, there is no sleep for me
> I only think of you day and night.

They continued communicating for three months, but then one day Babul's letters stopped. Frantic with worry, Kajol wrote many letters to Babul without receiving any reply. Finally, she came to Dhaka to look for Babul. Her first stop was at Babul's old address, but she found that he no longer lived there. Unable to ask anyone questions about Babul's whereabouts, since that would reveal their liaison, Kajol took up residence nearby and found a job at a local factory. Then one day, Babul showed up at his old address and they met again. Neither Babul nor Kajol wanted to talk about Babul's sudden disappearance. In my assessment, it was probably due to a debt that he owed. A few months later, they were married.

While speaking to me, Kajol and Babul would look at each other with evident fondness and often break into smiles. They said that their life together was beautiful, although they added that they had to struggle to get there. In their married lives, they do not hide anything from one another. They emphasized that they know each other so well that they could never lie. Babul added, "Better to be truthful."

Asked to explain how their relationship worked, Babul said, "When I buy fish from the market and I come home with it, I find that Kajol has also bought the same fish. It is as though she read my mind." Kajol replied, "If I think I want egg curry tonight, I come home and find that Babul has cooked egg curry for dinner. We communicate without verbalization." Babul added, "Our love puts us inside each other's minds. We just know what the other person wants."

Babul and Kajol have two sons. The older one is eighteen and works at a box-making factory for taka 3,000 a month. He gives his salary to his mother to help with household expenses. The younger son is fourteen and is in grade 7. Their hope is that their younger son will finish high school and attend a vocational college. Babul said that at his factory, most of the male workers over forty years old have been let go because of age. As for him, his manager has kept him on because he is a skilled worker, but Babul fears that he will lose his job within the next three years. Since his workday ends before Kajol's, he takes charge of household duties. When he gets home in the evening he makes sure that their younger son starts his lessons. He prepares the evening meal. Babul said that he did it every day because he knew that his wife would come home late, and if he waited for her to cook, then all of them would have to wait for dinner. He also recognized Kajol's need to relax after a long day at work.

I asked their opinion about the crises that garment workers face, such as divorce, abandonment, and domestic abuse. Babul replied that these behaviors come from social and family pressures. At a social level, he said, we do not try to prevent such issues from occurring; at the family level, these incidents occur but no one speaks about them or educates the children about respectful gender relations. They added that their children were being raised to be decent men.

Babul and Kajol have planned for their future. Together they have saved taka 300,000 and purchased a small plot of land in their village. Once the younger son graduates from high school, they plan to build a small cottage there and return to the village to live out the remainder of their lives. I was moved and touched by Babul and Kajol's story and their long journey to domestic happiness, which was so rare among the workers I interviewed. I wondered, what was their secret? Kajol said that factory work gives many people a lifeline for survival. Without the garment factory, many people would just die from hunger. Previously, people couldn't eat well, have good clothes, or send their children to school. Now those things are a possibility. They said that garment work has given them the opportunity for a better life, although they were aware that many people do not benefit as much as they have. Babul and Kajol saw a future together. Their secret was their love and respect for each other, and their ability to work together as a cohesive unit. Their life seemed to be outside the reach of almost all the other workers I met.

AT RAINBOW'S END: MONI'S STORY

Finally, I turn to Moni, a woman I never had the opportunity to meet but whose life story profoundly shook me. Her life is that of a "trespassing" woman who challenged social conventions around sexuality and marriage and sought sexual relations outside the accepted bounds of society. In her story, gender, class, age, and desire intersected in devastating ways, offering us a glimpse of Berlant's cruel optimism at play.

One day I was sitting at the workers' café in Mirpur and chatting with Sahanaj, a labor organizer. She is a woman in her early forties. Less than five feet tall, Sahanaj is feisty in her speech and action. Smiling, she said to me, "I know the internal veins [*nari nokhotro*] of these garment workers. They tell me their stories. I am like a big sister to them. I advise them on how to get out of difficult situations."

We were discussing some of the older workers' life histories. I was intrigued by how their private lives were changing through industrial wage economy. Sahanaj said that she had long experience with the affective lives of garment workers. Intrigued by what Sahanaj was saying, I asked her to speak more.

Sahanaj said: "The problems facing our girls is that they believe, or perhaps they want to believe, what the man tells them because they want to get married and have some social security. But the man betrays their trust. To gain the trust of these young girls, he may find an older woman to whom he pays a small sum of money to pose as his mother in front of his garment worker girlfriend. This older woman claims that he is her son and that he has no previous wife or children. This woman assures the young girl that she can marry him without any fears. But the garment worker does not realize that this woman is not her boyfriend's mother and does not ask this woman more probing questions."

Sahanaj continued: "These young women make these decisions on their own. In the city, the family support structure has weakened, and it allows, or perhaps forces, these women to make decisions on their own using their judgment. The city is treacherous. In the villages, most of these women do not have to make calculations about social behavior on their own. Their parents, uncles, and older family members intervene to make decisions on their behalf. So, they lack the social knowledge of how to navigate relationships, how to avoid pitfalls, and how to recognize deceptions." Sahanaj then shared the story of Moni, an older garment worker who had retired and returned to her village. Sahanaj knew Moni's story intimately, because Moni had once lived in her house as a subletter.

Moni was married in 1994 and moved with her husband to Dhaka from a village in northern Bangladesh. They both worked in a garment factory in Dhaka. Her first child was a boy, and that made her husband very happy. The following year she had a daughter. Then his attitude changed. He lost interest in his family and started gambling. Soon he abandoned the family. Without her husband's support, Moni's only option was to leave her children with her relatives in the village. She returned to the city and soon became a sewing operator, working shifts of twelve to fourteen hours. After some time, Moni met a younger man called Polash, who worked as a bus supervisor. At the time, Moni was thirty-six and Polash was twenty-four.

Moni rented a room in Sahanaj's house that she shared with two other garment workers. One day, Moni brought Polash to the house at night. Moni told her roommates that he was her husband. That night, the two girls slept on the floor while Moni slept on the bed with her lover. The following morning, the two girls came to Sahanaj to complain. They said, "As a labor leader, you adjudicate dispute resolutions for people, and yet in your own house, immoral things are happening. Moni brings a young man into the house and claims that he is her husband. How can a man who is young enough to be her son claim to be her husband? We demand judgment from you." Hearing this, Sahanaj became angry. As a feminist, Sahanaj retorted that if an eighty-year-old man could have a twenty-year-old wife, why couldn't it be the other way around?

Sahanaj then asked Moni to explain the previous night's events. Moni admitted that she had indeed married Polash. Then Moni showed her a piece of paper they had both signed. Polash had written, "Without any pressure from anyone, I have married this woman." Moni also wrote, "I have married this man without any pressure from anyone." When Sahanaj saw this, she said, "What kind of marriage is this?" Moni told her that Polash said their marriage was legal, and she refused to believe Sahanaj when she said that this was a sham marriage. As a formerly married woman, Moni probably knew that this was a fake marriage, but her moral subjectivity prevented her from accepting that she was not legally married and was engaged in extramarital sex, which is considered a sin in Islam and society.

Moni had also taken a personal loan of taka 150,000 to help Polash start a business. The loan was from a revolving credit group that the garment workers had formed at their factory. Within a few months of receiving the money, Polash stopped communicating with Moni. When she called him, he spoke very harshly to her, "You are a whore, why do you call me? I don't know you." After that, Moni became very depressed. She would cry a lot, stopped taking proper meals, and could not sleep at night. The credit union began to pressure her to pay back the loan. She could not go to work regularly at the factory. She would often weep at work. Due to her poor work performance at work, she faced a lot of verbal abuse from management. Her supervisors would publicly humiliate her and say, "What do you do all night long that you cannot meet your target? You are an old whore. All night long, who do you hang out with?" Male supervisors would taunt her by saying, "Hey, old woman, have you not fulfilled your desires yet? Is there no end to your amorous needs?" These public taunts made her more depressed and ashamed.

One day, Moni came to see Sahanaj and started to cry, saying that they were speaking very vulgarly with her at work. Sahanaj called Moni's line supervisor and asked him why they reprimanded her so harshly. He told her that Moni used to be an excellent worker, always on time with her target, but recently she could no longer meet her target. He further added that she was often absent or came in late to work. He said that he had not taken any steps to fire her because she was an old-timer and a proficient worker. He warned Sahanaj that if Moni's work performance did not improve, he would have to let her go.

Sahanaj then called Polash to ask him to return Moni's money. But Polash said, "If someone calls me to her house, takes off her clothes, then lets me do with her what I please, what is wrong in my taking advantage of this situation? Moni called me over and enticed me with her cooking. Do you know how many eggs she fed me the last time I stayed with her? Every night she fed me five to six eggs, one liter of milk, apples, oranges so I could become physically strong. She used to say to me, 'A strong man can fulfill all my desires.' I left because I couldn't satisfy all her desires all the time." When Sahanaj asked him to return Moni's money, he hung up and did not return her calls.

Sahanaj then asked Moni to get her Polash's home address, but Moni could only provide his friend Munir's phone number. Sahanaj knew this person would not reveal Polash's address unless she used some subterfuge. She decided that she would entice Munir into a romantic relationship, and that would perhaps make him reveal Polash's whereabouts. Sahanaj said that she developed a fake romance on the phone with Munir. "After slowly building our relationship on the phone," she said, "I finally persuaded him to give me Polash's address." Once she had the information, she terminated their phone relationship. Sahanaj said:

> Once I got Polash's address, Moni and I went by bus to Sirajganj where he lived. At Sirajganj, we went to Munir's pharmacy. I did not reveal to him that I was the woman who had the fake romantic relationship with him on the phone. When we arrived at his shop, an emotional Moni began to cry. Then I explained the full extent of Moni's predicament to Munir. Hearing her story, Munir said that Polash often took advantage of women. He suggested that we meet with the local chairman of the area and lodge a complaint against Polash to recover the money that he owed Moni.
>
> Then we went to the chairman's house and petitioned our case. Instead of showing empathy, the chairman had the opposite reaction. He said, "How can a woman live with another man without getting married? She deserves severe punishment. She is a morally corrupt woman."
>
> I told the chairman, "It is the fault of the man."
>
> He asked in an annoyed voice, "Who are you to talk about men?"
>
> Then I said, "Did Moni go from Dhaka to Sirajganj, or did Polash come from Sirajganj to Dhaka?" I wanted the chairman to recognize that it was Polash who had started this relationship by taking advantage of an older woman.
>
> The chairman then said, "Even if a man does one hundred bad deeds, I can't do anything. What kind of a woman is this? She didn't have any fear in her heart. Why did she mix with this young man? You support this woman, so you [Sahanaj] too must have a problem [here "problem" stands in as a code word for sexually loose woman]."

I said to him, "If I have some problem, that is not your concern. This girl worked in a garment factory from 8 a.m. to 8 p.m. Do you know how hard that work is? Earning this money is like selling your blood and sweat. How will she repay this money that he borrowed through her goodwill and now refuses to return? She also has a son and a daughter."

The chairman got even angrier and said, "This woman has two children and had a relationship with another man without getting married. She should be beaten with shoes."

I did not want to lose complete control over the situation. We were two women in a strange town. Moni was crying and was no help to me. I was trying to resolve this issue about marital infidelity and unpaid debt on my own.

I said to the chairman, "Whatever you want to do, do it later. First, bring him here." The chairman finally relented and asked Polash to come to his house. Upon hearing from the chairman, he arrived but he would not admit to his wrongdoing. Then I told him that I had a phone recording of his voice. That is when he got frightened and confessed. The chairman decided that both parties were guilty, and he resolved that they would have to pay fines. Polash would only have to return taka 50,000 to Moni, the remainder she had to pay from her funds. Polash paid Moni taka 10,000 that day and agreed to repay taka 10,000 every month until he paid off the debt. Then on a legal paper, they signed this agreement. After this, the chairman asked us all to leave since it was already getting late. With that agreement, we returned home.

After listening to this long story, I asked Sahanaj, "What happened to Moni? Did she get her money?"

Sahanaj said that Moni never received the remainder of her money from Polash. She added, "Moni's heart was so broken, she could no longer work. After losing all her money to pay off the debt she took for Polash, her only recourse was to return to her village."

I asked, "What does she live on?"

Sahanaj sadly replied, "She received a small plot of land from her father; she lives off the produce of that. There is a small vegetable garden that provides her with some vegetables. She gets some small fish from the local ponds and canals. It is a hand-to-mouth existence."

The room became heavy with sadness. For a few minutes, neither of us spoke. It was getting late, so we both had to leave. On my way home, I watched garment workers heading home from their long day at work. They walked steadily, with purpose, with hope. As I watched them, I knew that in those women's lives many similar stories resided.

In Moni's life story, we find her first husband's abandonment (a frequent occurrence among these women) enabled her to pursue her amorous desires. Moni believed that love and passion would fill the empty spaces of her life. Her aspirations went against the social norms of women's comportment in Bangladesh, which remain strictly patriarchal. She knew that Polash, a much younger man, would never love her, but she wanted to believe against all odds that he would. She fed him well, satisfied his sexual needs, and even procured a loan on his behalf. In fact, it was Polash's intention to use Moni instrumentally to get the loan that he had no intention of paying back. Berlant has written that "all attachments are optimistic." Moni's "incoherent" attachment to Polash as "the object of desire" overrode practical considerations. She probably knew that he did not love her, yet she continued to strive for Polash as a cluster of promises of a sexually satisfying relationship, and perhaps love too would be possible through their sexual intimacy.[25]

At work, Moni became the object of ridicule for being "an old hag" with sexual desires. Her emotional precarity and lack of concentration put her at risk at work, eventually getting her fired. Her private life and her work life intersected in devastating ways; one is not independent of the other, although we are made to think that they can be separated. Her inability to pay off the debts she had incurred for Polash increased her mental stress, since the credit union would not forgive the loan. For Moni, it took a lot of courage to travel by bus to another town to recover her money and, perhaps more significantly, her lover. There, too, Moni was abused as morally corrupt by the local chairman. Moni's life is a tapestry of the risks and dangers she formed through attachments in the lonely and treacherous city in the blind hope of a happier life. This is a crystallized example of "cruel optimism," an attachment we believe will work, but not only will it not work, it will damage and injure us gravely. Yet we welcome this cruel attachment because it fills a void in our empty, modern lives.

Sahanaj's story is equally revealing about her aspirations and subjectivity. Her courage to travel to Sirajganj and speak to the chairman, a local authority figure, came from her long-term activism with a labor rights group. She empathized deeply with the betrayals endured by women like Moni. In the narrative, Moni's and Sahanaj's lives converge. She traveled with Moni to another town where she fearlessly advocated for Moni. She asked the chairman to adjudicate a fair judgment—a man who instead saw Moni as an "adulteress" and Sahanaj as "a fallen woman doing a man's work." Socially, both of them were deemed trespassing women. In Sahanaj, the human desire for justice existed within the human desire for empathy. These lives were at the nexus of Freeman's neoliberal excitements, which had overtaken the lives of women in the city, and Berlant's cruel optimism, which crushed those stirrings that women felt in their hearts and loins as they sought more independence in their private lives.

"Did Moni ever find happiness?" I asked. Sahanaj looked at me and then away in the distance, and her eyes misted over. In a gentle voice, she replied, "No, Apa, how was that possible? In this joyless city, love and its embrace are denied to us, working-class women."

I planned to visit Moni in her village. Sahanaj made the arrangements. Moni was excited to meet us, especially Sahanaj, who was like a big sister to her. They had not seen each other for many years. Then work intervened for Sahanaj; her boss at the labor organization felt that my research had gone on for a long time, and she wanted Sahanaj, a highly valued worker, to join a new research project immediately. Without Sahanaj, it would be difficult for me to visit Moni. While I was pondering my options, an urgent message came from the United States that required my immediate return. Moni's life, like all these women's lives, was lived in a tsunami of betrayals. Alas, I, too, became part of that betrayal, lives lived in the sea of broken promises.

Ah, Moni, I hope you found your embrace at last.

CONCLUSION

In comparing the older and younger workers discussed in chapters 3 and 4, the following factors become evident. First, the older workers had lower levels of education, wages, and social knowledge. Hence their lives were more compartmentalized compared to the younger workers. Second, these older workers had less exposure to labor rights organizations that would have taught them about their rights. While they recognized the manifold indignities of factory work, the older women had fewer resources with which to resist factory-level oppression compared to the younger generation, who are better informed about their marital and labor rights. Third, the low wages earned by these older workers did not allow them to enjoy consumer culture in the same manner as the younger workers. Given the choice, these older women would have participated in consumerism. Instead, they invested in the children's education hoping to move them into middle-class status. Fourth, during the work lives of the older women, globalization had not yet penetrated the work environment of factory women. By 2005, however, younger workers were integrated into the global flows of migrant factory labor. The older workers did not have the same access to travel and earn higher wages. Overseas migrant work is a precarious world of sudden loss of employment or worker abuse. Many families mortgage their land to send a child overseas, and they often end in serious debt when their child is fired or defrauded by the employer. Knowing all that, the older women still wanted to experience this shiny, new world of possibilities.

This chapter offered an intimate look at the changing world of romance, marriage, and divorce among garment workers as well as how their spouses, their families, and the men in their lives have exploited those dynamics, sometimes with care, and at other times with intense cruelty and disdain. It also examines how work (public) and nonwork (private) lives intervene, reshaping the limits of possibilities especially for women on the lower economic strata. Despite the constraints of patriarchy and morbid social attitudes toward their lives, the women continued to craft lives that made their existence meaningful. The human longing for happiness—to love and to be loved, to care and to be cared for—gives these women, and for that matter all humans, a motive with which to craft lives, to imagine possibilities, and to invite Krishno the lover into their lives. It is an ephemeral dance of cruelty and optimism where these women are moving objects in search of love, an anchor, and an embrace.

5

AFTER WORK
LIFE IN THE SHADOWS OF CAPITAL

> No one has ever asked me about my love life. They always ask me about my work life, wages, health, exploitation. But I came as a young girl to work in the city. My eyes were full of hope. A good life meant the ability to earn wages, so I could send money home, eat and live well, but also to have a better marriage than what I could hope for in the village. But that did not happen.
> —Older garment worker

IN THIS CHAPTER I return to a question I posed in the Introduction: What did these women achieve after twenty-plus years of work in the factory? As mentioned in earlier chapters, garment workers were glaringly absent in the world of cultural production: TV serials, plays, songs, and novels are not written about their lives. My goal in this book has been to see these women in the fullness of life with all its complexities, cruelties, and pleasures. While Carla Freeman's neoliberal sentiments were more evident in the lives of younger workers who had entered the job market at higher levels of literacy and wages, the older workers remained trapped inside Lauren Berlant's cruel optimism and a more dismal world, as Moni's story showed in the last chapter.

Anthropologists have a long tradition of writing about their ethnographic interlocutors in the first person and documenting oral life histories that cover a wide spectrum of identities and lifeworlds. In anthropology the first-person narrative is an accepted form of writing. Examples include Ruth Behar's *Translated Woman: Crossing the Border with Esperanza's Story* (1993), where the author writes about Esperanza, a peddler, and translates her life story for us; and Lynn Stephen's *We Are the Face of Oaxaca: Testimony and Social Movements* (2013), which uses activists' testimonials to document local politics and resistance. Collectively, their work shows the important role ethnography can play in documenting women's voices for social change.[1] My work fits into this narrative genre.

While I am an anthropologist trained in ethnographic methods, I was exposed to historian Tamara Hareven's life-cycle approach to industrial work during my fellowship at a labor history research center at Humboldt University. Hareven applied the life-cycle approach to the history of the family in U.S. and European contexts.[2] Noting the importance of family life to social history, she wrote: "Historians now have to approach previously neglected dimensions of human life such as growing up, courting, getting married, bearing and rearing children, living in families, becoming old, and dying, from the perspectives of those involved."[3] In my study of the life cycles of older workers, I took an abbreviated approach to Hareven's life-cycle method.

The rural woman who becomes a garment worker now has more life choices than a domestic worker, because domestic workers are still facing the same exploitative conditions. The garment worker lives independently, her wages are higher, some have access to labor rights activists, and she can move around the city, whereas the domestic worker is trapped 24/7 inside the home and her rights are frequently violated by the people who hire her.[4] These dynamic changes are essential to our understanding of how women's lives are rapidly transforming through work in the formal labor market.

As stated in the introduction, I interviewed sixteen older and aged-out female workers in 2017 and 2018. My research assistant and I met with each of the sixteen women for three-hour open-ended interviews. We followed these up in 2018 with two interviews spaced six months apart; that is, interviews were staggered over a period of twelve months. In August 2020 my research assistant contacted these sixteen women to determine the effects of Covid-19 on their lives. Appendix II gives an outline of these updates of all sixteen women workers. These four meetings revealed the patchwork of their life cycles. The women were between forty-five and fifty-five years old. Appendix I gives a fuller picture of their marital statuses, literacy levels, number of children, and children's education. From this group of sixteen, I have selected three case studies to elucidate these women's aspirational dynamics—their search for the good life—a motif that ran through all the conversations I had with them. While each life story was singular, my objective was to find patterns that connected these women's lives and provided a window into their post-industrial lives, that is, life after they were laid off from factory work. I have bookended the three case studies with brief summaries of two workers, Sheuly and Sheema, who were at opposite ends of the spectrum of the good life that these workers desired.

All of the sixteen workers interviewed were born in a village. All had faced intense poverty and deprivation during their childhood years. A couple of them moved to the city as children with their parents due to debt and loss of arable land. Nine of these women were illiterate, five had between a grade 3 and grade 5 education, and one had studied up to grade 10. Fourteen of them came alone to the city between eleven and eighteen years of age. Thus, at a very young age, they had to adapt to urban rules, often without support from their parents to guide them through sticky situations that they confronted daily. Marriage, abandonment, cohabitation with the husband's second wife, remarriage, and intense spousal abuse were everyday aspects of their life cycles. Of the sixteen women, nine had been abandoned, two of those nine later remarried, one was a widow, and six were married at the time of my interviews. There were rare instances when a woman left her husband because of spousal abuse and neglect. In most cases the husband disappeared after the woman became pregnant or gave birth to a child, making her the de facto head of household.

The onslaught of globalization, migration, and rising unemployment has weakened the durability of rural married life, as discussed in previous chapters. This change becomes obvious when we compare an older generation tied to agricultural production with a new generation connected to migration and industrial work. All the parents of the sixteen women had remained married despite poverty, whereas their factory daughters faced marital dissolution soon after their marriage. Thus poverty, while a critical factor, was not the sole cause of the rise in marital separations. Marital instability was brought on by these women's new sense of self as wage-earning factory workers who exercised some control over their income, by the stress of factory life, and by men's loss of social power in the new economy unfolding in Bangladesh. I found that these men's inability to find gainful employment led them to feel emasculated and resulted in violence against their spouses. Women became objects of hate because they could shame and speak back to the men ("It is my money, I will spend it as I please"), forms of speech that were new and threatening to male authority. It was common for men to abandon their wives. This is not to suggest that all rural Bangladeshi men abandoned their wives and families. Far from it. Rather, it is to seriously engage with this dynamic that is on the upswing in this demographic. It could be argued that if men had secure employment and could meet their familial responsibilities, the number of these abandonments might fall considerably.

Once laid off from factory work, these women first tried to re-enter another factory on a short-term basis or joined the unregulated subcontracting operations as part-timers. Their work options were few. A few women operated day cares for garment workers' children or provided cooked meals for single workers in the slums, but most of them worked as day laborers or domestic workers. Some of them had adult children who assisted them financially, but this support fell short of what these women had anticipated receiving in their old age. When all opportunities dried up, the women returned to their village to live out the remainder of their lives. After years of work stitching clothes for the global fashion industry, these older and aged-out workers returned to the lives they had left.

Writing about private life is a messy and difficult process. In writing these women's life stories, I found more gaps and absences than linear narratives. These stories have contradictions writ large, and there are many elisions. In telling their stories, these older women would forget dates, confuse chronology and events, and contradict themselves. They were not accustomed to narrating their personal life histories; that this was a new mode of discourse for them should be kept in mind when reading the case studies. The idea of time is structured differently for these older women who grew up before globalization had penetrated rural society. Important dates are remembered in terms of major events (war, cyclone), not in the European sense of chronological time. The older women could not remember the date of their birth, because birthdays are not major social events in rural society. In Bangladesh, when you ask a rural person about her age, she usually gives an estimate and not an exact figure, such as "My age is probably between forty-five and forty-seven years." Sometimes the older women say *Apni diya daan*, which translates to mean you enter an age that you think is appropriate. This is due to the lack of importance attached to age outside of reproductive functions. Social security benefits that are tied to a person's age are not available in Bangladesh. Answers to questions of when they arrived in the city to work were given similar responses. Thus, a European understanding of the life course structured around precise dates does not fit these women's lives. Freeman has asked us to consider, "How are new inclinations toward feeling and interiority bound up in and/or circumscribed by language and other cultural modes of expression?"[5] Some of these gaps remained unbridgeable, but following the ethnographic method, I have contextualized their comments within the discursive field they inhabited.

The women used simple language to tell their stories. I have kept the translation close to their original texts, without introducing complex terms that were not part of their vocabulary. My goal is to know these women through their terms of reference, not Western academic terms. In telling their life stories, the women also wanted to indicate to me, the researcher, that factory work had earned them respect. They said they were "well regarded at work," which often contradicted what they said about their workplace environment. Most of them did not participate in workers' protests due to the absence of trade union activism during the formative years of the garment industry. Lack of participation in workers' protests made them realists, not fatalists. They were aware that without a viable trade union movement that protected them, factory management would fire them for demanding their rights. They had a strong sense of oppression at work from coerced overtime, low wages, inability to take sick leave, the constant threat of being fired, and the bullying by managers who berated them for not working hard enough. In the absence of an industry that followed labor laws, their answer was, "I had to feed my child. What else could I do?"

For these sixteen older women, Freeman's affective life—the life of care, love, and affection—was one they longed for, and one that was denied to them. Berlant's cruel optimism entered their lives through a meshwork of betrayals. The loss of their attachments was always imminent in their lives, but Berlant's formulation of optimism as seductive penetrated every aspect of their desires. Their optimisms endured temporarily because optimisms were laced with traces of hope—the nostalgic memory of a life left behind, the love of a mother who held them in her arms, and the less hectic rhythm of rural life. Their life histories are poignant stories of hope and loss where Berlant's cruel optimism and Freeman's neoliberal excitement collide and collapse into a torrent of toxicities. I begin with a short anecdote about an older woman.

SHEULY'S STORY

Sheuly was one of the few older women I met who had left her husband voluntarily. She is forty-five years old. When we met in March 2018, I was immediately struck by her appearance. She was dressed in a white sari with a pink border (garment workers tend to wear brightly colored saris) and wore gold-colored rimmed glasses and a thin gold chain around her neck. She was soft-spoken and used refined Bengali language. Her appearance was that of a middle-class Bangladeshi woman. I was surprised to learn that she was illiterate. She said, "I did not have an opportunity to study. I cannot even write my own name." As a result of her exposure to urban life and her aspirations for middle-class status, Sheuly had adopted middle-class aesthetics.

Sheuly had fair skin, which is considered a mark of beauty in Bangladesh. She said that in her youth her arms were round like "balloons," meaning that she looked well fed. She was married at the age of twelve years in the village. When she was twenty years old she had her first child, a boy. When her son was five years old, her husband took a second wife. Around that time, Sheuly had a second child, a girl, and lived with her husband and co-wife for another three years in the village. The two wives argued constantly. Then they moved to the city to find better opportunities. Sheuly found work in a factory. In the city, the family situation further deteriorated. Within two months, Sheuly left her husband. She said, "We constantly fought, and I could not bear it any longer. Since I had a factory job, I decided to move out with my two children." Sheuly continued to work for seventeen years at the same factory. After her separation, many men wanted to marry her, but she was adamant: "I was married once, I have children. I will not marry again." Sheuly also expressed a refreshing sense of humor. When asked if she still received marriage proposals, she replied with a laugh, "Yes, but I tell them, I will need you in my old age, you should come at that time."

A distinguishing feature of her work life was that she had remained at the same factory for seventeen years, developing a good working relationship with management that prevented her from getting laid off. So, at age forty-five she was still employed, but she knew that she would be laid off soon due to age and her failing eyesight, noting that "I have to wear spectacles to thread the needle." She mentioned that there were only two other women her age at the factory; all the other women were below thirty years of age. Her son worked as a driver for a private firm and helped her financially. Together, they had bought a plot of land and built a small house in the village where she plans to retire one day. For Sheuly, factory work helped her have a better life. She mentioned that had she remained in the village, her parents would have forced her to marry another man, and her children would have suffered.

"City life and factory work has made me much smarter and stronger," she added. "I was not able to achieve everything, but I was able to get much of what I had desired—long-term employment, a son who cares for me in my old age, and a piece of land to call my own." In Sheuly's case, three factors helped her to have a good life: she left an abusive relationship early and did not allow her husband back into her life; she worked in a factory where the management appreciated her and kept her on; and she and her son worked collaboratively to build a durable life. She says she was satisfied with what she had achieved through factory work.

From the brief story of Sheuly, I turn to the extended case studies of three older, aged-out workers: Mahmuda, Aleya, and Monoara. Mahmuda was married to her second husband at the time of our interview and had a comparatively good life for an older garment worker, but Aleya's and Monoara's lives were more precarious. These two women had limited social support networks, putting them at high levels of economic and social vulnerability. Each of the case studies shows multiple strands in the making of the women's private lives within a landscape of shifts in family structures, migration, age, and work. The cases cover five aspects of workers' lives—childhood, married life, children, factory life, and old age and aspirations—that sketch the arc of change in their life cycles from factory work. They show how women construct new lives at the intersection of work, age, and emotions that structure their aspirational worlds.

CASE 1: MAHMUDA

Mahmuda, a fifty-two-year-old woman at the time of our first interview, in October 2017, lived in Mirpur, an industrial neighborhood adjacent to Dhaka. She had been married twice. Her second husband, Anwar, was a fifty-five-year-old automobile driver with a grade 9 education. She had two sons and a daughter. Mahmuda was born in 1968 in Barisal, a coastal province of southern Bangladesh. She had vague recollections of her childhood. She was the third child of seven children. Her father had studied up to grade 9. According to her, his schooling made him disinterested in agricultural work. He did not have any land and worked for other people. The family always faced poverty. After the war of 1971 the family became even more impoverished, and they came to Dhaka in search of work. Mahmuda had an uncle in Dhaka who helped her father find a job. The family has lived in Dhaka since 1972.

Childhood

Mahmuda said, "I used to be very pretty. I was fashionable as well. I liked to wear nice clothes. I was talented, and I knew how to sew and crochet. Since we were so many brothers and sisters, my father couldn't educate the first four of us, but my mother had studied to grade 5, so she taught me Bengali at home."

When she turned thirteen, in 1981, Mahmuda realized that she had to support her family financially. Next to their house was a factory, and with encouragement from her older sister, she went to the factory seeking employment. According to Mahmuda, "The managers were very impressed with my interview, and they gave me a job on the spot for taka 100 a month. I was offered twice what all the other workers were making at taka 50 a month." It was 1981, just three years after the establishment of the first garment factory in 1978. At that time the industry was in its initial phase of growth, and factories were unregulated. Wages were very low and were uneven across the factories that were opening. In its early years, the garment industry used child labor extensively.

Married Life

Mahmuda was married twice, and both times she faced severe complications. Her first marriage occurred at age sixteen. Her father had arranged a match for her with an older man who already had a wife and two children. Mahmuda had a boyfriend at her factory, though, and she refused to accept the marriage proposal. She said, "I was in the garment factory earning money. I thought I had a bright future. My future looked very bleak on the day my father informed me of my upcoming marriage." When she told her father about her boyfriend, he became furious and severely beat her. Mahmuda and her boyfriend decided that she would run away to her neighbor's house when the groom's family came to see her that evening. When the groom's family arrived, her family could not find her. Later her father told her, "I will marry you to whoever wants to marry and take you away from my house, because you made me lose face today." That day her boyfriend came over and asked for her hand in marriage. After the wedding, they went to live with her older sister temporarily.

Mahmuda and her first husband were together for only six weeks. Then he left for his village for the Muslim Feast of the Sacrifice. He said that he would return in a few days, but he never returned. Soon after his disappearance, Mahmuda learned that she was pregnant. When she told her family of her pregnancy and abandonment by her husband, they recommended that she get an abortion, but she would not agree. Her father told her that if the child were a son, he would allow her and the child to stay at his house, but he would throw them out if it were a girl. Mahmuda said, "I was lucky that I had a son. Otherwise, I would be on the street with my child." She named her son Tanjil.

Her second marriage happened five years later, to Anwar. For four years she would not agree to his proposal, but Anwar was persistent. He would wait for her outside the factory gates. He would give her small gifts of peanuts and chocolates. Finally, she agreed to marry him, but she laid down two conditions. Her first condition was that Anwar could never beat her. Her second condition was that he had to love and accept her son as his own. Mahmuda said with a whimsical smile, "Anwar is a good man, and he has been like a father to Tanjil." But life was not easy for them. She was not aware that Anwar had a gambling addiction, which resulted in his inability to hold a job. They lived on Mahmuda's income, which put them under tremendous financial stress. Seeing her predicament, her uncle helped Anwar get a job and gave him money to get a driver's license. He now works at a local bank as a driver; this is considered a good job in the local job market and pays taka 15,000 a month. Working cooperatively, Mahmuda and Anwar turned their fortunes around. Mahmuda's family networks, a father who provided housing at a critical juncture in her life, and an uncle who found a job for Anwar helped them build a stable family life.

She said that for the last twenty-five years they had had a good life. Anwar never beat her, and she considers this to be her "good fortune." She said that her husband doesn't physically abuse her, because when she found out about his gambling and his occasional attraction to another woman, "I would always punish him by throwing water in his face." Then, shyly, she told me the following story. One day, she was sorting clothes for washing when she found a folded love letter and a woman's photo in the pocket of Anwar's shirt. She said, "I could not get that woman's picture out of my mind." That day at work she began to cry. Mahmuda was very skilled at her job and liked by her manager. When her manager saw her crying, he asked her about it, and she told him the whole story. That evening, the manager went with her to her house to speak with Anwar. According to her, her manager told Anwar, "If you write a letter to another woman again, you will find that your wife will be going around with me in my car." When Anwar heard his threat, he touched Mahmuda's feet and asked for her forgiveness.

Needless to say, this is an unusual story, because such a threat would make most husbands assume that their wife was having an affair with the manager at the factory. The story offers several possible interpretations: the manager was fond of Mahmuda; the manager was a good man and helped his workers; Mahmuda was a skilled worker, so the manager did not want her grief-stricken and unable to work. Perhaps, by telling me that the manager, a powerful local figure, came to her house to admonish her husband on his errant ways, she was asserting that she was respected at work, was admired by the powerful factory manager, and had some authority over her husband. Whatever may have been the intentions of the manager or Mahmuda, his actions saved their marriage.

Mahmuda said that Anwar loved her very much. He always bought the food she liked, and on Valentine's Day he gave her flowers and monetary gifts. She also added that Anwar never prevented her from enjoying her life. In many ways, he was different from most men of his generation. He helped with household chores, and on days when she worked late he cooked the meal, fed the children, and cleaned the house. On every Eid (the Muslim high holidays) he gave her new clothes. She also gave him gifts such as shirts and trousers. When the kids were young, they would go as a family to the cinema. He also got along with his in-laws and did not object if she stayed with her father's family for a week. They shared household expenses. Anwar took care of the day-to-day expenses of the family; Mahmuda paid for rent and the children's education. Apart from that, she could spend money without asking his permission. When Anwar lost his job due to gambling, he stayed at home and took care of the kids, so she could sometimes take a day off and see a movie with friends.

Mahmuda was very forthcoming about their sexual life. She said that Anwar was responsive to her needs. She said, "If my husband wanted to have relations with me and I was not feeling well, I just had to tell him once that I was not well. But if I ever feel the need for sexual intimacy, I cannot go to him. If I go to him, then he will say I have no shame. We used to live in one room before, and we all slept on the floor. Now we have two rooms, and that gives us more privacy." Mahmuda said that they always discussed whether they wanted to have children. She used contraceptives to regulate her pregnancies. Anwar did not want to use contraception. In terms of her family life, she was self-reliant and independent. She sent her children to school. She didn't feel it necessary to ask Anwar's permission to purchase commodities that she liked. In all these respects, Anwar stood out as a model husband, and their life story is singular among the garment workers I met.

Children

Mahmuda mentioned that her older son, Tanjil, from her first marriage, was her favorite, although she was no longer on good terms with him following his marriage. She said, "I married Anwar on the condition that he had to love my son in the same way he loved me. I turned my blood into water to raise this son. I sent him to a good school. My relatives used to mock me and say that a garment worker's child will not amount to much. I used to feel bad when I heard those comments. When my son was in grade 9, my sister's son was also studying in the same class. She was rich and could afford a private tutor for her child. I asked her, 'Can Tanjil also attend these private lessons?' My sister laughed and said, 'If my son studies with your son, he will not be a good boy.' But Tanjil would stand outside the door and listen to the tutor teaching his cousin. That is how he studied for his exams. I had this one wish that my son would one day become a big officer. My son now works for taka 50,000 a month in a company as a finance manager." From her marriage to Anwar, she had a daughter and a son. Her daughter was studying in an English honors program at a private university prior to her marriage. Her third child, a son, was studying in grade 12, and she wanted him to study computer engineering. Mahmuda had lofty ambitions for all three of her children.

When I asked her how she had accomplished all this, Mahmuda replied that she did not purchase a TV, sofas, or any fancy furniture. She put her earnings into educating her children. She thought of education as an investment. She said to me, "Money can be stolen; education is yours for life. My lack of education is a pain I carry all the time. When I started to work at the garment factory, I had a decent production manager. I followed his instructions. He showed me how to do quality work and meet factory targets. That is how I became a skilled worker. I followed all his instructions, but I knew I could never become a production manager because I didn't have an education. I didn't know any English. That's why I thought if I could educate my children, they would provide for me. To educate my children, I took loans from people. I asked my relatives for help. While I was sending them to school, I was always at least taka 30,000 in debt."

Tanjil passed his honors exam and got a good job at a company. But then he fell in love with a young girl at his office and married her. He now lives independently with his wife. Mahmuda didn't agree to his marriage, and she didn't speak to him for two years. Although her son has a very good income, she has never accepted any money from him.

Mahmuda had married off her daughter while she was still enrolled in the university. She put her severance pay from the factory (taka 57,000) toward her daughter's wedding, which cost almost taka 100,000.

The wedding was held at a local Chinese restaurant, and in Dhaka this is a sign of middle-class status, which garment workers aspire toward but very few can afford. While Mahmuda denied herself many small pleasures in order to educate her children, she had spent all her severance money on her daughter's lavish wedding. When I asked her if she had regretted spending her severance on the wedding, she said no. She described it as a rich person's wedding. Grand weddings are noteworthy events in the life cycles of garment workers. In villages, the richer farmer has a grand wedding to which the entire village is invited. In the city, these women watch rich people's weddings from the outside. Thus, even for one day, the chimera of wealth was deeply meaningful for Mahmuda.

Factory Life

Mahmuda was fired from her job in 2017. For her, factory work meant independence, the ability to earn a living, an increase in courage, and social skills. She said, "Factory work has meant a lot to me. Without a factory job, I would have to listen to my husband, bear the punishments of my father and brothers. I wouldn't be able to raise my children in the way I wanted." At the factory, she had to face many struggles because she would speak on behalf of other workers. When she saw a supervisor verbally abusing another worker, she intervened and mediated on the worker's behalf. When somebody fell ill at work, she would go with that person to the hospital. When she came across firing documents and noticed that the paperwork listed an incorrect amount due to the worker, she would explain that worker's rights to her. At the last factory she worked, she was a member of the harassment committee. Their line manager had kicked a worker who was two months pregnant, and the fetus died. The line manager had also threatened and shamed the same female worker publicly by saying that he would put his penis into her through her "backside." Mahmuda took on this case and made the factory harassment committee investigate. The worker was compensated for her injuries, and the line manager was given a warning.

Then Mahmuda told me the story of how she got fired. There were two young women who worked in her assembly line, and both were pregnant. They had worked for seven years in the same factory. When they tried to apply for maternity leave, the production manager accused them of becoming pregnant to make money by receiving maternity leave pay. Mahmuda said she defended them against the accusations of the manager. She said, "If they had gotten pregnant to get some material benefits from the factory, they could have done this much earlier since they have worked here for seven years." Listening to the production manager's rant against these two women, she realized that he intended to terminate them during the upcoming Eid holidays when workers leave for their villages. So, she told these two women not to mention anything to management, and she would take care of their situation. During lunchtime, she made a phone call to their local trade union leader and asked for her assistance. Unbeknownst to her, the trade union leader was in the pay of factory management, and she communicated Mahmuda's call to them.

The following day, Mahmuda was supposed to get paid. When she went to get her wages, the accountant told her, "I do not have your money. You have to talk to the manager." She said, "I immediately knew something was wrong." Then she went to see the female officer in charge of compliance at the factory. This female officer pretended that she didn't know anything about Mahmuda's case. Then Mahmuda went to the manager's office. They kept her waiting outside for a very long time. Finally, someone told her to come back the following day. When she tried to punch her timecard, she saw that the card would not punch. She again went back to the compliance officer and asked what was going on. Then all the managers came out and accused her of being at fault for advocating for those two pregnant workers. She told them, "When I see something is wrong, I cannot accept it."

Then the managing director said that because she was old, they were going to lay her off. She said, "Fine, you can fire me, but you have to give me all the money that is due to me. Otherwise, I will not sign any paperwork." For the next few hours, they negotiated how much money was due to her. Mahmuda said that she received severance pay of taka 57,000.

OLD AGE AND ASPIRATIONS

After Mahmuda lost her job, the family was entirely dependent on her husband's income. At the time of the first interview, Mahmuda was still looking for work at another factory, but at fifty-two years of age, nobody would hire her. She had learned tailoring while she worked at the factory.

She wanted to own a boutique shop, but that required a big investment. When I reminded her that the severance pay could have gone toward a down payment for her store, she brushed aside my comment and said, "My daughter's wedding had to be grand."

Then I asked, "What are the major changes in your life?" She said that her most important achievement was turning her husband away from gambling and illicit affairs with other women. As a result of her hard work, he now respected her and loved his children. She went on to add that although factory work had given her economic independence, she had to come up with the initiative and courage to make it all work. Otherwise, she said, "One is simply a cog in the wheel." Mahmuda's economic and aspirational subjectivities were pronounced; she believed in her ability for self-improvement. In that respect, she was Freeman's neoliberal subject.

In April 2018 we did a follow-up interview with Mahmuda to assess how she was doing. Mahmuda came to the labor office for her meeting and complained of severe pain in her lower abdomen. When we asked her if she had seen a doctor, she said that they now live on her husband's income and cannot afford to pay her medical expenses.

Hearing her comment, I said, "Can't Tanjil help you?" Mahmuda went quiet, then she said, "I will see the doctor next week." It was a veiled way of signifying that she did not want money from her son and that we should refrain from probing. In our earlier interview she was excited to speak about her son, but now a darkness came over her face when his name was mentioned.

She told us that her younger son had taken up a night-time job at a local call center to pay for his education. However, the work at the call center was affecting his ability to concentrate on his schoolwork, and his grades were suffering. Her daughter had been sent back to Mahmuda's house by the husband and his parents, who were demanding more dowry. Mahmuda no longer worked and whatever savings she had was exhausted, so she was unable to pay them.

From long-term factory work, Mahmuda had a developed a political and legal subjectivity that was absent in most of the older workers I met. She said that she learned about labor laws and took a proactive role in the anti-harassment committee at her factory. She mentioned that she was not a member of any labor organization and did not attend labor rights training workshops. What helped her navigate the hazards of the factory were her "life experiences." She said, "It is not sufficient to know the law; one needs courage to demand the implementation of the law. In trying to make changes at the factory level, workers face harassment and layoffs."

She said, "When they tried to fire me, I said to them, I will sign the paperwork only after you give me what is due to me. If they tried to force me out of the factory, I would go to the minister of labor and demand my rights."

Somewhat taken aback by her comment, I asked, "Why would you go to the ministry of labor and not the labor court?"

She said, "The courts are confusing places, full of red tape. They give ordinary people like me the runaround. The lawyers are the ones who make money." In all likelihood, she would not be able to get past the gate of the ministry of labor in the city. However, the fact that Mahmuda now believed that the labor minister would listen to her demands showed that she had developed an increased sense of self-worth.

On September 3, 2018, we did a second follow-up with Mahmuda. She was still unemployed. Her younger son had left his call-center job and withdrawn from his university in order to find a full-time job to help the family. Her daughter had gone back to her in-laws, but they were not treating her well. Mahmuda wanted her younger son to enroll at German Technical School, a local institute that trains workers for overseas employment. Within the course of a year that I tracked Mahmuda, her life of aspirations had substantially narrowed and fragmented. She wanted her children to climb up the economic ladder, but that ladder was broken with the eldest son absent in her life, the younger son forced to withdraw from college, and the daughter's university-level education did not amount to much.

In the Covid follow-up in August 2020, I learned that Mahmuda's younger son now supported them financially, but her older son did not. Her husband was still employed, so the family had a steady income. What helped Mahmuda survive was how her family had cohered as a unit to survive, but her older son had separated himself from the family. While Mahmuda's older son had moved into the new middle class through his education and occupation, he had accomplished that by abrogating his responsibilities to his natal family. Despite all her effort and investment in education and a lavish wedding, her younger son and daughter remained trapped in their working-class environment.

CASE 2: ALEYA

We met Aleya one evening in October 2017 in the labor rights office. She was fifty-two-years old, short in stature with a merry face. She came rather diffidently into the room where my research assistant and I were sitting. When we explained to her that we wanted to write her life story (*jibon kahini*), she laughed and said, "My life story will remain folded inside me. But we can talk." By her comment "folded inside me," Aleya indicated to us that she would share her life events selectively.

Childhood

Aleya was from Mirjapur village in Tangail district. She was the second of four children. Like millions of Bangladeshi cultivators, her father lost his small plot of land to creditors. Her recollection of her father was vague, since he passed away when she was seven years old. With the death of her father, Aleya's mother did not have the financial resources to send Aleya to school, so she helped with household chores. Her older sister lived in Dhaka with her husband. When Aleya was thirteen years old, her sister brought her to Dhaka to work in the garment industry.

Married Life

Once Aleya moved to the city, her sister and brother-in-law arranged for her to meet a young man named Belayat, a day laborer. After meeting him, she agreed to the marriage proposal. Aleya's mother was happy to approve of her marriage, since Belayat did not ask for a dowry. After her marriage, Aleya returned to live with her mother in the village while her husband worked in Dhaka. The following year she came to the city and moved into a one-room unit that her husband rented in Mirpur, a hub of smaller garment factories. In her first year in the city, she did not work. After a year, she noticed that Belayat would forget to buy food or would bring rotten fish and vegetables home. He told her that he did not have the money to buy higher-quality food. Aleya said that she lost weight from lack of nutritional food. Seeing her look so thin, one of her neighbors suggested that she should join a garment factory.

Belayat did not prevent Aleya from working at a factory. Once she started working, though, he would take away her wages. She said that if she didn't hand over the money, he would become enraged and physically hurt her. After that, she added with a sigh, he would never take her anywhere. He did not even give her a sari on Eid, the Muslim high holiday. Aleya said that he forced her to have sex whenever he felt like it. Even when she was exhausted from work after a long night shift, she had to succumb to his sexual needs.

After two years of marriage, she gave birth to a daughter. She took time off from work to raise her child. Then Aleya returned to factory work, and life went on for several years. One day, Aleya found a letter written to Belayat by a woman who claimed to be his wife. Aleya confronted him about it the same day. When he heard her accusations, he became incensed and physically assaulted her. Later he confessed that he had married the other woman. She realized that this had occurred around the time he had stopped buying good food for the family. He was transferring his resources from Aleya to his second wife. The following day when Belayat returned home from work, Aleya shut the door and would not let him in. She said, "I was morally outraged by his behavior. I loved him, did everything he asked, and he betrayed me." After this, Aleya and Belayat separated but did not legally divorce.

What was remarkable about her story was her courage in forcing her husband out of the house. Aleya had indicated to us that she was terrified of her husband because he was physically abusive. Yet she found the strength to lock him out of the house, to separate from him and take her life into her own hands. When asked to explain this, Aleya said that through factory work she had developed a sense of mental strength in her ability to survive on her own. Her moral and economic subjectivities had converged. She would not accept the immoral behavior of her husband, and her factory wages, although meager, allowed her to separate from him.

Children

After her separation, Aleya left her daughter in the village with her aunt and uncle and returned to work. Her kin network was supportive and fulfilled their care obligations, and this helped to maintain a tie between Aleya and her family. When her daughter was older, she brought her to the city. Her daughter completed her grade 10 examination, known as the Secondary School Certificate Examination. Aleya said with tremendous pride, "In the city, I saw opportunities for young women that were absent in the village. I did not want her to be like me. I did not want her to suffer the hard work and indignities of factory work. I wanted to educate her." Aleya's daughter had an arranged marriage. Aleya and her sister together had saved taka 60,000 for her dowry. What helped Aleya survive on her own was her supportive kin network, an aunt and uncle who became surrogate parents to her daughter, and her sister's help with her daughter's dowry. These kin networks are essential for survival for these garment workers. Those who are without these familial networks of support fall through the cracks.

Factory Life

Aleya had started at the lowest rung as a helper. After eight years, she became a sewing operator at taka 6,000 a month. Over her work life, which was staggered over twenty years, Aleya had changed factories four times. The first time it was because she refused to adhere to the dress code, the second time because she could not do night duty, the third time because she fell sick, and her fourth job was her last factory job. Aleya said, "Inside the factory, we are all workers, we all do similar work." She said that she never faced any negative comments about her work from relatives or neighbors. These women live in the slums that adjoin factories, so the slum dwellers have a shared understanding of these workers' lives. When a factory worker comes home past midnight, they do not think that she is a sex worker. They understand that the women have to work late when a shipment is due. Aleya saw her slum as a caring community. She said that the landlady often sent food, saying, "You are alone, and you work so hard."

When I asked her about working conditions inside the factory, she said, "In the beginning, I made mistakes and was verbally abused. Supervisors would often say 'daughter of a whore.' That was very humiliating. But once I became a skilled worker, line supervisors did not verbally abuse me. When another worker got reprimanded in front of me, I feel pain but I do not say anything because that could get me fired." Aleya said that through her factory work she became aware of workers' rights organizations and began to attend meetings of a local labor organization. But she also added that due to age, she could not remember much of what was taught. For her, these workshops were a place away from the slum where she could meet other factory workers and exchange ideas. She admired the trainers, who were well-dressed, middle-class women who spoke with confidence. She added that she gained social knowledge from meeting these trainers. More than the information that the trainers taught through flip charts and posters ("What I learned, I would soon forget"), she enjoyed the relaxation and community building that these meetings offered.

She said that at the time she was let go, factory management provided her with taka 12,000 as severance. although they were supposed to give her taka 16,000. When I asked her why she did not claim her full severance pay, she said, "I was tired. The factory managers make it very difficult for workers to get their severance pay." Apart from the taka 12,000 she received as severance pay, Aleya did not have any money saved.

Old Age and Aspirations

At the end of our conversation, I asked Aleya how factory work had changed her life circumstances. She thought for a while and then said, "Now I know a lot more about the world. I could educate my daughter. Had I lived in the village, I would not be able to do that. Beyond that, I have not achieved much."

In our first follow-up interview in 2018, Aleya said that she initially had returned to her village due to lack of work. Once there, though, she felt like a burden on her relatives and returned to Dhaka, hoping to find work again. Finally, she found work at a small tailoring shop that made women's clothes for the domestic market. The hours were long, from 9 a.m. to 9 p.m.; sometimes she had to work through the night, but they did not pay overtime. She said that the work environment at this shop was better than the garment factory, but if she was late or missed work due to sickness she was harshly reprimanded. She made taka 6,000 a month. Aleya said that she was making enough money to pay for her room and board, but working twelve hours a day took its toll on her body.

We did a second follow-up interview five months later. Aleya told us that she had been laid off from the tailoring shop because they did not get enough work orders. After getting laid off she lived for a few months with her daughter in Dhaka, taking care of her granddaughter. Then she left her daughter's house and rented a room for taka 1,000 per month from the severance pay she had received from the factory. That money was almost exhausted, and she had no savings to fall back on. In our final interview, in August 2020, she informed us that she had been unable to find work and had returned to her village to live with her sister. At the end of her life, it was her sister, not the factory or her married daughter whom she had raised as a single mother, who gave her a lifeline to live out the remainder of her life. By living frugally in the village she was able to meet her minimal expenses—a place to sleep and basic meals of rice and lentils. She said that although she had no savings left, she had learned a lot from living in the city. She was able to be a good mother, educate her daughter, and marry her off. She then said, "What more can we older female workers expect of life? I had dreams of many beautiful things, but they all perished with time. I waded through life in muddy water. I am lucky to have reached the shore without too many injuries."

CASE 3: MONOARA

I first met Monoara in October 2017, when she was forty-eight years old. She is a short woman with a smiling face. Also abandoned by her husband, she had raised two daughters as a single mother.

Childhood

Monoara came from the district of Dinajpur in northern Bangladesh. Her father was a sharecropper. The eldest of six children, Monoara had studied up to grade 3, when she had to leave school in order to help her family. She said that she was very sad for her "lack of education." Monoara said, "If I were a son, then we would not have so much poverty in our household. I would work alongside my father in the fields. These days girls can work everywhere. In my childhood, girls didn't work in the fields because society thought it was unacceptable."

When Monoara was thirteen years old, Alamgir, a thirty-three-year-old man who lived next door to her, sent a proposal to her father. Her father would not agree to a marriage with Alamgir, because he was

Figure 19. Monoara in the kitchen she shares with ten garment worker families.

a man of questionable morals. Failing to secure her father's approval, Alamgir abducted Monoara and forcibly married her.[6] Given the circumstances, her father had to accept the marriage. She remembered the early days of her marriage as "carefree." "I was too young to understand what marriage meant," she said. "All day long, I would run between my father's and my in-laws' houses. Everybody was very affectionate toward me."

Married Life

Monoara recalled that in the initial phase of her married life her husband loved her very much. When she first had sexual relations with her husband, she did not feel that he mistreated her. Alamgir would take her to the market on his bicycle and buy her sweets. At night they would sleep together. Monoara said that she loved her husband. After seven months, she had her first period. Soon after that, she became pregnant and gave birth to a daughter.

Alamgir was a vegetable vendor and operated his business in another village. After their daughter's birth, he began to spend days away from Monoara at the village where he had his business. This behavior went on for three years, and then Monoara found out that Alamgir had married another woman in that village. Monoara's father was very angry when he heard the news, and it led to an altercation between the two families. Her in-laws then sent her back to her father's home, saying, "Since our son no longer wants to be with her, we cannot pay for her and her daughter's maintenance." Then after two years, Alamgir returned and said that he had divorced his other wife and wanted to take her back. Her family sent her to live with Alamgir. Within a few months, she became pregnant. After the birth of a second daughter, Alamgir disappeared again, and she did not see him for twelve years.

For the second time, Monoara returned to her father's home, but he could no longer provide for her and her two children. In her village, the local rice-processing mill was hiring workers, and she found work there. During the rice harvest season, she worked all through the night at the mill, pulling large bags of rice and processing them. According to her, "This is when I realized how much my life circumstances had changed. For ten years, I stayed awake all night working at the rice mill. At the end of the month, I would get taka 1,500, which I would give to my father. This period was the most difficult time of my life, far more difficult than garment factory life."

After twelve years, Alamgir returned and wanted to take her back to his new home in another village. Monoara was very angry with him because she had raised her daughters alone, But her parents forced her to return to Alamgir's house. When she arrived there she saw that he already had another wife—this was wife number three, with whom he had three children. She had to live with a co-wife. She said that she shook that off and tried to make a life with Alamgir. He had given up his vegetable business and now operated a cycle-van to ferry people and goods around. It was tough for him to support a family of eight. He told his wives that they would move to Dhaka because garment factories hired women, and they could both work and help provide for the family. So, Alamgir, Monoara, the third wife, and the third wife's children came to the city. Monoara's children remained with her parents in the village. Monoara began her new life in a slum near a garment factory in Dhaka. Within a month, both of Alamgir's wives had factory jobs. At the end of the month, they would hand over their wages to him. The family lived in a one-room unit. As senior wife, Monoara slept on the veranda with Alamgir, and the co-wife slept inside with her children. She said that Alamgir would often have sexual relations with his other wife, and she felt very offended and hurt by his actions.

After three months of working at the factory, she asked her husband for money from her wages to pay for her daughters' expenses in the village. On hearing this, Alamgir became very angry. Then both he and the co-wife beat Monoara very badly, cutting her forehead with a sharp knife. The following day Monoara went to work as usual. When she returned home in the evening she found that the house was empty of furniture and food. Alamgir and his third wife had decamped with everything. The incident occurred in the middle of the month, and Monoara did not have any money to pay for food. After searching through her house, she found some wheat and wheat husk. She ate wheat for five days by soaking it in water. Later, she borrowed some money from the local moneylender to cover the remainder of the month's expenses. During this time, she was so mentally distressed that she could not concentrate at work. She would make mistakes and get verbally abused. Later she found that her husband had returned to their village. He again asked her to join him. This time around, an older and more financially independent Monoara refused. That was the end of her relationship with Alamgir. She continued to work in the factory for another sixteen years.

I asked her to explain why she had returned to Alamgir so many times. She did not answer the question directly, but instead said, "I had a loving relationship with Alamgir in the early stages in our marriage." I wondered whether that was that an attachment of optimism that profoundly shaped how she wanted to think of love in her otherwise loveless life. She then added that she was "emotionally broken." She said that later Alamgir stopped loving her. He never spoke kindly to her or gave her gifts on Eid holiday. Her two daughters were Alamgir's children, yet they never received any affection or gifts from their father. To this day, Monoara is still very sad about the lack of love in her life. She pointed to her heart and said, "There is an empty space here that will never be filled."

Children

Monoara had only studied up to grade 3. She repeatedly said, "If I were able to study, my life would have been better. I did not want my daughters to experience the same fate." Her daughters stayed in the village until they were eighteen years old. Then they came to the city to work at a garment factory, where they met their future husbands. Before agreeing to the men's proposals, Monoara made them promise her that they would never allow her daughters to work in a garment factory and that they would never beat them. She arranged a simple wedding in the village and invited thirty of her relatives. But soon after the weddings, one of the sons-in-law broke his promise by putting her daughter to work at the factory. The other daughter moved to her husband's ancestral village, where she had a difficult life doing all the household chores from fetching water to helping with rice processing. With a deep sigh, Monoara said, "I left the rice mill to find a better life in the city. My daughters studied up to grade 10. Yet today they have ended up doing exactly what I tried to escape. Can people like us ever hope for a happy life?"

Factory Life

When Monoara first entered factory work, her wages were taka 700 as a helper. From that she paid her rent, sent money for her daughters, and took care of her living expenses. After paying for her living expenses, there was no money left to save. At the end of her sixteen-year career, her income was taka 6,500 as a sewing operator. She described her life in the following terms: "I lived alone, so I didn't want to cook much. I would quickly make vegetable curry and have it with rice. Because of my frugal life, I could pay for my daughters' schooling."

Once she joined the factory, she witnessed verbal and physical abuse of workers. She added that factory managers did not discriminate between male and female workers. They were all equally abused. She mentioned that supervisors would forcefully remove workers from their workbenches and put them outside the factory to shame them publicly. Monoara participated in the 2013 wage increase movement, but she was not in a leadership role. When I asked if she wanted a leadership role, she said that factory owners kept workers under strict supervision and that management fired workers who participated in protests on some pretext. She did acknowledge that workers' movements were necessary, adding, "Otherwise, how will we get improved wages or work conditions? Factory owners will not give us better conditions out of their goodwill."

When asked about the circumstances of her being laid off, she said that the factory relocated from an older building that failed factory inspections after the 2013 upgrades were initiated. When management made this decision to move, Monoara and fifty other older workers, both men and women, were all let go. According to Monoara, she should have received taka 18,000 as severance pay, but she was given only taka 12,000. She said that she fought for this money for several months. Finally, she gave up due to sheer exhaustion. Her factory did not have a trade union representative who could advocate on behalf of workers' interests.

Old Age and Aspirations

Due to her age, Monoara could not find work at another factory, although she has continued to look for one. At our first interview we learned that for the last seven months she had been living off the money she received as severance pay. She knew that taka 12,000 would not last long. Her room rent alone was taka 1,000. I went to meet her in the workers' slum where she lived. She took me inside a small, windowless room. We sat in her tiny room, facing each other.

"So, what will you do now?" I asked.

Monoara said, "I have not learned anything about tailoring garments from factory work. Assembly line work does not teach you how to make a full garment. We make parts of a garment, like stitching cuffs, hemlines, and so forth. When I started to work in the factory, I just thought about the wages at the end of the month, and that money helped me live. I had no time to think about my future. Now I do not know how I will live."

We were silent for a few minutes, letting her words sink in.

She continued, "At least I was able to escape the conditions of the rice factory. I have worked at a factory for sixteen years, yet I have no savings. I don't see much improvement in my life." After a pause, she added, "I could not speak easily with strangers before. Now I can. I walked alone from the factory to my house. Nobody said anything to me, nobody touched my body. I could not do this in the village. Factory work gave me courage, I suppose."

In our first follow-up interview with Monoara we learned that she had found temporary work at a subcontracting factory. Factories often get rush orders from larger factories, and they hire seasoned workers like her on a short-term basis. In the second follow-up interview, six months later, we learned that she was no longer employed there.

In August 2020, during Covid, I heard that Monoara had found employment with another subcontracting factory but that her wages were low and paid irregularly. Sometimes she had to wait for two months before she got paid. She described herself as "living on the edge." Monoara said, "All my life I worked and supported myself. I have married off my daughters. I will not accept charity from anyone. As long as I have eyes and my fingers, I will work." While her positive attitude was remarkable, it also made me question why Monoara did not assign blame for her penurious circumstances to the factory owner or the state. (The global buyers do not come into the worldview of garment workers because that world is too distant.) Was it because she experientially knew that was the behavior of capitalists and the neoliberal state? In all probability, the answer is yes.

Monoara had a spark in her. She smiled even when she was sharing the darkest moments of her life. While it is true that she did not achieve financial security from factory work due to the low wages she received during her work life, she had "life experiences" that she saw as valuable. Would her life have been any better in the village? In all likelihood, no. In her, the moral and economic subjectivities were pronounced. She exhibited pride in her work ("I will not accept charity") and a belief that she could take care of herself. At the same time, Monoara exhibited an alone-ness that was extremely heartbreaking in the bustling slum where she lived. She was surrounded by people, noise, and the hustle and bustle of city life, but she stood apart like a lone figure walking the streets in search of work.

I bookend this chapter with the brief story of Sheema, who started as a child worker and had the most broken body among the older workers

I met. Her life was on the extreme end of the spectrum of the good life that all these workers sought to create.

SHEEMA: A CHILD WORKER'S STORY

I met Sheema on a winter evening in April, 2017. She was forty-seven years old and had a disheveled appearance. Her body was thin and her eyes were sunken. After sitting down with my research assistant and me, Sheema said that she had lost her factory job a few months ago because of her age and ill health. Then she added, "I started work at eleven years of age. My body was too young to do the heavy industrial work for eight hours a day. You may not believe it by looking at me today, but I was pretty when I was young."

Sheema had started working in a garment factory as a child in the early 1990s. One day the factory owner saw her working on the floor. When he found out that she was underage, he told the floor manager that if a buyer walked into the factory and saw her, they would get into trouble for using child labor. This was during the time of the U.S. Child

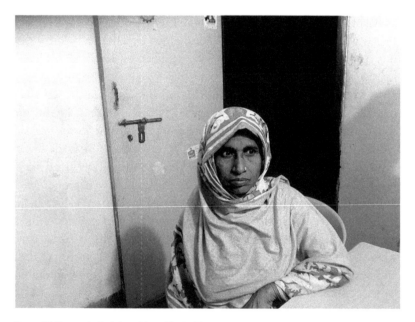

Figure 20. Sheema in the labor rights office in Mirpur.

Labor Deterrence Act, which made many factory owners let go of child workers for fear of losing contracts. The manager defended Sheema by saying, "Although she is young, she is a hard worker and can read numbers in English. We do not find workers who can read English." Workers have to match pieces of clothing by numbers in order to stitch them together, so her ability to read was a useful skill. Finally, the owner relented, but he told Sheema that she was to tell everyone that she was sixteen years old.

Sheema had been married twice. Her first marriage occurred at the age of twelve. Her husband was a mechanic and was much older. He used to fix the refrigerator at her landlady's house, and that is how they met. She found him an "unattractive, old man." She was enjoying her factory work, earning good money, and had no plans of getting married. She claimed that her husband married her by using "black magic." At that time, she was living with her sister and two other garment factory workers. Her sister went to their village to give birth to her child, leaving Sheema alone with the two girls. Sheema described her first marriage in the following terms, "One day, my two roommates gave me a nice sari to wear. They dressed me up. I was young, so I thought it was all for fun. Then they took me to a different house. Once there, a man uttered some words and I was asked to repeat the word 'kobul' three times. 'Kobul' translates into 'I accept.'" According to Islamic law, this is the expression of free will and verbal consent of the bride and groom to the marital contract and takes place in front of two witnesses. It is how an Islamic marriage gets validated.

"After that," she continued, "my roommates laughed and said that I was now married to the mechanic. Bewildered, I kept on asking, 'When did I get married?' They said that once you say the word 'kobul' you are married according to Islamic custom. I was very angry. I said, 'I married that man who looks like a skeleton? Are you crazy?' There you see, I was tricked into marrying him."

After three months, her husband took her to his village home. Once there, she found out that he already had two wives. After seeing Sheema, his second wife asked for financial compensation or she would file a complaint against him under the Prevention of Women and Child Repression Act. Her husband made Sheema hand over all her savings to pay his second wife. Sheema lived with her husband for two years in the village and gave birth to two daughters, but she found this life unbearable. After the birth of her second child, she left her children with her parents and went to the city to live with her sister. She said, "I was like a madwoman for six months. I did not cut my hair and took no news of my daughters." Sheema may have been suffering from postpartum depression that was aggravated by her family situation.

After six months, she said, she came to her senses and her sister helped her find a factory job. She divorced her husband and brought her daughters to the city. Her husband went on to marry nine women after her, but none of his wives stayed with him. Sheema said, "My husband had limited sexual abilities, and that is why no woman wanted to stay with him." Twelve years later, she heard that he had been murdered and his body thrown into a pond. After that, she married her second husband and had another child with him. He too was abusive and would take away her money. Like many men in this social demographic, he left after the birth of their daughter. Sheema was unable to educate her daughters, and all three of them became garment workers.

Sheema continued work for twenty-five years in seven different factories, making lateral moves without any increase in wages. She described her work life as "haphazard." She said that from the havoc wrought on her body from child labor, she had lost all physical ability to work in her later years. She added that her body was extremely weak and she was in constant pain "in her bones." She probably suffered from osteoporosis from bone loss. At the time of our first and second follow-up interviews, Sheema was doing minor tailoring jobs at home to provide for her basic needs. With a deep sigh, she said, "Had I been able to study, perhaps I would not be in this situation. I am too old and broken. Factory work took away my health, my future." In August 2020, Sheema was doing odd jobs as a domestic worker, but due to Covid her income was precarious. Employers would often tell her not to come to work because they were afraid of exposure to Covid. Her daughters sometimes helped her out. She described her condition as "dire."

SUMMARIZING THE OLDER WORKERS' LIVES

These case studies offer a microscopic view of how the work and nonwork lives of these older women intersected in diverse and devastating ways.

All these women came to the city as young girls full of hope. They felt that the new global economy of manufacturing would help them enter a life of comfort that they lacked in their village homes. Their lives show a patchwork of wants and aspirations, love and tribulations, hopes and despairs, triumphs and struggles. Like Esperanza in Ruth Behar's *Translated Woman,* these women showed courage and broke the stereotype of the self-abnegating Bangladeshi garment worker. What also came across was that all of them saw education as the step toward upward mobility and social recognition. They did not seek to become neoliberal entrepreneurs. Instead, they wanted a secure job with a guaranteed income that is increasingly unavailable to the precariat labor force.

These lives should not be read as failed lives trapped in the cruelty of neoliberalism, although that is where an uncritical reading of their life stories takes us. I invite the reader to reflect on these stories with empathy and nuance. These women moved from village to city, from nonwork to work, and from marriage to abandonment and remarriage. All these lives are lived in *difference* within sameness. Their lives are circulating within Freeman's neoliberal optimisms (I can eat better, I can work, I can make more money than my predecessors, I have mobility, I can educate my children, and I can enter into middle-class status and leave poverty behind), where a new world of increased possibilities was overtaking the old. Their attachment to objects that only harmed and injured them, Berlant's "cruel optimisms"—marriage to men who betrayed them and children who would not or could not support them in old age—was like an open sore in their lives. As Berlant noted, "All attachments are optimistic," even when they injure us, because the idea of a possibility (I could be loved and held even if for a day) is what lures us toward the object of attachment.[7] These older women clung to the idea of the good life of material comfort and love from their husbands and children. Sarah White, in her study of rural family life, notes that "conformity with the moral order extends even to the level of emotions. At a discursive level, if not necessarily at the level of actual experience, 'what is' thus elides with 'what should be.'" In her study, she heard statements like "The love of a husband for a wife is unique, as is women's love for their husbands," "All women feel tenderness for their husbands," and "This has come from God, it cannot be questioned."[8] The garment factory women I met did not speak of marital love as ordained by God, but they did mention that love from their husbands/lovers was absent from their emotional lives and something they desperately desired.

These women had earned some limited form of sovereignty over their lives. Their circumstances forced them to take responsibility for their lives and create possible futures. They left abusive spouses, stood up to factory management when they faced workplace injustices, and tried to create better lives for their children through education. In his work, Guy Standing notes how class and social prejudices block poor people's aspirations: "In most societies, a working-class child would be laughed at for aspiring to be a banker or lawyer; a middle-class child would be frowned on for aspiring to be a plumber or a hairdresser."[9] For these factory women, class mobility was a cherished goal that they saw as worth sacrificing for. Their goal was to help their children reach the new middle class that was unfolding through industrial capitalism. But many of these older women also recognized the limits of upward mobility in a deeply hierarchical society due to their lack of social capital. As one older woman said to me, "My son has received his bachelor's degree. He wants to work in a government office, but I do not have the contacts to help him. He has ended up working at a store." But their voices were laced with traces of hope—if not for them, then for their children.

The Bangladeshi government bureaucracy is a labyrinth of byzantine rules and procedures and endless bribery for file processing that is beyond the scope of ordinary people like garment workers. Given their fragile lives, most of these women's children ended up as garment workers or in similar occupations. Only two children of the sixteen garment workers went on to the new middle class, one as an accountant, the other as a technical engineer. Failing to secure higher-status jobs, their daughters became garment workers, and their sons became vendors, store clerks, day laborers, private car drivers, security guards, and rickshaw pullers, professions that did not require higher education. Neoliberal ideas of upward mobility were not realizable in their lifeworlds. Children of these garment workers entered and reproduced the socioeconomic class of their garment factory mothers, or to adapt the subtitle of Paul Willis's book on the British working class, "Garment Workers' Kids Get Garment Worker Jobs."[10]

In these women's lives, work and nonwork intersected in a tangible structure of their consciousness as semi-autonomous subjects. They had a new identity. They were worthy and capable in ways that society, families, and spouses/lovers had not deemed them to be. "I am respected at work" was a recurring theme in their conversations. This is how they wanted society to see them. Beyond work, most of these women's search for the erotic life of an enduring and loving embrace remained a mirage. There existed a missing object in their lives called love. As mentioned in the introduction, love had multiple meanings in their lives. The missing object called "love" in their lives was replaced by ideas such as "I am a good worker," "I am honest," "I educated my children," and "I can work and do not want charity." These ideas signify dignity and respect. Similarly, hope as residue existed like a dim glimmer in their lives. It was an architecture of being, a circular existence between their village lives, no matter how harsh, and their new lives that were lived in the anonymity of factory work and urban slums. Their village remained a place of clean air and the love of their parents. That is, there was something *out there* for them like an invisible lifeline.

I repeat what I had outlined in the introduction about female garment workers' lives. Within capitalist oppression and exploitation, love was one emotion that gave meaning to their lives that was intimately theirs. Love here in the broadest sense meant recognition from the state as its citizens; love from their families as valued and recognized family members; respect from their employers as workers; and finally, affection and care from their husbands/lovers. In all these domains of affection and care, these older women were brutally thwarted. In their life histories, loss of their attachments was always imminent, yet they strove to create meaningful lives. In the age of excitement that is overtaking Dhaka through television forecasts on economic growth and weekly NGO seminars that measure GDP modernity from garment exports, aged-out workers do not measure as even a tiny blip on that screen. They scaled the imaginary ladder of neoliberal class mobility, only to fall to the bottom in their old age. Yet these lives lived as castoffs of capital have much to teach us about human resilience, subject formations through migration and industrial work, women's precarious emotional lives, and the sentiments of the good life formed in the shadows of capital.

CONCLUSION
POLITICS OF THE PRECARIAT

IN THIS CONCLUSION I address the following questions: What is the political future of garment workers in Bangladesh? Will they form Standing's precariat as a "dangerous class" that can become a source of unrest and destabilize society?[1] Will they develop a working-class consciousness that will help them organize collectively and fight for their rights? Or will they become Freeman's neoliberal subjects and pursue individual goals of consumerism and upward mobility? At the core of garment workers' precarious work and life conditions is the absence of a viable trade union movement that has the power to represent their concerns at a national level and engage in meaningful collective bargaining. So, what is the culture of trade unions in the garment industry?

The history of trade unions in Bangladesh is deeply imbricated in national politics over labor. These unions exist in a triadic relationship between political parties, unions, and workers, where workers are mobilized in the interest of the political party that controls their union. They first developed during British colonial rule in the jute and cotton industries in Bengal. Since factories had large labor pools, national political parties targeted trade unions as a steady source of workers to fight against the British. Consequently, a process developed in colonial Bengal that "represented a particular type of politicization of labour unions: factory-based trade unionism was virtually absent and unions were key organizations on the national political stage."[2] This process continued during

Pakistani rule from 1947 to 1971. The Pakistani government banned the Communist Party in 1954, accusing East Pakistani Communist leaders of trying to topple the newly formed government.[3] As a result, Communist Party leaders were persecuted and arrested. Many went into hiding, leading to a fragmentation of left political parties that could no longer cohere as a political force. The situation was further exacerbated in the 1960s when the Pakistani dictator General Ayub Khan "introduced factory-level unionism as part of an anti-communist campaign and with the aim of extending the military regime's hegemony over the working class."[4] This close alliance between trade unions and major political parties continued after the independence of Bangladesh. A noticeable change in trade union politics from the 1960s to the present was that "whereas the leftist parties prior to the 1960s had used politicized unions to promote their oppositional political agendas, the ruling parties of recent decades have used politicized unions to support their hold on power."[5]

While trade unionization came late to the garment industry, a small oppositional labor politics emerged after the 1990 Saraka garment factory fire killed twenty-seven workers. But "unionization of RMG workers remained stagnant into the 2000s, despite the fact that employment in the industry grew by an astounding 500 percent between 1990–91 and 2006–7."[6] There are several reasons for this. First, the garment industry grew under neoliberal policies in the 1980s that did not encourage trade union activities. To enable private enterprise to flourish unregulated, the "labor activism that emerged [was] suppressed through legal restrictions and violence and intimidation against workers attempting to unionize."[7] Second, many foreign-owned factories are inside the Export Processing Zones, where trade unions are not allowed to operate. Third, its workforce is primarily women who are recent urban migrants with little social knowledge about industrial work and politics. Their politicization occurs on the factory floor, but only a small fraction has access to trade unions. There is also a gender dimension to trade unions. While a male worker can attend a union meeting in another part of town late at night, a female worker is constrained in her physical movements and by her caregiver role as a mother. If trade unions are active in the area where the women work, women can become exposed to unions and learn about their rights as workers under labor laws. But in most areas, legitimate trade unions that genuinely represent workers' interests are nonexistent. A report of Solidarity International showed that, between 2010 and 2020, in the RMG sector, 1,123 unions applied for registration, 593 were approved for registration, 487 were denied, and 22 applications were withdrawn.[8]

Within the wider labor movement, many "national union federations are more closely tied to political parties than to the shop floor, while smaller and under-resourced labor groups (including unions too small to be formally registered) attempt to organize garment workers amidst threats of violence by factory owners and hired thugs."[9] Many of these unions at the national level can be termed as "collaborationists" who work to advance the factory owners' agendas and profits, as we saw in the 2006 wage negotiations described in chapter 2.[10] The smaller trade unions and labor groups associated with left political activists have a different objective. While they want to protect workers' rights, they also see the four million garment workers as a way to capture some political power at the national level. Their ideology and rhetoric are steeped in ideas of the proletariat that will rise to fight capitalist oppression.

Figure 21. Workers from Dragon and Imperial Sweater factories stage a demonstration in front of the Labor Ministry to demand arrears, September 8, 2020. Courtesy: *New Age* newspaper, Bangladesh.

The following sections outline two approaches to workers' protests in 2016: first, a small left labor organization's negotiations on behalf of workers; and second, the heightened police repression of workers and trade union activists during the 2016 Ashulia strike, the new normal. I was not in Bangladesh at the time of either of these incidents. My information is taken from newspaper reports and interviews with workers and trade union leaders who were involved in these events.[11]

TWO STRIKES, DIFFERENT OUTCOMES
Rezaul Factory Strike, 2016

On September 18, 2016, garment workers from Rezaul Properties came to the labor rights office in Mirpur (the organization that assisted me with my research) to seek advice over the sudden announcement of relocation of the Rezaul factory from Mirpur to Gazipur. The workers did not want to relocate to Gazipur, that was located eighteen miles from their current domicile. At this factory there were some simmering issues over nonpayment of back wages and workers' vacation and maternity benefits. Workers felt that relocation would give management an opportunity to defraud them of what was due to them. In their meeting, the labor rights group informed them that the 2006 Labor Act requires that owners give workers two months' advance notice before relocating or closing a factory.

Armed with that information, the workers met with factory management to discuss the issue of relocation. At that meeting, factory management said that the factory would not be relocated immediately and that when they did relocate, they would do so according to the provisions of the Labor Act. Furthermore, they agreed to fulfill all the demands of the workers. More than two months later, on December 2, Rezaul factory management put up a sign that said that the factory would be relocated to Gazipur on February 28, 2017. The pending issues of back pay and benefits had not been resolved. Concerned workers met with factory management and asked them to explain the reasons for relocating the factory. Later, management posted a revised notice that the factory was being closed due to safety issues, especially from fire hazards. The notice mentioned that all the workers would receive their benefits as mandated by law.

Workers were still not satisfied with the closing of the factory, because most of them could not relocate due to jobs held by other family members and the schools their children attended. They feared that management knew that most workers would not be able to relocate and planned to hire new workers at lower wages in Gazipur. They were also concerned over the unpaid wages and benefits. On December 4, 2016, representatives from the labor group along with some workers went to the BGMEA office to meet with the factory owners for a resolution. Even after three hours of negotiations, management and workers could not come to an agreement. At that point, the workers left the meeting. When the workers at the factory heard of the failed meeting, they got very agitated. They padlocked the main gate of the factory, locking several managers inside the factory. Workers said that they would let the managers go only after their demands were met. This led to another round of meetings between workers, their representatives, and management. Finally, the factory owner announced over a loudspeaker to the gathered workers that he had agreed to their demands. But when he was asked to sign the paperwork, he refused, saying his word was good enough. That same night, management asked workers to work overtime to fulfill the quota that was affected by work interruption during the bargaining, and the workers complied. After work that night, several workers kept vigil outside the factory gates. Late at night they saw large lorries going inside the factory. They feared that the lorries were being packed with factory equipment to be relocated to Gazipur. The workers realized that the management had no intention of fulfilling their financial commitments.

The following day, the workers came to the factory and found that the gate was closed. A notice was posted on the door that the factory was closed indefinitely. Following this incident, the labor rights group helped organize the workers to sit outside the factory gates. Workers and labor activists distributed leaflets and held banners. They stood in front of the factory in peaceful protest. The police tried to break them up by charging them with sticks and spraying tear gas. As the situation got more serious, the labor group contacted the various labor federation leaders working in the area. As a result, twenty labor federations came together in support of the workers. They contacted the BGMEA head office and asked them to resolve the situation. BGMEA asked the owner of Rezaul to come to their office. The labor group and federation leaders took one hundred workers in five buses and went to the BGMEA office for a solution. After discussions with all groups concerned, the parties signed a memorandum of understanding that prior to closing a factory, the following conditions must be met:

a. Workers must be given one month of bonus pay for each year worked.
b. They must receive two months' notice prior to a factory closure.
c. They must receive paid leave as mandated by law after one year of work.
d. Wages and overtime accrued until December 16, 2016, must be fully paid.
e. Those workers due maternity benefits must receive maternity leave pay.
f. Workers must receive free medical treatment at work.

Based on this understanding, on December 8, 2016, about twelve hundred workers finally received their back wages and benefits.

Ashulia Strike, 2016

The strike in Ashulia, an area where I also conducted research, occurred in December 2016 as well. The strike involved many more workers and factories. It received widespread coverage in Western media that resulted in global retailers pressuring the Bangladesh government to stop persecuting trade unions and address the ongoing labor concerns in these factories. But the Ashulia strike was different from the Rezaul strike. In Ashulia, workers demanded higher wages; at the Rezaul strike, workers demanded back pay, not a pay increase. The Ashulia incident involved a broader range of left political activists; in the Rezaul strike, workers sought the help of a local labor rights organization that was known to the factory owners. In the Mirpur incident there was only one labor rights organization involved that had worked for many years with workers and had developed a relationship of trust with them. The organization was also known to the factory owners. In the Ashulia area there are multiple labor organizations representing different viewpoints, and they do not always cohere as a group on a united platform. As a result of these differences, the outcomes were also different.

According to several trade union leaders, the strike was instigated by a meeting of Garments Sramik Front, a workers' left-oriented union, on November 25, 2016. At the meeting, they distributed leaflets demanding a wage increase for workers from $67 (the wage set in 2013 after the Rana Plaza factory catastrophe) to $200, citing increased housing and food costs. Between 2013 and 2016, food and housing expenses had increased considerably, putting workers and their families in severe economic hardship. Two weeks later, workers walked out of the Windy Apparel factory, demanding higher wages. There were simmering issues at Windy over nonpayment of wages to workers. Many workers were also angry with management over a very sick female worker who was not allowed to go home, fainted on the factory floor, and was taken to the hospital where she was pronounced dead. Soon workers from nearby factories (Setara and Ha-Meem) joined Windy workers in demanding higher wages. Each group of workers from these factories had their specific set of grievances against management, but they were united in viewing wages as too low to survive on.

The response of the factory owners to the striking workers was swift and decisive. They took punitive measures to crush the strike and retaliate against the leftist trade union organizers. They immediately closed sixty factories, putting 200,000 workers out of work. They called in the industrial police, who began to attack protesting workers. Factory owners fired sixteen hundred workers whom they identified as the instigators. Then they hung their pictures outside factory gates so these workers could be publicly known. Owners also made this information available to factories located nearby, thereby making it difficult for the fired workers to find new jobs. The police arrested seven trade union leaders and thirty workers. It was the first time in the history of Bangladesh that police arrested trade union workers under the draconian Special Powers Act of 1974, which was created to charge people for treasonous acts against the state.[12] They threatened two of the arrested leaders with "crossfire," a code word for killing people in a staged shootout with the police. The police also charged a journalist from a local TV channel (ETV) under the Information and Communication Special Technology Act (2015) for inciting violence by reporting on the strike. The reporter spent fifty-two days behind bars before he was released on bail. Two leftist trade union leaders involved in organizing the strike mentioned that the police officer in charge had invited the union leaders to meet them at a local restaurant. These two decided against going to the event, but many others went. Once there, they were arrested and taken to the local jail in a police van. The trade union leaders said, "This was the first time in the history of left politics, that the police did not have to search for the leaders. The leaders came to them voluntarily to get arrested." Their behavior could be interpreted either as the political naïveté of these leaders or as a strategy to bring attention to workers' grievances.

The Ashulia strike lasted from December 11 to December 18 and received widespread international coverage due to the large number of international labor and human rights organizations monitoring the garment industry. Global retailers (H&M, Next, C&A, Inditex, Gap, Primark) also pressured the government to address these labor code violations.[13] However, I would assert that their concern was not for the workers but their loss of a cheap production site from which they have sourced clothes at cutthroat rates. As noted in earlier chapters, these multinationals were aware of the work conditions inside these factories from workers' protests since the 1990s. Finally, the prime minister asked the factory owners to reopen the factories on December 19. On TV, the prime minister threatened the striking workers by saying that she had raised their wages in 2013, and if she wanted she could lower their wages as well. Not only was this an offensive remark, but it also showed the paternalistic relationship of the state to the workers. The workers are deemed as serfs working for the state; their labor belongs to the state and not to them. The state can, if it chooses, confiscate their hard-earned wages. Finally, given no option, the workers returned to the factories on December 23 without having any of their demands met.

In my interviews with workers, I found that although many were unaware of what had sparked the strike initially, they were united in the opinion that wages were too low. As one worker said to me, "I heard that workers at Windy were on strike. Initially, I did not want to join. Then I thought, why not? So, I joined. We cannot live on such low wages." However, in contrast to the 2006, 2010, and 2013 mass uprisings when workers did receive a raise in wages and several other long-overdue benefits, in 2016 they received no wage increase but only an assurance from the labor minister that garment owners would work with landlords to put a cap on rents in the area. Why did Garments Sramik

Front circulate a leaflet demanding a wage increase to $200 without discussing the matter with local labor leaders? Surely, they knew from long-term immersion in labor politics that the workers would suffer should a strike be called. What was the outcome of the strike for the workers? Over sixteen hundred workers lost their jobs, many trade union leaders were arrested, and many unions were busted. The winner was the factory owners. By 2016, the factory owners, with state complicity, had organized resources from industrial police to the courts to weaken opposition to the way they ran the factories.

WORKERS' POLITICS AND FUTURES

Modern politics in Bangladesh is crowd-based politics. As Nusrat Chowdhury mentions, "Protesting crowds have been the media of change in the democratic culture of Bangladesh."[14] In the absence of a functional democracy where dissenting parties can debate issues, street protests are the instrument of choice of the disenfranchised. Crowd politics, then, is the oral artifact of the voiceless. Although garment workers are not organized under the umbrella of a sustainable labor movement, they have become strategic in occupying major streets and closing off vehicular traffic to bring attention to their grievances. Bringing part of the city to a standstill causes enormous upheaval—buses cannot move, people cannot get to their offices, shops cannot open. It forces factory owners and BGMEA and state officials to negotiate with workers and their representatives and reach an understanding. But such tactics do not move the dialogue beyond the immediate goal of getting some of their demands met. It does not change the culture of factory work or the precarious conditions of workers' lives. Once some of those grievances are met even partially, the insurgency fizzles away.

Ching Kwan Lee's findings on Chinese factory labor parallel much of what I have outlined here. In analyzing the workers' protests of Liaoyang in 2002, Lee discovered that behind "the façade of multifactory participation, the protest organizers from one factory insisted on excluding other factories' workers from participating in planning meetings and meetings with the leadership."[15] That is, at the micro level, leaders from different factories had different motivations for organizing labor protests, what Lee calls "cellular activism." As she argued, "The massive multi-factory turnout was a chance incident that portended the specter of unintended radicalization rather than the result of workers' strategy or capacity for lateral mobilization."[16] She goes on to say, "While there is no lack of references to 'working-class interests' and 'citizens' legal rights' among workers in these protests, the validity of these insurgent identities is negated by the workers themselves in the process of labor disputes."[17]

In the Tuba factory strike of 2014, sixteen hundred workers went on strike over nonpayment of wages and Eid holiday bonus. Moshrefa Mishu, a female left political leader of the Garment Workers Forum, joined the movement and attempted to take their grievances to a national level. In an interview, she said to me that the strike was "a trigger of a nationwide workers' movement."[18] The workers occupied the factory, and some of them even went on a hunger strike initiated by Mishu. She exhorted the workers not to accept any watered-down proposal from the factory owners. But once an agreement was brokered between the factory owners and the workers' representatives for a staggered payment of back wages and holiday pay, the workers took the money and went home to celebrate Eid with their families. They returned to their villages to enjoy a Muslim holiday when they meet with extended family, offer gifts and money, wear new clothes, eat festive food, and get renewed through their familial bonds. Clearly, the workers rejected a revolutionary identity imposed by left political leaders. Commenting on the same event, trade union leader Lovely Yesmin said that these left political parties make the work of trade unions difficult because "a trade union is not a political party."

What motivates the workers to strike is not a revolutionary political spirit but the oppression that they are subjected to in the workplace. They strike primarily over nonpayment of wages that often coincides with ongoing oppressive behavior of management. It is important to note that workers strike because they do not get living wages; they do not strike if they are paid well and on time. Will repressed workers fight over the nonpayment of wages? Yes. Will the workers continue to agitate after they have received their payment for a broader labor rights movement? In all probability, no. Factory management's lack of compassion, verbal abuse, and inhumane behavior result in pent-up anger among workers, and a raw incident of abuse acts as the instigator. However, most strikes are short-lived and fail because of what Lee has called "cellular activism," that is, work disruptions at the factory level that fail to translate into a broader movement for workers' rights.[19]

Beyond fair wages and job security, what else do workers want? From conversations with workers and trade union leaders, I found the following needs: workers' colonies where they can live in affordable apartments for families and hostels for single women; low-cost day care and schools for their children; skills retraining for aged-out workers so they can reenter the economy; financial management classes so they learn to save and invest. Once these basic needs of shelter, education, training, and savings have been met, and the workers can flourish in the fruits of their labor, other questions can enter their discourse. The politics of the present is a politics of anger and disenfranchisement, but it is also a politics dwelling in neoliberal optimism of class mobility and consumer goods. A politics of the future must consider all these aspects of workers' sentiments. Failure to do so results in temporary gains and long-term losses.

In a public rally for garment workers organized by a left political party in Ashulia in November 2015, I saw that on the roster of speakers there was only one female leader in a list dominated by left male political leaders for an event that was addressing female garment workers. There was no entertainment for the workers. I mentioned to the organizers that these workers live joyless lives and that after a long day at work they weren't interested in coming to a rally to be reminded of how miserable their lives are. I suggested, "Why not have some music or a skit about workers' lives to entertain them, to bring some joy into their lives? Perhaps then they might listen to what you have to say." The organizers summarily dismissed my comments. My research assistant later went to the rally, which we videotaped. There were only a few women present, and almost all were wives and sisters of the organizers. Their target audience, the garment workers, had opted out of attending. There could be a variety of reasons for this, and I did not interview the local garment workers, but had the organizers recognized the need for pleasure alongside politics, they might have had more success with the workers. Life bereft of pleasure does not beckon hope.

To return to the question of labor politics, I found that the trade unions, whether left or mainstream, saw these factory women as one-dimensional subjects, that is, either as working-class revolutionaries or as disciplined workers helping to build the national economy. Thus, there is an ongoing conflict between these two ideologically distinct factions; they both represent the workers, but with very different objectives that are played out with the bodies of workers. The workers themselves are aware of these ideological motivations, but they remain voiceless in the game of chess played with their identities as factory workers. Trade union leaders fail to recognize that these working women are human subjects with a range of feelings for the good life that do not correspond to how they envision them. This misrecognition results in the failure of left political parties to bring the workers into their ideological universe as proletarian revolutionaries. The language of left politics and the language of neoliberalism do not merge; they are separate streams.

While these factory women participated in protests demanding higher wages and bonuses, conversations with workers revealed that they were not seeking to become working-class subjects or the foot soldiers of a workers' revolution. Within their restricted social world, these women attempted to make a good life possible through the limited choices available to them regarding work, marriage, family, children's education, and seeking partners who might help to move them out of joyless life, although these choices often backfired, as the previous chapters have detailed. These factory workers aspire to a middle-class life because it offers them security from economic precarity, but it also grants them status in a deeply hierarchical society. Gifts of money, music, clothes, jewelry, toys, trips home—all convey meaning-making and enjoyment with family and others that regenerate these women in more ways than their work lives. This new subject of neoliberal aspirations contains the seeds of a political subjectivity that straddles the contradictions of being an industrial worker and an aspirational subject who rejects the working-class subject position.

For a political culture that advances economic equality and opportunity for the children of the garment workers, the left political leaders must recognize these women not only as workers but in the fullness of their identities and aspirations, as mothers, daughters, lovers, sisters, friends, and political agents. These women have repeatedly said, "I do not want my daughter to be a garment worker. I want something better for her." So, what do these women want? Who do they want to be? A middle-class subject, or a revolutionary working-class actor? Or are they trapped in the seductive promises of a neoliberal tomorrow? Perhaps answering that question requires that we know these women through their life histories, in their words, thoughts, and actions. My aim in this book is to humanize these women, to show that they are not working machines and cold statistics but rather human subjects seeking a good life of decent work, opportunity, fantasy, commodities, education, fun, laughter, sex, and love—the whole universe of what makes us human. Becoming their allies would also mean dwelling with them in their precarity, in their dreams and desires, in their longings, and in their lost embraces. Perhaps the way forward is to break the arrogance of the educated middle class—left leaders, researchers, and policy makers—of having the right answers to complex social problems and not leave the task of political transformation to be borne by the oppressed garment workers. What that politics will be is for history to decide.

Epilogue

AFTER DEATH
A BODY WITHOUT A HOME

The deaths of hundreds of workers brought me to this research, and thus I end with the story of the death of a worker named Nilufa. Her life encapsulates the essence of what it means to be an older female worker in the garment industry in Bangladesh. I heard of Nilufa at the beginning of my research with older female workers. So, in concluding the book, I return to her story.

On an afternoon visit to a labor rights advocacy office, I met with Sahanaj, their café coordinator. We were discussing why many rural women conceal their names when they come to work in the city. Sahanaj mentioned that many workers did not have the national identity cards that were introduced in 2008. They often borrowed a card from a relative to find employment, hence the name change. Many other workers had run away from abusive situations at home, whether from parents or husbands. "These workers often have no idea where such actions can lead," said Sahanaj with a knowing nod. My interest piqued, I asked her to explain her comment further. Then she told me the story of Nilufa, a garment worker who had hidden her identity when she came to Dhaka to work in the garment industry in the late 1990s. At that time Nilufa was in her mid-thirties and a member of a workers' group through their labor organization. A woman called Anju was the coordinator of the workers' groups, the position now held by Sahanaj.

Nilufa had married at a young age. Her family had agreed to pay a dowry of taka 50,000 ($600 in 2018 figures) to her husband's family, but they were too poor to pay that amount. Unable to pay the dowry, Nilufa faced tremendous domestic abuse from her husband. Finally, she left the village without his knowledge and came to Dhaka to find employment in the garment industry. After a few years, her husband tracked her to the city and forcibly took her back to their village. There he poured kerosene over her and lit her on fire. Nilufa survived her burn injuries, and Anju brought her to Dhaka for medical attention. Anju also filed a case against Nilufa's husband for domestic violence, and the judge sentenced him to three years in prison. From this point onward, her first husband disappeared from Nilufa's life. After she recovered from her injuries, Nilufa returned to work at a garment factory. Her widowed mother came to the city to take care of her small son, so her daughter could start a new life. Her mother worked as a domestic worker, and Nilufa's young son lived with her.

Nilufa soon met a man with whom she started a romantic relationship, and they got married. She hid her first marriage from him, but he soon discovered that she had been previously married and had a child from that marriage. When he discovered her deception, he began to severely abuse her. While Nilufa's deception was the ostensible cause of the domestic violence, financial motivations were also at play. Advised by the labor rights group, she saved $6 a month in a bank account. When her husband found out about it, he demanded that she hand over the money to him. When she refused, he became incensed and accused her of being a deceitful wife. As a result of the beatings and abuse, Nilufa would frequently fall ill. During this time she contracted jaundice that attacked her liver, and her stomach swelled from the disease. One day her husband kicked her in the abdomen, causing severe hemorrhaging. Anju took her to the hospital, where the doctors determined that she had developed a severe infection in her uterus. In their opinion, she was at the last stage of her life. The labor rights group paid for her medical care, but eventually Nilufa died. Her second husband escaped prosecution by running away.

The story takes an interesting turn at this point. Anju and Nilufa's mother accompanied her corpse in an ambulance to her village for burial. When they arrived, Anju told the villagers who had assembled that this dead woman was Nilufa, a woman from their village, who worked as a garment worker in Dhaka. Anju had brought the death certificate and other documents to prove Nilufa's identity. Then the villagers asked Nilufa's mother, "Is this your daughter?" She said, "Yes, this is my daughter, and her name is Nilufa." Her mother was in a state of shock from the death of her daughter. She was not coherent in her speech and often contradicted herself. That made the villagers suspicious. They said that they recognized Nilufa's mother as a woman from their village, but her daughter's name was not Nilufa. Her daughter had a husband, but she did not live with him. So, who was this dead woman that Anju had brought to their village? Already Nilufa's body had swollen from her disease and death, and her face was unrecognizable. Her corpse was beginning to smell as well. The villagers accused Anju of human trafficking and trying to bury Nilufa in their village under false pretenses. Then the assembled villagers raised another issue. They said that they did not know if this woman was Hindu or Buddhist. Therefore, how could they bury her? The villagers considered Nilufa a fallen woman who lived in the city engaged in dishonorable work. Then they threatened Anju by saying, "What kind of a woman are you? Taking care of a corpse is a man's job, not a woman's job."

During this controversy, Nilufa's mother lost consciousness several times. Finally, she was able to state that her daughter's real name was Nurjahan, who had gone to the city to escape her abusive husband and find work to support herself. To hide her whereabouts from her husband, she changed her name to Nilufa and eventually married another man. The local imam who was present at the meeting then remarked, "This woman [Nilufa/Nurjahan] already had a husband. She lived with another man against Islamic law. According to sharia, she should have been beaten 101 times for committing adultery. This corpse should not be buried anywhere in our village."[1] At this time, the headmaster from the local school arrived on the scene. As a man of learning, the headmaster is a respected figure in the village. After listening to all sides, he said that this woman had gone to the city to save her life. He added that they should bury her in the graveyard and that her identity could be determined later.

Finally, Nilufa/Nurjahan was buried at the edge of the village burial grounds at 10 p.m. After the burial, Anju returned to the city. Within four days, several villagers filed a case against Anju for human trafficking. The local police investigated the case and concluded that Nilufa was indeed Nurjahan and that she had changed her name to escape an abusive husband. Nilufa's mother lived the remaining years of her life in the village in poverty doing odd jobs. As to what happened to Nilufa's young son, nobody kept track of him. Nilufa, her mother, and her son are all nameless and faceless humans in the wheel of capitalism.

In this case, the necropolitics of marginalized female subjects enters through the dead body of Nilufa. Achille Mbembe builds his notion of necropolitics on Foucault's critique of sovereignty and its relationship to war and biopower. According to Mbembe, "Sovereignty resides, to a large degree, in the power and capacity to determine who may live and who must die."[2] Gender and cultural politics determine whose death is celebrated and whose is not. While Mbembe's notion of necropolitics does not explore gender, it offers a cultural frame through which we can analyze how power and the social construction of the female body as deviant come into play over the corpse of a worker. Garment workers lack sovereignty over their bodies once they enter factory work. Their right to a safe work environment is taken away by factory owners who deem them "disposable bodies" who can be exploited at very low wages for profit.[3] And as the 2013 Rana Plaza industrial catastrophe showed, "workers fearful of entering a visibly cracked building had no capacity to refuse unsafe work," since they were rendered voiceless.[4] What are the politics of death for a garment worker like Nilufa? Who mourns her death, who identifies her body, what forms of respect are shown to her corpse, what is a proper burial for her, and who decides where to bury the body? All are socially sanctioned norms followed by the community, and deviance from those norms is not tolerated in Bangladesh.[5]

Nilufa trespassed village expectations of a married woman's role—she ran away from an abusive husband, worked in a garment factory (which was considered shameful for women in the 1990s), and remarried and attempted to create a new life, all external to the moral code of her village society. Thus, her body is excised from the collective by burying it at the edge of the graveyard. The harshness of capitalism and the unforgiving nature of social norms have rendered these factory women faceless and nameless, and in the case of Nilufa, a body without a home. Garment workers are rendered into working machines, and when they die, whether from sickness or in a factory fire where their bodies are burned beyond recognition, society sighs and counts them as mere statistics. The life stories recounted here are the jagged narratives of women's broken lives. While Nilufa's story is at the extreme edge of the stories recounted in this book, it shows the spectrum of the dystopic lives of these female workers in Bangladesh. Nilufa's story brings together Lauren Berlant's "cruel optimism" in the face of betrayals and one's hopeless faith in illusions, and Carla Freeman's neoliberal "swirl of affects," where ideas of the good life are made seductively (un)attainable while neoliberalism pushes one to the brink of precarity and death.[6] The Nilufas of this world exist in "sacrifice zones" where state, factory owners, global retailers, and family members benefit from their labor and love, but the women themselves remain uncared for.[7]

If we were to ask who and/or what was responsible for the death of Nilufa/Nurjahan, what answer would we get? In the immediate analysis, her two husbands were responsible for her death. But if we analyze the situation further, we see a range of actors who were directly or indirectly responsible. The state's disinvestment in the agricultural economy and the long-term environmental degradation have forced many to migrate to the city for work. Yet once in the city, they are trapped by the greed of factory owners who keep workers' wages abysmally low. Global buyers are equally responsible for manufacturing clothes in such bleak conditions. The Bangladeshi state is similarly liable, for it views these workers as disposable bodies whose sole purpose is to create economic growth. And finally, Western consumers remain responsible for their demand for cheap clothes used once and then thrown away. In life and in death, these women remain unknown and ungrieved by a global society that reaps enormous profits from their backbreaking and life-diminishing work. All of us are part of this global chain of manufacturing—the race to the bottom—and the creation of a global precariat labor force with toxic effects on the lives of female workers.

APPENDIX I
SIXTEEN GARMENT WORKERS IN 2017–2018

Name	Age	Marital Status	Education	Number of Children	Children's Education/Work
Aleya	55	Married/abandoned	Illiterate	1 daughter	Daughter studied up to grade 10
Alima	46	Married/husband married 4 times	Grade 10	2 sons	1st son (illiterate), day laborer; 2nd son, grade 5, rickshaw puller
Bilkis	53	Separated	Illiterate	2 sons, 1 daughter	1st son, garment worker; 2nd son, BA in accounting; daughter, garment worker
Bodrun	55	Widow	Illiterate	1 daughter	Daughter, grade 5, garment worker
Hajira	45	Married/abandoned	Illiterate	1 daughter, 2 sons	Daughter, grade 8, married; 1st son, grade 5, garment worker; 2nd son, vendor
Hena	53	Married/abandoned	Illiterate	2 daughters	1st daughter (illiterate), garment worker; 2nd daughter, studying in grade 10
Jahanara	45	Married	Grade 5	1 daughter, 1 son	Daughter, grade 10, married; son, grade 5, garment worker

Name	Age	Marital Status	Education	Number of Children	Children's Education/Work
Johura	50	Married/abandoned	Illiterate	5 daughters, 1 son	1st and 2nd daughters, no schooling, garment workers; 3rd daughter, grade 12; 4th and 5th daughters, grade 8; son in technical school
Latifa	52	Married	Grade 5	1 daughter, 2 sons	Daughter, grade 10; 1st son, diploma in engineering; 2nd son, grade 10
Mahmuda	52	Married twice	Grade 5	1 daughter, 2 sons	Daughter, BA in English; 1st son, BA in finance, accountant in a garment factory; 2nd son studies computer engineering
Monoara	48	Married/abandoned	Grade 3	2 daughters	Both daughters studied to grade 10; 1st daughter, garment worker; 2nd daughter returned to the village
Morjina	45	Married	Illiterate	2 daughters, 1 son	1st daughter, grade 10; 2nd daughter, BA; son, grade 12
Sheema	45	Married twice	Grade 4	3 daughters	No education, all three garment workers
Sheuly	45	Married	Illiterate	1 daughter, 1 son	Daughter married; son, grade 5, private car driver
Sufia	50	Married/abandoned	Illiterate	2 daughters	1st daughter, grade 5, garment worker; 2nd daughter, grade 10
Yasmin	45	Married/separated	Grade 5	2 daughters	Both daughters educated in madrassa, married

APPENDIX II
FOLLOW-UP ON SIXTEEN GARMENT WORKERS IN 2020

After Aleya lost her factory job, she initially worked as a domestic worker. Then her health deteriorated, and she could no longer work. During Covid she was unable to pay her expenses in the city and returned to her village to live with her sister. Her case study is included in chapter 5.

Alima still worked, but she feared that she would lose her job any day. Her daughter-in-law worked at a garment factory in Mauritius and sent money home every month. With that money, Alima had built a four-room house in their village. Alima believed that even if she lost her factory job, she would have a comfortable life from her daughter-in-law's income. In her case, the family had cohered as a unit to build some working capital.

Bilkis was out of a job in 2018. Her husband had abandoned her. Her oldest daughter worked in a garment factory, and the family lived off her income. The younger daughter had tested positive for Covid and was unable to work. Bilkis described her financial situation as grim.

Bodrun lost her job due to old age. Her health was so weak that she could no longer find any work. Her only child, a daughter, was supporting her in her old age.

Hajira had returned to her village, since she could not find any work due to old age.

Hena lost her job due to old age. She could not find any work in Dhaka, so she returned to her village. She received some financial assistance from the local Union Council chairman, who is an elected officer at the village level. She termed her living condition as precarious.

Jahanara had worked for a total of eight years at the same garment factory. Unlike most workers, her work life was episodic. She would work for a couple of years and exit work to raise a child. Consequently, she worked most of her life as a helper at very low wages. In 2017, Jahanara had mentioned that the most satisfying aspect of her work life was her ability to educate her son and daughter. However, financial circumstances had forced her son to enter a garment factory at the age of fourteen. Her husband was a sugarcane beverage vendor. In 2020 he had tested positive for Covid and could no longer work. She described her family life as "a hand-to-mouth existence."

Johura was the only woman in my study group with six children, five daughters and one son. Her husband was a rickshaw puller. Out of her six children, she was able to educate her son and the three younger daughters. In our interview in 2017 she said that she considered the education of her children her most significant accomplishment. In 2020 she was no longer employed at the factory and was working as a domestic worker. She was not receiving any financial help from any of her adult children.

Latifa's factory had closed in 2018. She received taka 95,000 from her provident fund at the factory. Her son invested that money to start a small business, and she was living off that income. She was able to meet her basic needs.

Mahmuda was fired from her job at the time of our first interview. Her older son worked as an accountant at a garment factory. Her younger son supported her. Her financial situation was reasonably comfortable. Her case study is included in chapter 5.

Monoara was working at a subcontracting factory where the wages were low and paid irregularly. She had developed many health problems. Most of her earnings went toward her medical bills, leaving very little money for her expenses. Her case study is included in chapter 5.

Morjina had worked in a sweater factory for seventeen years. The pay at a sweater factory is much higher than at a factory making jeans and shirts. Since 2013 her monthly income had ranged from taka 8,000 to 14,000. She was able to educate all her four children to grade 12. In 2018 she took out a loan to build a three-room house in her village.

In 2018 her prospects looked positive by garment worker standards, but in 2020 she lost the house due to nonpayment of the loan. Her husband was also unemployed due to Covid. Although she had educated her four children, none of them could financially help her. She said that she was living like "a destitute."

Sheema lost her factory job due to old age. In 2020 she was working as a domestic worker with irregular wages. She described herself as "living on the edge." Her story is included in chapter 5.

Sheuly was still employed. Her financial situation was reasonably comfortable. Her story is included in chapter 5.

Sufia was fired from factory work due to old age. She has two daughters and no husband. The family lived on the income of the older daughter, who worked in a garment factory. The younger daughter had no work. Sufia was struggling financially.

Yasmin remained employed in 2020. Her husband had tested positive for Covid and could no longer work. They lived on her income. She said that they had very little money to survive on.

NOTES

INTRODUCTION

1. The exchange rate in 1995 was taka 40:1 USD. Unless otherwise noted, subsequent calculations use the 2018 exchange rate of taka 80:1 USD. The Bangladeshi currency taka has been devalued multiple times since 1971. The devaluations of the taka lowered the costs of production for Western buyers, making Bangladesh into a very lucrative location for apparel production. For the garment workers, the devaluations reduced the purchasing power of their wages. It should be noted that workers' wages are not adjusted for inflation. All exchange rates are calculated against USD.

When the first garment factory opened in 1978, the exchange rate was taka 15:1 USD. By 1994 the first wage board was set in the industry, the taka was devalued to 40.2 against USD 1. In 2006, 2010, 2013, and 2018 workers' wages were increased. The corresponding exchange rates were taka 68.9, taka 69.6, taka 78.1, and taka 83.5. Information provided by Dr. Ahmad Ahsan, Policy Research Institute, Dhaka. Source: *World Development Indicators*, World Bank, Washington, D.C.

2. The actual number of workers is probably much higher, since workers in the outsourcing industry are not accounted for. Four million is a number popularized by the apex organization of garment factory owners known as the Bangladesh Garment Manufacturers and Exporters Association (BGMEA). Since the 2013 collapse of the Rana Plaza factory, many substandard factories were closed and workers were laid off, so the number of workers in the organized ready-made garment industry in Bangladesh is lower than four million.

3. Carla Freeman, *Entrepreneurial Selves: Neoliberal Respectability and the Making of a Caribbean Middle Class* (Durham, N.C.: Duke University Press,

2014); Arjun Appadurai, *Modernity at Large: Cultural Dimension of Globalization* (Minneapolis: University of Minnesota Press, 1996); Lauren Berlant, "Cruel Optimism," in *The Affect Theory Reader,* ed. Melissa Gregg and Gregory J. Seigworth (Durham, N.C.: Duke University Press, 2010), 93–117; Guy Standing, *The Precariat: The New Dangerous Class* (London: Bloomsbury, 2011); and personal conversation with Bhuiyan.

    4. Paul Kennedy, *Vampire Capitalism* (London: Palgrave Macmillan, 2017), 8.

    5. Florence L. Denmark, Hillary Goldstein, Kristin Thies, and Adrian Tworecke, "Older Women, Leadership, and Encore Careers," in *Women and Aging: An International, Intersectional Power Perspective,* ed. Varda Muhlbauer, Joan Christler, and Florence Denmark (New York: Springer, 2015), 71–88.

    6. International Labour Organization, "The ILO at a Glance," December 2007, https://www.ilo.org/public/english/download/glance.pdf.

    7. I have refrained from framing these women's aspirations in Aristotelian terms of the individual's capacity to reason as the signature of a good life. Bangladeshi rural women should be analyzed through the native terms that shape their ideas of the good life. Their moral compass is formed in village society through folk views regarding Islam. In Islam, the good life means following the commands of Allah as laid out in the Quran.

    8. Freeman, *Entrepreneurial Selves,* 3.

    9. George Marcus, "Ethnography in/of the World System: The Emergence of Multi-sited Ethnography," *Annual Review of Anthropology* 24 (1995): 95–117.

    10. Micaela Di Leonardo, "Oral History as Ethnographic Encounter," *Oral History Review* 15, no. 1 (Spring 1987): 4.

    11. Nazli Kibria, *Becoming a Garments Worker: The Mobilization of Garments Workers in the Garments Factories of Bangladesh* (Geneva: United Nations Research Institute for Social Development, Occasional Paper, 1998).

    12. Sherry Ortner, *Anthropology and Social Theory: Culture, Power and the Acting Subject* (Durham, N.C.: Duke University Press, 2006), 16–17.

    13. Tamara Hareven, *Families, Histories, and Social Change: Life-Course and Cross-Cultural Perspectives* (Boulder: Westview Press, 2000).

    14. Hareven, 4.

    15. *Nari Sramik* (Dhaka: Bookline, 2022).

1. THE DISORDER OF WORK AND LIFE

    1. Suzanne Bergeron, "Political Economy: Discourses of Globalization and Feminist Politics," *Signs* 26, no. 4 (2001): 983–1006.

2. Dina Siddiqi, "Do Bangladeshi Factory Workers Need Saving? Sisterhood in the Post-sweatshop Era," *Feminist Review* 91 (2009): 156.

3. Annette Fuentes and Barbara Ehrenreich, *Women in the Global Factory* (Boston: South End Press, 1983); June Nash and María Fernández-Kelly, *Women, Men, and the International Division of Labor* (New York: SUNY Press, 1983); Diane Wolf, *Factory Daughters: Gender, Household Dynamics, and Rural Industrialization in Java* (Berkeley: University of California Press, 1992); Lourdes Beneria and Martha Roldan, *The Crossroads of Class and Gender: Industrial Homework, Subcontracting, and Household Dynamics in a Mexico City* (Chicago: University of Chicago Press, 1987).

4. Diane Elson and Ruth Pearson, "'Nimble Fingers Make Cheap Workers': An Analysis of Women's Employment in Third World Export Manufacturing," *Feminist Review* 7 (1981): 87–107.

5. Helen Safa, "Runaway Shops and Female Employment: The Search for Cheap Labor," *Signs* 7, no. 2 (Winter 1981): 418–33.

6. Naila Kabeer, *The Power to Choose: Bangladeshi Women and Labour Market Decisions in London and Dhaka* (London: Verso, 2000), 71.

7. Samita Sen, *Women and Labour in Late Colonial India* (Cambridge, UK: Cambridge University Press, 1999), 21.

8. Chitra Joshi, "Notes on the Breadwinner Debate: Gender and Household in Working-Class Families," *Studies in History* 18, no. 2 (2002): 261–74.

9. Shahidur Rahman, *Broken Promises of Globalization: The Case of the Bangladesh Garment Industry* (Lanham, Md.: Lexington Books, 2013); Sanchita Saxena, ed., *Made in Bangladesh, Cambodia, and Sri Lanka: The Labor behind the Global Garment and Textile Industries* (New York: Cambria Press, 2014); Hasan Ashraf and Rebecca Prentice, "Beyond Factory Safety: Labor Unions, Militant Protest, and the Accelerated Ambitions of Bangladesh's Garment Industry," *Dialectical Anthropology* 43 (2019): 93–107.

10. Carla Freeman, *Entrepreneurial Selves: Neoliberal Respectability and the Making of a Caribbean Middle Class* (Durham, N.C.: Duke University Press, 2014).

11. Sandya Hewamanne, "Sewing Their Way up the Social Ladder? Paths to Social Mobility and Empowerment among Sri Lanka's Global Factory Workers," *Third World Quarterly* 39, no. 11 (2018): 2173–87.

12. Aihwa Ong, *Spirits of Resistance and Capitalist Discipline: Factory Women in Malaysia,* 2nd ed. (New York: SUNY Press, 2010).

13. Aihwa Ong, "The Gender and Labor Politics of Postmodernity," *Annual Review of Anthropology* 20 (1991): 280.

14. Wolf, *Factory Daughters,* 10.

15. Johanna Lessinger, "Work and Love: The Limits of Autonomy for Female Garment Workers in India," *Anthropology of Work Review* 23, nos. 1–2 (2002): 18.

16. Sandya Hewamanne, *Stitching Identities in a Free Trade Zone: Gender and Politics in Sri Lanka* (Philadelphia: University of Pennsylvania Press, 2008), 14.

17. Caitrin Lynch, *Juki Girls, Good Girls: Gender and Cultural Politics in Sri Lanka's Global Garment Industry* (Ithaca: Cornell University Press, 2007).

18. Kabeer, *The Power to Choose.*

19. Freeman, *Entrepreneurial Selves;* Sandhya Hewamanne, "Performing 'Dis-respectability': New Tastes, Cultural Practices, and Identity Performances by Sri Lanka's Free Trade Zone Garment Factory Workers," *Cultural Dynamics* 15, no. 1 (2003): 71–101; Saxena, *Made in Bangladesh*; Priti Ramamurthy, "Material Consumers, Fabricating Subjects: Perplexity, Global Connectivity Discourses, and Transnational Feminist Research," *Cultural Anthropology* 18, no. 4 (2003): 527.

20. For example, see Ashraf and Prentice, "Beyond Factory Safety"; Zia Rahman and Tom Langford, "International Solidarity or Renewed Trade Union Imperialism? The AFL-CIO and Garment Workers of Bangladesh," *Working USA* 17, no. 2 (2014), https://doi.org/10.1111/wusa.12106; and Marilyn Rock, "The Rise of the Independent Garment Workers Union (BIGU)," in *Organizing Labor in Globalizing Asia,* ed. Andrew Brown and Jane Hutchinson (London: Routledge, 2001).

21. Naila Kabeer, "Cultural Fools or Rational Dopes? Women and Labour Supply in the Bangladesh Garment Industry," *European Journal of Development Research* 3, no. 1 (1991): 133–60; Naila Kabeer, "Globalization, Labor Standards, and Women's Rights: Dilemmas of Collective (In)action in an Interdependent World," *Feminist Economics* 10, no. 1 (2004): 3–35; Sarah Ashwin, Naila Kabeer, and Elke Schüßler, "Contested Understandings in the Garment Industry after Rana Plaza," *Development and Change* 51, no. 5 (2020): 1296–1305.

22. Nazli Kibria, "Culture, Social Class, and Income Control in the Lives of Women Garment Workers in Bangladesh," *Gender and Society* 9, no. 3 (June 1995): 289–309.

23. Saxena, *Made in Bangladesh.*

24. Dina M. Siddiqi, "Miracle Worker or Womanmachine? Tracking (Trans)national Realities in Bangladesh Factories," *Economic and Political Weekly* 35, nos. 21/22 (May 27–June 2, 2000): L11–L17.

25. Dina Siddiqi, "Before Rana Plaza: Towards a History of Labor Organizing in Bangladesh's Garment Industry," in *Labor in the Clothing Industry*

in the Asia Pacific, ed. Vicki Crisnis and Adrian Vickers (London: Routledge, 2016), 60–72.

26. Sanchita Saxena, ed., *Labor, Global Supply Chains, and the Garment Industry in South Asia: Bangladesh after Rana Plaza* (London: Routledge, 2019), 14.

27. Saxena, 14.

28. Shelley Feldman and Jakir Hossain, "The Longue Durée and the Promise of Export-Led Development," in Saxena, *Labor,* 21–44.

29. Chaumtoli Huq, "Opportunities and Limitations of the Accord: Need for Worker Organizing Model," in Saxena, *Labor,* 65–83.

30. Dina Siddiqi, "Spaces of Exception: National Interest and the Labor of Sedition," in Saxena, *Labor,* 100–114.

31. Naila Kabeer. "The Evolving Politics of Labor Standards in Bangladesh: Taking Stock and Looking Forward," in Saxena, *Labor,* 231–60.

32. Sanchita Saxena and Dorothee Baumann-Pauly, "Off the Radar: Subcontracting in Bangladesh's RMG Sector," in Saxena, *Labor,* 45–62.

33. Alessandra Mezzadri and Sanjita Majumdar, "The Afterlife of Cheap Labor: Bangalore Garment Workers from the Factory to the Informal Economy," FEDI Network, Working Paper No. 12.18.1 (2019): 2.

34. David Harvey, *Spaces of Global Capitalism: Towards a Theory of Uneven Geographical Development* (London: Verso Press, 2006), 12.

35. Guy Standing, *The Precariat: The New Dangerous Class* (London: Bloomsbury Academic, 2011), 1.

36. Robert Miles, *Capitalism and Unfree Labor: Anomaly or Necessity?* (Alameda: Tavistock Books, 1989); Raka Ray, *Cultures of Servitude: Modernity, Domesticity, and Class in India* (Stanford: Stanford University Press, 2009); Rhacel Salazar Perreñas, *Servants of Globalization* (Stanford: Stanford University Press, 2015); Michele Gamburd, *Kitchen-Spoon's Handle: Transnationalism and Sri Lanka's Migrant Housemaids* (Ithaca: Cornell University Press, 2000).

37. Guy Standing, "The Precariat: Today's Transformative Class?," A Great Transition Initiative Essay, October 2018, 6, https://greattransition.org.

38. Standing, *The Precariat,* 12.

39. Judith Butler, *Notes toward a Performative Theory of Assembly* (Cambridge: Harvard University Press, 2015), 33.

40. Lauren Berlant, "Cruel Optimism," in *The Affect Theory Reader,* ed. Melissa Gregg and Gregory J. Seigworth (Durham, N.C.: Duke University Press, 2010), 93–117.

41. Berlant, 93–94.

42. Berlant, 93–94.

43. Freeman, *Entrepreneurial Selves,* 2–3.

44. Arjun Appadurai, *Modernity at Large: Cultural Dimension of Globalization* (Minneapolis: University of Minnesota Press, 1996), 5–6.

45. Freeman, *Entrepreneurial Selves*, 8–9.

46. Fauzia Ahmed, "The Rise of the Bangladesh Garment Industry: Globalization, Women Workers, and Voice," *National Women's Studies Association Journal* 6, no. 2 (Summer 2004): 38.

47. Sherry Ortner, *Anthropology and Social Theory: Culture, Power, and the Acting Subject* (Durham, N.C.: Duke University Press, 2006), 70.

48. Berlant, "Cruel Optimism," 93–95.

49. Carla Freeman, "Feeling Neoliberal," *Feminist Anthropology* 1, no. 1 (2020): 3.

50. In an email dated January 23, 2021, Bhuiyan communicated to me that he did not want to take credit for "residue of hope" as an analytical construct. He wrote: "I am thrilled to know that the expression residue of hope had impressed you. However, we both know that the expression was merely a bubble that grew out of my reading of 'your' materials. Therefore, I just can't claim any credit for the term or any such concept beyond this simple literal expression. It is your insights that told you to pick it up, your intellectual depth that wove it into a theoretical frame and finally made it workable. Apa, I am moved by your generosity and also by the fact that you kept me in your thoughts but this is all what I have to say in response. Maybe in future, if I get a chance, to work with you or for you then you could always guide me to explore the idea further and more closely. Looking forward to only that for now." I was both humbled and impressed by Bhuiyan's words. In this neoliberal age where we try to copyright thought, we all have much to learn from his grace.

51. Ortner, *Anthropology and Social Theory*, 107. For a longer discussion on the topic of subjectivity, see pages 107–28.

52. Ortner, 111.

53. Ortner, 111.

54. James Scott, *The Moral Economy of the Peasant: Rebellion and Subsistence in Southeast Asia* (New Haven, Conn.: Yale University Press, 1976), viii.

55. Sarah White, "Beyond the Paradox: Religion, Family, and Modernity in Contemporary Bangladesh," *Modern Asian Studies* 46, no. 5 (September 2012): 1442.

56. A significant segment of garment factory women adopts the Islamic attire of the burqa. There are several reasons for it. Many women wear the burqa for physical security reasons, because men tend not to harass women who wear Islamic attire. Others wear the burqa because that is how they were socialized in rural society. A third faction adopts it as an expression of their faith.

57. White "Beyond the Paradox," 1442.

58. Sandya Hewamanne, *Sri Lanka's Global Factory Workers: (Un)disciplined Desires and Sexual Struggles in a Postcolonial Society* (London: Routledge, 2016), 24.

59. Hewamanne, 24; Lynch, *Juki Girls, Good Girls*.

60. Freeman, *Entrepreneurial Selves*, 8.

61. Standing, *The Precariat*, 25. For an extended reading of the formation of the precariat, see 1–25.

62. Siddiqi, "Before Rana Plaza," 61.

63. Examples include the Convention on the Elimination of all Forms of Discrimination against Women (CEDAW, 1979) and the 1995 Beijing Conference.

64. Jean Comaroff and John Comaroff, *Law and Disorder in the Postcolony* (Chicago: University of Chicago Press, 2009), 27.

65. Julie Taylor, *Paper Tangos* (Durham, N.C.: Duke University Press, 1998), 66.

66. Dilip Gaonkar, "Alternative Modernities," *Public Culture* 11, no. 1 (1999): 1–18.

67. Gaonkar, 1.

68. Partha Chatterjee, "Our Modernity" (Rotterdam: South-South Exchange Program for Research on the History of Development and the Council for the Development of Social Science Research in Africa, 1997), 8, https://ccs.ukzn.ac.za/files/partha1.pdf.

69. Tani Barlow, "On Colonial Modernity," in *Formations of Colonial Modernity in East Asia*, ed. Tani Barlow (Durham, N.C.: Duke University Press, 1997), 6.

70. Barlow, 6.

71. I came across this term at a conference in Singapore but do not recall the name of the speaker.

72. For further details see Mahmudul Hasan, "Commemorating Rokeya Sakhawat Hossain and Contextualizing Her Work in South Asian Muslim Feminism," *Asiatic* 7, no. 2 (December 2013): 39–59.

73. Sofa quoted in Ahmad Ibrahim, "Ahmed Sofa in Posterity: Muslim Anxiety in a 'Muslim World,'" *Daily Star*, April 28, 2017, https://www.thedailystar.net/star-weekend/ahmed-sofa-posterity-muslim-anxiety-muslim-world-1397431.

74. Ibrahim.

75. Personal communication with author.

76. Personal communication with author.

77. Personal communication with author.

78. In 1998, when I was conducting research in Bangladesh, the clergy of Yunusia Madrassah attacked a women's rally organized by the NGO Proshika. The clergy claimed that these shameless rural women had come on the streets wearing denim shorts (they called them "jeans–half pants") and Sandoz undershirts. The clergy's reference to jeans indicated the inclusion of female labor into the garment industry where women sewed jeans and T-shirts. Similarly, the Sandoz brand, a longtime manufacturer of men's undershirts, was traditionally worn by upper-class men. These were the new anxieties that were getting unleashed—the rural power structure was gradually dissolving and weakening social hierarchies as women became industrial wage earners and the sharecropper's family now had a new roof, could send their children to school, and had some disposable income. See Lamia Karim, "Democratizing Bangladesh: State, NGOs, and Militant Islam," *Cultural Dynamics* 16, nos. 2 and 3 (2004): 291–318.

79. Julfikar Malik, "Sermon Shafi Style," *Daily Star,* July 11, 2013, https://www.thedailystar.net.

80. White, "Beyond the Paradox," 1441.

81. After the Quran, the Hadith, the collected sayings of Prophet Muhammad, is the most important religious document in Islam, and it is incumbent upon observant Muslims to follow its moral guidance.

82. Appadurai, *Modernity at Large*, 3–5.

83. Syed Waliullah, *Tree without Roots,* ed. Niaz Zaman (Dhaka: University Press Limited, 2005), 3–4.

2. THE AGE OF EXCITEMENT

1. "Overseas Employers Asked to Increase Wages of Bangladesh Workers," *New Age,* September 10, 2018. Over 100,000 skilled workers work overseas in the apparel production industry, and 50 percent of them were sent by the country's only state recruiting agency, Bangladesh Overseas Employment and Services Limited. While the remittances from the migrant workers provide a stream of much-needed foreign exchange for the government, the Bangladeshi state offers little support services for these workers often trapped in dehumanizing work conditions overseas. See https://www.newagebd.net.

2. Mohammad Rezaul Bari, "The Basket Case," *The Forum* 3, no. 3 (March 2008), https://archive.thedailystar.net/forum/2008/march/basket.htm.

3. https://bracinternational.org.

4. "Bangladesh Shows Development Is the Best Resilience: World Bank CEO," *bdnews24.com,* July 9, 2019, https://bdnews24.com.

5. World Bank, "The World in Bangladesh: Overview," https://www.worldbank.org/en/country/bangladesh/overview.

6. David Lewis, *Bangladesh: Politics, Economy, and Civil Society* (Cambridge, UK: Cambridge University Press, 2011), 4–5.

7. Ester Boserup, *Woman's Role in Economic Development* (London: Earthscan, 1970).

8. See Irene Tinker and Michelle Branson, *Women and World Development* (Washington, D.C.: Overseas Development Council, 1976); and Caroline Moser, *Gender Planning and Development: Theory, Practice, and Training* (London: Routledge, 1993).

9. Adrienne Germain, "A Major Resource Awaiting Development," *New York Times*, August 26, 1975, https://timesmachine.nytimes.com/.

10. Lamia Karim, "Analyzing Women's Empowerment: Microfinance and Garment Labor in Bangladesh," *Fletcher Forum of World Affairs* 38, no. 2 (Summer 2014): 155.

11. Meena Khandewal and Carla Freeman, "Pop Development and the Uses of Feminism," in *Seduced and Betrayed: Exposing the Contemporary Microfinance Phenomenon,* ed. Milford Batemen and Kate Maclean (Santa Fe: School for Advanced Research Press, 2017), 57.

12. Sandra Harding, "Just Add Women and Stir?" in *Missing Links: Gender Equity in Science and Technology for Development* (Ottawa, N.Y.: UNIFEM, 1995), 295.

13. Harding, 295.

14. Nazli Kibria, "Becoming a Garment Worker: The Mobilization of Women into the Garment Factories in Bangladesh," in *Women's Employment in the Textile Manufacturing Sectors of Bangladesh and Mexico,* ed. Carol Miller and Jessica Vivian (New York: United Nations Research Institute for Social Development, 1998), 151–77.

15. Elisabeth Porter, "Rethinking Women's Empowerment," *Journal of Peacebuilding and Development* 8, no. 1 (2013): 3.

16. World Bank Source Book on Empowerment, Chapter Two: Empowerment, 10. Also cited in Mac Darrow, *Between Light and Shadow: The World Bank, International Monetary Funds and International Human Rights Law* (London: Bloomsbury Academic Publishing, 2003), 155.

17. Naila Kabeer, "Gender Equality and Women's Empowerment: A Critical Assessment of the Third Millennium Development Goal," *Gender and Development* 3, no. 1 (March 2005): 13–14.

18. Chaumtoli Huq, "Women's Empowerment in the Garment Industry through Labor Organizing," *Wagadu: A Journal of Transnational Women's and Gender Studies* 20 (Fall 2019): 138.

19. Jamie Peck and Adam Tickell, "Neoliberalizing Space," *Antipode* 34, no. 3 (December 2002): 380–81.

20. Just Faaland and John Parkinson, *Bangladesh: The Test Case for Development* (Boulder: Westview Press, 1976), 5.

21. For an extended discussion on this topic, see Fahimul Quadir, "The Political Economy of Pro-market Reforms in Bangladesh: Regime Consolidation through Economic Liberalization," *Contemporary South Asia* 2, no. 4 (2007): 199.

22. For a detailed discussion on the formation of Bangladesh, see Ali Riaz, *Unfolding State: The Transformation of Bangladesh* (North York: de Sitter, 2005).

23. Quadir, 200.

24. Rehman Sobhan, "Structural Maladjustment: Bangladesh's Experience with Market Reforms," *Economic and Political Weekly* 28, no. 19 (May 8, 1993): 929.

25. Anu Muhammad, "Bangladesh—A Model of Neoliberalism: The Case of Microfinance and NGOs," *Monthly Review*, March 1, 2015, http://www.monthlyreview.org.

26. Quadir, "Political Economy of Pro-market Reforms," 201.

27. Quadir, 203.

28. Muhammad, "Bangladesh."

29. "182 Businessmen Elected to Parliament," *Prothom Alo* (English), January 7, 2019. https://en.prothomalo.com.

30. Muhammad, "Bangladesh."

31. Alexandra Rose Caleca, "The Effect of Globalization on Bangladesh's Ready-Made Garment Industry: The High Cost of Cheap Clothing," *Brooklyn Journal of International Law* 40, no. 1 (2014): 283.

32. Naila Kabeer and Simeen Mahmud, "Rags, Riches, and Women Workers: Export-Oriented Garment Manufacturing in Bangladesh," in *Chains of Fortunes Linking Women Producers and Workers in Global Markets,* ed. Marilyn Carr (London: Commonwealth Secretariat, 2004), 133–64.

33. See Pietra Rivoli, *Travels of a T-Shirt in the Global Economy: An Economist Examines Markets, Power, and Politics of World Trade* (Hoboken, N.J.: Wiley, 2005); Sanchita Saxena, *Made in Bangladesh, Cambodia, and Sri Lanka: The Labor behind the Global Garment and Textile Industries* (New York: Cambria Press, 2014).

34. Aihwa Ong, "The Gender and Labor Politics of Postmodernity," *Annual Review of Anthropology* 20 (1991): 279.

35. "Nixon and Kimchi: How the Garment Industry Came to Bangladesh," *Planet Money T-Shirt Project,* National Public Radio, December 2, 2013, https://www.npr.org.

36. Shahidur Rahman, *Broken Promises of Globalization: The Case of the Bangladesh Garment Industry* (Lanham, Md.: Lexington Books, 2013), 21.

37. Caleca, "The Effect of Globalization," 284.

38. Shelley Feldman and Jakir Hossain, "The Longue Durée and the Promise of Export-Led Development," in *Labor, Global Supply Chains, and the Garment Industry in South Asia: Bangladesh after Rana Plaza*, ed. Sanchita Saxena (London: Routledge, 2019), 24.

39. https://www.bgmea.com/bd.

40. Marten van Klaveren, *Wages in Context in the Garment Industry in Asia* (Amsterdam: Wageindicator Foundation, 2016), 18.

41. Anu Muhammad, "Bangladesh RMG: Global Chain of Profit and Deprivation," *bdnews24.com*, May 17, 2013, https://opinion24.com.

42. Gunseli Berik, "Revisiting the Feminist Debates on the International Labor Standards in the Aftermath of Rana Plaza," *Studies in Comparative International Development* 52, no. 2 (2017): 3.

43. For an extended discussion on this topic, see Berik.

44. Achim Berg, Saskia Hedrich, Sebastian Kempf, and Thomas Tochtermann, *Bangladesh's Ready-Made Garments Landscape: The Challenge of Growth* (Frankfurt: McKinsey Consulting Inc., 2011), 6.

45. Van Klaveren, *Wages in Context*, 18.

46. Zia Rahman and Tom Langford, "Why Labour Unions Have Failed Bangladesh's Garment Workers," in *Labour in the Global South: Challenges and Alternatives for Workers*, ed. Sarah Mosoetsa and Michelle Williams (Geneva: International Labor Office, 2012), 98.

47. Adva Saldinger, "5 Years after Rana Plaza, Worker Safety Has Improved, but More Needs to Be Done," *Devex*, April 24, 2018, https://www.devex.com.

48. European Commission, press report, "Joint Statement by HR/VP Catherine Ashton and EU Trade Commissioner Karel de Gucht Following Factory Fires in Bangladesh," January 29, 2013, https://ec.europa.eu/commission/presscorner/detail/en/IP_13_79.

49. https://bangladeshaccord.org.

50. Posner quoted in Elizabeth Paton, "Fears for Bangladesh Garment Workers as Safety Agreement Nears an End," *New York Times*, May 28, 2021, https://nytimes.com.

51. Chaumtoli Huq, "Opportunities and Limitations of the Accord: Need for a Worker Organizing Model," in Saxena, *Labor*, 69.

52. Ashraf Hasan and Rebecca Prentice, "Beyond Factory Safety: Labor Unions, Militant Protests, and the Accelerated Ambitions of Bangladesh's Garment Industry," *Dialectical Anthropology* 43 (2019): 99.

53. Sanchita Saxena and Dorothee Baumann-Paul, "Off the Radar: Subcontracting in Bangladesh's RMG Industry," in Saxena, *Labor,* 45–63.

54. Saxena and Baumann-Paul.

55. Website of Ha-Meem Group of industries, http://www.hameemgroup.net/about-us.aspx.

56. Trade union leaders and labor activists have communicated this fact to me. It is common knowledge in Bangladesh that many trade union representatives work for factory owners although an accounting of that has not taken place.

57. Rahman and Langford, "Why Labour Unions Have Failed," 90.

58. Personal communication to author by several labor activists who attended the meeting; none of them would go on the record for fear of reprisals by factory owners. However, this is a well-known fact among labor groups in Bangladesh. See also Rahman and Langford, "Why Labour Unions Have Failed," 91.

59. Dhiman Chowdhury, "Obstacles to Contributory Provident Fund in the Private Sector: Bangladesh Experience," *Journal of Business Administration* 37 (September and December 2016): 1.

60. "Bangladesh Sets Minimum Wage for Garment Workers," *Associated Press* in Dhaka, July 29, 2010, https//theguardian.com.

61. Shikha Bhattacharya, "Fashion, Targets, and Violence in Asian Garment Supply Chains," in Saxena, *Labor,* 210.

62. Jim Yardley, "Bangladesh Pollution, Told in Colors and Smells," *New York Times,* July 14, 2013, https://www.nytimes.com.

63. Naila Kabeer, *The Power to Choose: Bangladeshi Women and Labour Market Decisions in London and Dhaka* (London: Verso, 2000), 71–72.

3. THE ARC OF CHANGE

1. Carla Freeman, *Entrepreneurial Selves: Neoliberal Respectability and the Making of a Caribbean Middle Class* (Durham, N.C.: Duke University Press, 2014).

2. Bangladesh Institute for Labour Studies Report, unnamed report (1995), Dhaka, 6.

3. In real estate development, women are used for breaking pieces of brick into smaller fragments that are mixed with cement to build houses. This low-paid work is arduous.

4. Sarah White, "Beyond the Paradox: Religion, Family, and Modernity in Contemporary Bangladesh," *Modern Asian Studies* 46, no. 2 (September 2012): 1444.

5. Nazli Kibria, "Becoming a Garments Worker: The Mobilization of Women into the Garments Factories of Bangladesh," United Nations Research Institute for Social Development (UNRISD), Occasional Paper no. 9, Geneva, 1998.

6. Shelly Banjo, "Bangladesh Garment Factories Often Evade Monitoring," *Wall Street Journal,* October 3, 2013.

7. Sohel Mahmud, Vinay Rajath D., Rayhan Mahmud, and Mst. Nusrat Jahan, "Health Issues of Female Garment Workers: Evidence from Bangladesh," *Journal of Population and Social Studies* 26, no. 3 (July–September 2018): 1.

8. Nazma Akter is also the president of Sommilito Garments Sramik Federation, one of the largest union federations in Bangladesh, which has a membership of seventy thousand garment workers. She started working in the garment industry at age eleven. http://awajfoundation.org/staff/nazma-akter/.

9. Sarah Labowitz and Dorothee Baumann-Pauly, "Beyond the Tip of the Iceberg: Bangladesh's Forgotten Apparel Workers" (New York: NYU Stern Center for Business and Human Rights, 2015), https://pages.stern.nyu.edu. See also "Participatory Factory Mapping Research: Planning Phase," research brief (Dhaka, Bangladesh: BRAC University Center for Entrepreneurship Research Development, 2016), https://ced.bracu.ac.bd.

10. "Gender Based Violence in the GAP Garment Supply Chain: Workers Voices from the Global Supply Chain," A Report to the ILO, Asia Floor Wage Alliance, 2018, https://www.globallaborjustice.org.

11. White, "Beyond the Paradox," 1443.

12. Sherry Ortner, *Anthropology and Social Theory: Culture, Power, and the Acting Subject* (Durham, N.C.: Duke University Press, 2006), 25.

13. Ortner, 25.

14. Ortner, 70.

15. Leela Fernandes and Patrick Heller, "Hegemonic Aspirations: New Middle Class Politics and India's Democracy in Comparative Perspectives," *Critical Asian Studies* 34, no. 2 (2006): 497.

16. Raka Ray and Seemin Quayum, *Cultures of Servitude: Modernity, Domesticity, and Class in India* (Stanford: Stanford University Press, 2009), 15.

17. GDP per capita (USD) for Bangladesh, https://data.worldbank.org/indicator/NY.GDP.PCAP.CD?locations=BD.

18. Freeman, *Entrepreneurial Selves,* 9.

19. Lecture by Sheikh Abdur Razzak Bin Yousuf, https://www.youtube.com/watch?v=O01QEcVBkwY&t=125s.

20. Freeman, *Entrepreneurial Selves,* 3.

21. Freeman, 9.

22. Freeman, 16.

23. Sandya Hewamanne, "From Global Workers to Local Entrepreneurs: Sri Lanka's Former Global Factory Workers in Rural Sri Lanka," *Third World Quarterly* 41, no. 3 (2020): 548.

24. Abrar Apu, "Subcontracting in Textile and Clothing Sector in Bangladesh," *Textile Today,* February 1, 2013, https://www.textiletoday.com.bd.

4. CHANGING NORMS OF ROMANCE, MARRIAGE, AND SEXUALITY

1. Arjun Appadurai, "Disjuncture and Difference in the Global Cultural Economy," *Theory, Culture and Society* 7 (1990): 295–310.

2. Nicole Constable, "The Commodification of Intimacy: Marriage, Sex, and Reproductive Labor," *Annual Review of Anthropology* 38 (2009): 49–65.

3. Denise Brennan, *What's Love Got to Do with It? Transnational Desire and Sex Tourism in the Dominican Republic* (Durham, N.C.: Duke University Press, 2004).

4. Constable, "The Commodification of Intimacy," 50.

5. Constable, 50.

6. Carla Freeman, "Feeling Neoliberal," *Feminist Anthropology* 1 (2020): 2, https://doi.org/10.1002/fea2.12010.

7. Freeman, 3.

8. The rise in dowry demand among the poorer classes increased after the independence of Bangladesh in 1971, when Bangladeshis encountered India.

9. Muslim Family Laws Ordinance, 1961, http://bdlaws.minlaw.gov.bd/act-305/section-13539.html.

10. Arjun Appadurai. *Modernity at Large: Cultural Dimensions of Globalization* (Minneapolis: University of Minnesota Press, 1996).

11. Lauren Berlant, "Cruel Optimism," in *The Affect Theory Reader,* ed. Melissa Gregg and Gregory J. Seigworth (Durham, N.C.: Duke University Press, 2010), 97.

12. Julie Taylor, *Paper Tangos* (Durham, N.C.: Duke University Press, 1998).

13. Taylor, 85.

14. Freeman, "Feeling Neoliberal," 3.

15. Freeman, 3.

16. Freeman, 3.

17. For a discussion of some of Taslima Nasrin's erotic novels, see Lamia Karim, "The Transnational Politics of Reading and the (Un)making of Taslima Nasrin," in *South Asian Feminisms,* ed. Ania Loomba and Ritty A. Lukose (Durham, N.C.: Duke University Press, 2014), 205–23.

18. Shakeel Mahmood, "The Status of Female Garment Workers' Health on STIs/HIV and the Role of Garment Factory Owners in Bangladesh," *European Scientific Journal* 16, no. 23 (August 2020): 23–56.

19. Bonnie Crouthamel, Erin Pearson, Sarah Tilford, Samantha Hurst, Dipika Paul, Fahima Aqtar, Jay Silverman, and Sarah Averbach, "Out-of-Clinic and Self-Managed Abortion in Bangladesh: Menstrual Regulation Provider Perspectives," *Reproductive Health* 18 (2021): open access, https://doi.org/10.1186/s12978-021-01123-w.

20. Emran P. Khan and Abdullah Karim, "The Prevention of Women and Child Repression Act 2000: A Study of Implementation Process from 2003 to 2017," *Journal of Humanities and Social Science* 22, no. 7 (July 2017): 34–42.

21. Personal communication with author.

22. Moon Moon Sen is the daughter of the late Indian actor Suchitra Sen, a legendary beauty of the Indian/Bengali silver screen in the 1950s and 1960s. Suchitra Sen was very popular in Bangladesh because she was originally from East Bengal (Bangladesh). Her daughter, a Bengali actor working in India, also became very popular, because Bangladeshi viewers identified with her ethnic roots and took pride in her as one of their own.

23. Personal communication with author.

24. Pierre Bourdieu, *The Bachelor's Ball: The Crisis of Peasant Society in Bearn* (Chicago: University of Chicago Press, 2008).

25. Berlant, "Cruel Optimism," 93.

5. AFTER WORK

1. Ruth Behar, *Translated Woman: Crossing the Border with Esperanza's Story* (Boston: Beacon Press, 1993); Lynn Stephen, *We Are the Face of Oaxaca: Testimonial and Social Movements* (Durham, N.C.: Duke University Press, 2013).

2. Tamara K. Hareven, *Families, Histories, and Social Change: Life-Course and Cross-Cultural Perspectives* (Boulder: Westview Press, 2000).

3. Hareven, 1.

4. See Raka Ray, *Cultures of Servitude: Modernity, Domesticity, and Class in India* (Stanford: Stanford University Press, 2009); and Rhacel Salazar Parreñas, *Servants of Globalization: Migration and Domestic Work* (Stanford: Stanford University Press, 2015). In Bangladesh, most of the studies on domestic work are on child workers, which is a result of development policies that seek to abolish child workers; little work is available on adult domestic workers. See Emma Seery, "Securing Protection for Domestic Workers in Bangladesh" (London: Oxfam Publications, 2020), https://oxfamilibrary.openrepository.com/handle/10546/621102.

5. Carla Freeman, "Feeling Neoliberal," *Feminist Anthropology* 1 (April 2020): 3, https://doi.org/10.1002/fea2.12010.

6. It was important for Monoara that I did not represent her marriage as a rape. She maintained that she was married according to proper Islamic protocols. I have respected her views.

7. Lauren Berlant, "Cruel Optimism," in *The Affect Theory Reader*, ed. Melissa Gregg and Gregory J. Seigworth (Durham, N.C.: Duke University Press, 2010), 93.

8. Sarah White, "Beyond the Paradox: Religion, Family, and Modernity in Contemporary Bangladesh," *Modern Asian Studies* 46, no. 5 (September 2012): 1442.

9. Guy Standing, *The Precariat: The New Dangerous Class* (London: Bloomsbury Academic, 2011), 23.

10. Paul Willis's *Learning to Labour: How Working Class Kids Get Working Class Jobs* (London: Routledge, 1978) analyzes the social reproduction of class in England.

CONCLUSION

1. Guy Standing, *The Precariat: The New Dangerous Class* (London: Bloomsbury Academic, 2011), 11–12.

2. Zia Rahman and Tom Langford, "Why Labour Unions Have Failed Bangladesh's Garment Workers," in *Labour in the Global South: Challenges and Alternatives for Workers*, ed. Sarah Motoetsa and Michelle Williams (Geneva: International Labour Office, 2012), 89.

3. For an extended discussion on the politics of 1954, see Layli Uddin, "'Enemy Agents at Work': A Microhistory of the 1954 Adamjee and Karnaphuli Riots in East Pakistan," *Modern Asian Studies* 55, no. 2 (2021) 629–64.

4. Rahman and Langford, "Why Labour Unions Have Failed," 89.

5. Rahman and Langford, 89.

6. Rahman and Langford, 90.

7. Hasan Ashraf and Rebecca Prentice, "Beyond Factory Safety: Labor Unions, Militant Protest, and the Accelerated Ambitions of Bangladesh's Garment Industry," *Dialectical Anthropology* 43 (2019): 97.

8. https://www.solidaritycenter.org/wp-content/uploads/2021/03/Bangladesh.Union-registration-information.December-2020.pdf.

9. Ashraf and Prentice, 97.

10. Rahman and Langford use the term "collaborationists" in "Why Labour Unions Have Failed."

11. "Bangladesh: Stop Persecuting Unions, Garment Workers," Human Rights Watch, February 15, 2017, https://www.hrw.org/news.

12. "Bangladesh: Stop Persecuting Unions, Garment Workers," *Human Rights Watch,* 2017.

13. "Bangladesh."

14. Nusrat Chowdhury, *Paradoxes of the Popular: Crowd Politics in Bangladesh* (Stanford: Stanford University Press, 2019), 8.

15. Ching Kwan Lee, "The Unmaking of the Chinese Working Class in the Northeastern Rustbelt," in *Working in China: Ethnographies of Labor and Workplace Transformation,* ed. Ching Kwan Lee (London: Routledge, 2006), 17–18.

16. Lee, 18.

17. Lee, 18.

18. "Tuba Workers Threaten to Close Down Clothing Factories across Bangladesh," August 6, 2014, bdnews24.com.

19. Lee, 17.

EPILOGUE

1. According to the Hanafi school of jurisprudence followed by Sunni Muslims of Bangladesh, if a husband is missing for an extended period, a woman can have the marriage dissolved on the grounds of presumed widowhood. Had Nilufa lived and wanted to rejoin her natal village, questions would arise about the legality of her second marriage under local interpretations of Islamic laws. The imam would be the final judge, and the interpretations of imams vary widely.

2. Achille Mbembe, "Necropolitics," trans. Libby Mientjes, *Public Culture* 15, no. 1 (Winter 2003): 11.

3. Lamia Karim, "Disposable Bodies: Garment Factory Catastrophe and Feminist Practices in Bangladesh," *Anthropology Now* 6, no. 1 (2014): 52–63.

4. Hasan Ashraf and Rebecca Prentice, "Beyond Factory Safety: Labor Unions, Militant Protests, and the Accelerated Ambition of Bangladesh's Garment Industry," *Dialectical Anthropology* 43 (2010): 99.

5. Mbembe, "Necropolitics."

6. Lauren Berlant, "Cruel Optimism," in *The Affect Theory Reader,* ed. Melissa Gregg and Gregory J. Seigworth (Durham, N.C.: Duke University Press, 2010); Carla Freeman, *Entrepreneurial Selves: Neoliberal Respectability and the Making of a Caribbean Middle Class* (Durham, N.C.: Duke University Press, 2014), 8.

7. "Sacrifice zones" refers to the work of Steve Lerner, who studied communities in the United States where poor people and people of color live in unhealthy environments of toxic chemicals. Lerner, *Sacrifice Zones: The Front Lines of Toxic Chemical Exposure in the United States* (Cambridge: MIT Press, 2012).

INDEX

Page numbers in italics refer to illustrations.

abandonment, 41, 80, 84, 85, 115, 123, 138–42, 155, 161, 167, 168, 173, 185, 195
abortion, 56, 173; banning, 133; clinics, 134; services, 134
abuse, 194; domestic, 38, 110, 136, 141, 155, 214; physical, 32, 91, 119, 135, 140, 141, 149, 182; sexual, 98; spousal, 117, 119, 137, 142, 167; verbal, 98, 140, 183; worker, 189
Accord on Fire and Building Safety, 27, 68–69, 70, 87, 88, 90
activism, 127, 162; cellular, 207–8, 209; labor, 200; political, 41; trade union, 2, 37, 169
ADR. *See* alternative dispute resolution
adultery, 162, 215
age, *82*, 129, 156, 171, 172; global economy and, 5; women and, 81; work and, 3
Agreement on Textiles and Clothing (1995–2004), 62
agriculture, 45, 53, 80, 167; female labor and, 78; state subsidies and, 59
Ahmed, Ahrar, 46, 151–52
Akhter, Nazma, 11, 93, 112, 237n8
Alexandra, Empress, 128
alimony, 42, 84, 141, 143, 144, 147
Alliance for Bangladesh Worker Safety, 69, 70, 90
alternative dispute resolution (ADR), 142, 143
Al-Zahid, 10, 148
Anjuman-e-Khawatin-e Islam, 45
anti-harassment committee, 179
Appadurai, Arjun, 3, 49, 79, 113, 128; globalization and, 7, 30, 33–34, 40, 123; modernity and, 46
Ashulia strike, 13, 202, 204–7, 209
aspirational subjectivity, 9, 37, 41, 78, 121, 137, 167, 179

aspirations, 33, 34, 36, 37, 39, 43, 114, 124, 161, 170, 178–81, 184–85, 190–92, 195; class and, 107–8; middle-class, 77–78
assembly lines, 4, 21, 30, 75, 90, 98, 120, 177, 190
attachments, 31, 32, 169, 195, 197; cruel, 33, 161
autonomy, 25, 29, 38, 46, 135, 136, 138, 140; female, 47, 151; financial, 148; sexual, 8, 123, 134; wages and, 148
Awaj Foundation, 92, 93
Awami League, 59
Azim, Firdaus, 46

Bachelor's Ball, The (Bourdieu), 152
Bangladesh Garment Manufacturers and Exporters Association (BGMEA), 5, 18, 66, 71, 72, 139, 203, 204, 207, 225n2
Bangladesh Institute for Labor Studies (BILS), 5
Bangladesh National Party, 60
Bangladesh Overseas Employment and Services Limited, 119, 232n1
Bangladesh Readymade Garment Workers Federation, 20
Barbados, 34; pink-collar workers in, 30; workers in, 114
Barlow, Tani, 43, 44
Baumann-Pauly, Dorothee, 27
Begum Rokeya Sakhawat Hossain, 44, 45
Behar, Ruth, 165, 195
behavior, 9, 190, 208; immoral, 182; misogynistic, 113; social, 156
Berlant, Lauren, 3, 165; cruel optimism, 7, 9, 30, 32, 33, 36, 51, 78, 129, 142, 156, 161, 162, 169–70, 195, 217; object of desire and, 32
betrayals, 12, 31, 78, 130
BGMEA. *See* Bangladesh Garment Manufacturers and Exporters Association
Bhagalpur, 45
Bhalobashar Din, 127
Bhuiyan, Nurul Momen, 30, 40, 230n50; hope and, 3, 7, 36, 78
birth rates, 45, 133, 137
Bollywood, 112, 127, 128, 145, 148, 149
bonuses, 204, 208, 210; nonpayment of, 31, 41
Boserup, Ester, 55
Bourdieu, Pierre, 152
BRAC University, 46, 54, 126
breadwinner argument, challenging, 24–25
Brennan, Denise, 124
Broken Promises of Globalization (Rahman), 26
bureaucracy, 2, 10, 196
Butler, Judith, 29

C&A, 65, 206
capitalism, 24, 30, 48, 57, 125, 151–52, 201, 216; change under, 152; consumer, 50; corporate, 25; developing countries and, 56; female labor and, 7, 23, 42; global, 31, 44, 125; harshness of, 216; industrial, 196; male domination and, 23; modernity and, 4–5; resistance to, 25; utilitarian terms of, 21–22; vampire, 5
cell phones, 48, 79, 108, 145
Chakmas, 12, 13

Chatterjee, Partha, 43, 44
child care, 20, 93, 105, 182
child labor, 70, 73, 194; garment industry and, 172; prohibition on, 65; using, 27, 192–93
child mortality, reducing, 55
childrearing, 149, 166
child support, 142
child welfare, 143
child workers, 193, 239n4
Chowdhury, Abdul Majid, 62
Chowdhury, Nusrat, 207
citizenship, industrial, 29, 68
city life, factory work and, 86, 110, 171, 191
class, 156; aspirations and, 107–8; business, 60; capitalist, 61; dynamics of, 105–11; economic, 35; garment workers and, 106; precariat, 41; social, 123, 151, 152, 240n10; solidarity, 25
class-in practice, concept of, 106
clothing, 39, 47, 92, 108, 136; manufacturing, 62, 217; sources of, 65
Comaroff, Jean and John: class struggle/class action and, 42
communication, 37, 90, 145
Communist Party, banning, 200
comportment, 39, 87, 161
Constable, Nicole, 124
consumerism, 8, 46, 78, 85, 111–13, 150, 163, 209
Covid-19, 18, 54, 166, 191, 194, 221, 222, 223
crime rates, 42, 88
cruel optimism, 7, 9, 30, 32, 33, 51, 78, 129, 142, 156, 161, 162, 169–70, 195, 217; neoliberalism and, 36

culture, 25–26, 37, 104; consumer, 105–13; democratic, 207; global, 45; lifestyle and, 46; lifeways of, 11; political, 210; popular, 127; work, 96

Daewoo, 62
day care, 15, 88, 168, 209; lack of, 93–95
day laborers, 81, 168
Day of Love, The, 127
debt, 2, 27, 81, 101, 112, 154, 161, 163, 167, 176; family, 79; unpaid, 160
Decade for Women, 56
deportation, 120, 121
deregulation, market, 59, 61
Desh Company, 62
desire, 6, 12, 32, 111, 156; sexual, 130, 134, 161
development, 44, 46, 48, 59, 80; national, 55; neoliberal, 78, 109; organizations, 56, 58; policies, 54, 56; women and, 55–58. *See also* economic growth
Dhaka airport, migrant workers at, 53
dignity, 6, 9, 22, 24; rural women and, 14
discipline, 61; factory, 25, 37, 98, 120, 121
diseases: waterborne, 91; work-related, 92. *See also* health issues
divorce, 41, 84, 104, 118, 123, 140, 144, 155, 163, 167, 182, 194; acceptance of, 136; education and, 135; fake, 147; marriage and, 135–37; middle class and, 137; registration of, 143; as social stigma, 136; verbal, 126

domestic work, 126; child workers and, 239n4
domestic workers, 1, 16, 20, 108, 109, 214; life choices for, 166; migrant, 29; working as, 168
dowry, 126, 135, 183, 238n8
Dragon Sweater Factory, workers from, *201*
dress code, Islamic, 47

economic growth, 32, 40, 43, 47, 54, 65, 107, 168, 180; labor and, 14; large-scale, 55
economic issues, 34, 46, 56, 64, 79, 101, 114, 171
economic liberalization, 49, 55, 60
economic subjectivity, 37–38, 132, 137
economy, 14, 48, 210; free-market, 111; gig, 116; global, 5, 195; industrial wage, 156; informal, 15, 57; knowledge, 5; rural, 17, 28, 33
education: children's, 167; democratization of, 109; divorce and, 135; health, 91; higher, 108, 121, 196; investment in, 181; lack of, 45, 176, 186; levels of, 81; primary/secondary, 45, 55; quality, 39; self-improvement and, 20; universal, 49; upward mobility and, 107
education sector, jobs in, 79
Eid holiday, 175, 178, 179, 182, 188, 208
employment, 40, 108, 168; factory, 16, 152; lack of, 79; limited, 45; long-term, 171; low-income, 81; non-unionized, 38, 79
empowerment, 58, 146; economic, 56; educational, 56; political, 56; women's, 44, 57

Entrepreneurial Selves (Freeman), 34
entrepreneurship, 57, 114–16; Bangladeshi, 63; neoliberal, 195
environment: degradation of, 79; socioeconomic, 30; toxic, 14; work, 10, 29–30, 98, 120, 169; working-class, 181
equality: economic, 210; gender, 56, 57
Ershad, Hussain Muhammad, 60
ethnography, 7, 9, 12, 125, 165, 166, 169; listening/observation strategies of, 11
exploitation, 24, 38, 166, 197; capitalist, 31; worker, 27
Export Processing Zones, 63, 200

Faaland, Just, 59
factories: subcontracting, 191; substandard, 30; upgrades for, 67–71
factory management, 2, 21, 71, 74, 84, 90, 169, 184, 192, 202; aging out and, 23; behavior of, 189, 190, 208; wages and, 73; women workers and, 5
factory owners, 63, 68, 75, 120, 207, 216, 236n56, 236n58; behavior of, 9, 190; inspections and, 88; monitoring and, 87; organization of, 5, 225n2; quota-free status and, 64; Rana Plaza and, 14; strikes and, 205; unions and, 201; wages and, 71
factory work, 16, 20, 88–93, 109, 114, 117, 121, 140, 170, 187, 196; benefits of, 107, 171; city life and, 86, 171; disadvantages of, 85, 163, 183; dynamics of, 77; impact of, 8, 80, 86–87, 191,

194; life cycles and, 172; urban life and, 81
factory workers, 1, 25, 30, *67*, 88–89, *92*, 107, 109, 149, 150, 183, 184, 193, *201*; abuse of, 189; aged-out, 16, 24, 168, 171, 197; challenges for, 95; Chinese, 207; as "debris" of capital, 21; desire for being of, 12; female, 6, 24, 28, *75*, 108, 150, 209–10; older, 194–97; sense of self for, 167; sexual needs of, 131
family, 144, 183; artisanal, 80; dynamics, 8, 37, 100–102, 104–5; fragmented, 17–18; life cycles and, 16–17; normative, 125; nuclear, 85, 104, 132, 138; organization, 77, 100, 171; patriarchal, 125; respect for, 98; surveillance of, 145
family court, 123, 142–44
farmers, 33, 35, 50, 60, 61, 80, 109
Feast of the Sacrifice, 173
"Feeling Neoliberal" (Freeman), 124
Feldman, Shelley, 27, 63
female workers: labor force and, 217; male attitudes toward, 148–52; marriage and, 143; sexual choices and, 144–48; stories of, 129; surveys of, 15–16
feminist studies, 7, 23, 36
Fernandes, Leela, 106
financial circumstances, 2, 110, 151, 203, 222, 223
financial issues, 2, 16, 21, 79, 138
firings, 12, 84, 180, 183
food, 19, 60, 73; cost of, 71, 205; improved, 39, 181; processing, 53; stalls, 111
Ford Foundation, 55

Foucault, Michel, 216
Fourth World Conference on Women, 56
freedom of association, 39, 44, 71
freedom of movement, 86
freedom of speech, 44
Freeman, Carla, 3, 30, 51, 57, 113, 130, 165, 179; affective life of, 169; aspirations and, 6, 9, 33, 34; entrepreneurship and, 114; on feeling/interiority, 169; female workers and, 25; feminist theory and, 36; globalization and, 40; neoliberalism and, 7, 124, 162, 170, 195, 199; swirl of affects and, 78, 217
free market, 25, 55–56, 58, 59
Free Trade Zones (FTZ), 25, 61, 114
FTZ. *See* Free Trade Zones

gambling addiction, 88, 94, 157, 173–74, 175, 179
Gaonkar, Dilip, 43
Gap, 69, 88, 206
garment factories, 10, 27, 61, *63*, 80, 109, 118, 196, 216; age of workers at, 81; fire/deaths at, 68; growth of, 79; importance of, 60; products from, 66; relocating, 64; safety at, 69–70; subcontractors and, 116; working at, 15, 18, 30, 60, 77, 118, 146, 160, 175, 181–82, 187–88, 189, 214
garment industry, 25, 38, 46, 105, 111, 132, 139, 145, 213; characteristics of, 61; decline of, 14; economic liberalization and, 55; global, 61–67; growth of, 8, 55, 63–65, 67, 68, 78, 88, 169;

neoliberalism and, 200; production by, 64, 65; regulating, 27; servicing, 77; studies on, 3–4, 26; subcontracting and, 15, 70–71; unionization and, 200; women and, 79, 80, 232n78; working in, 7, 10, 12–13, 14, 45, 66, 84, 88, 214, 225n2
Garments Sramik Front, 205, 206–7
garment workers, 1, 11, 31, *35,* 41, 48, 49, *66, 86,* 91, *95,* 101, 112, 117, 123, 127, 132, 133, 140, 145, 156, 158, 165, 170, 175, 186; aged-out, 3, 34; children of, 95, 149, 176; as class-in-practice, 106; crises for, 155; cultural nuances of, 125; entrepreneurial, *115*; environment for, 29–30, 163, 199; extended families and, 17; factory life and, 12; fate of, 216–17; interviews of, 8, 15, 195–96; labor of, 29, 149; lives of, 3, 27, 30, 112, 121, 129, 161, 166, 197; male, 5, 150, *150*; marrying, 138, 151; rally for, 209; social clause and, 65; survival for, 183
"Garment Worker's Cry, A" (Yesmin), text of, 95–96
Garment Workers Forum, 208
gender, 25, 56, 105, 129, 155, 156; age and, 3; dynamics, 88, 104; generation and, 38–39; necropolitics and, 216; roles, 14, 19, 113, 125; work and, 3
Generalized System of Preferences, suspension of, 68
Georgieva, Kristalina, 54
German Technical Training Center, 119, 180

GI Bill, 32
global capital, 7, 10, 22
globalization, 7, 10, 16, 26, 30, 40, 45, 47, 78, 79, 109, 111, 116, 127, 136, 151, 152, 163, 167, 168; competitive, 58; imagination and, 33–34; impact of, 8; notion of, 49; work and, 77
Grameen Bank, 54
Great Recession, 28
Green Revolution, 55

Hadith, 48, 232n81
Ha-Meem group, 71, 88, 205
H&M, 65, 206
harassment, 180; feminist notions of, 98; sexual, 96–100; verbal, 98; workplace, 87, 88–93
Harding, Sandra, 57
Hareven, Tamara, 16, 17, 166
Hasan, Ashraf, 70
health issues, 2, 9, 26, 118, 137, 179, 222; eye problems, 93; fatigue, 93; headaches, 76, 93; hearing problems, 93; hypertension, 93; jaundice, 214; kidney/urinary tract diseases, 91; leukorrhea, 133; maternal, 55; mental health, 95; osteoporosis, 194; prolapsed uteruses, 133; psychological troubles, 93; reproductive, 56, 91, 133, 134; slums and, 102; STIs, 131, 133; upper-respiratory problems, 76, 92. *See also* diseases; injuries
health sector, jobs in, 79
Hefazat-i-Islam, 47
Heller, Patrick, 106
henna, 113
Hewamanne, Sandya, 25, 40, 114

Hindus, 12, 126, 127, 139, 140
hope, residue of, 3, 7, 12, 36, 78, 101, 230n50
Hossain, Jakir, 27, 63
housework, 85, 104–5, 149, 150, 181
housing, 6, 73, 88, *100, 103*; affordable, 132; cost of, 71, 205; described, 102–3; improved, 39; nuclear, 104
"How Will Women Dress?" (Razzak Bin Yousuf), 113
human immunodeficiency virus (HIV), 133
human trafficking, 216
humiliation, 99, 158, 183
Huq, Chaumtoli, 27, 57–58, 70

"I Am a Machine Operator" (Yesmin), 127; text of, 21
Ibrahim, Ahmad, 46
identity, 16, 38, 39, 165, 215; age earning, 16; capitalism and, 25; cards, 72, 139; elite, 45; insurgent, 9; middle-class, 108; social, 43; women's, 26
ideology, 25, 43, 48, 58, 105, 201, 210; political, 11
illiteracy, 20, 59, 81, 90, 107, 167, 170
ILO. *See* International Labour Organization
imagination, 9, 20, 26, 32, 49, 95, 127, 128; globalization and, 33–34
Imperial Sweater Factory, workers from, *201*
income, 38; disparity, 25; per capita, 54; supplemental, 74, 115
Inditex, 206
industrialization, 3, 14, 17, 36, 61, 78, 104

industrial work, 9, 10, 20, 32, 77, 167, 192, 197; browning of, 24; feminization of, 24; global flows of, 14; hope for, 15; migration and, 42; politics and, 200
industrial workers, 5–6, 17, 19–20, 30, 40, 210; aging out of, 23; migrants as, 37–38; public lives of, 123
inflation, 71, 72, 225n1
Information and Communication Special Technology Act (2015), 205
injuries, 40; workplace, 30, 32, 68
injustice, workplace, 40–41, 196
insecurities, 9, 28, 60, 87, 116, 132; financial, 2, 29; marital, 45, 85; sexual, 97, 151
International Conference on Population and Development, 56
International Labour Organization (ILO), 5, 94–95; decent work and, 6; monitoring by, 206; safety standards and, 91
International Year of the Woman Conference, 55
Internet, 46, 49
intimacy, 34, 36, 40, 42, 124, 161, 175
Islam, 140, 193, 226n7, 232n81

justice: desire for, 162; notions of, 39; social, 11, 38, 46

Kabeer, Naila, 24, 25, 26, 27, 58, 66, 76; empowerment and, 57
Kamal, Ahmed: on divorce, 137
Kennedy, Paul: vampire capitalism and, 5
Khan, Ayub: on unionism, 200

Khandewal, Meena, 57
Kibria, Nazli, 26
kinship, 17, 100, 104, 144; obligations of, 36; reciprocity and, 36; support from, 182, 183
knowledge, social, 10, 109, 139, 147, 156, 162, 184
Kormojibi Nari, 13, *141*
Krishno, 128, 130, 163
"Krishno, the Lover" (Yesmin), 42; text of, 128

labor, 7, 144, 166, 199; cheap, 8, 28; conditions, 68; dignity of, 24; disputes, 204, 208; economic growth and, 14; exploited, 78; flexibility of, 28; forced, 65; garment, 66–67; industrial, 28, 29, 49; migrant, 163; non-unionized, 64; politics over, 199; precariat, 28–30, 60, 195, 217; unfree, 28–29; wage, 30, 33, 38, 40, 49, 57. *See also* child labor
Labor Act (2006), 8, 72–73, 202
labor activists, 5, 18, 96, 203, 207, 236n56, 236n58
labor codes, 65, 67, 116
Labor, Global Supply Chains, and the Garment Industry in South Asia (Saxena), 26–27
labor groups, 140, 201, 203, 236n58
labor laws, 85, 169, 200
Labor Ministry, 71, 180, 201
labor organizations, 9, 10–11, 27, 41, 58, 162, 163, 179, 201, 202, 204, 207; meeting of, 183–84
labor rights, 11, 15, 27, 48, 95, 143, 146, 163, 204, 208, 214; advocacy of, 144, 213; loss of, 64–65

labor rights office, 146, 181
labor unions, 72, 201, 207; factory level, 58; national, 58; politicization of, 199, 200. *See also* trade unions
landscape, 77, 121, 123; changing, 78–81; cultural, 7; factory, 22; urban, 16, 22
Language Movement, 106
least developed countries (LDCs), 62
Lee, Ching Kwan, 207–8, 209
legal subjectivity, 37, 41, 126
Lerner, Steve: sacrifice zones and, 242n7
Lessinger, Johanna, 25
Lewis, David: on development policies, 54
Liaoyang, worker protests of, 207
Liberation War (1971), 106
life: changing landscapes of, 78–81; erotic, 129, 197; factory, 38, 177–78, 183–84, 189–90; family, 18, 31, 37; good, 6, 19, 33, 36; married, 186–89; normative cycle of, 100; political, 41; post-industrial, 167; private, 42, 138, 168; rural, 81, 170; social, 34, 124, 135; urban, 81; work/nonwork, 6, 22, 76, 77, 123, 165, 194–95
life circumstances, 16, 180, 191
life cycles, 167, 169; family and, 16–17
life patterns, changing, 81, 84–88
life stories, 9, 39–40, 165, 168, 170; telling, 169; writing, 181
lifestyle, 37, 43, 46, 50, 108, 112, 114, 121
line supervisor, *69*

literacy, 44, 81, *82,* 84, 166
living conditions, 78, 93, 133
love, 9, 124, 161, 197, 211; experiencing, 8; marital, 195–96; need for, 3; romantic, 127–31; work and, 30–36
lower class, 35, 106, 109
Lynch, Caitrin, 25

Made in Bangladesh, Cambodia, and Sri Lanka (Saxena), 26
madrassas, 85, 113
Mahmud, Sohel, 92–93
Majumdar, Sanjita, 27
manufacturing, 32, 62, 91; apparel, 4, 7, 65, 66; global economy of, 65, 195, 217; low-skilled, 23; outsourcing of, 61; production costs and, 61; raw materials for, 63
Marcus, George, 11
marital disputes, 123, 138–42; resolving, *141*
marital status, 81, *83,* 84, 85, 136, 166
marriage, 8, 17, 42, 104, 117, 119, 122, 123, 124, 125, 126, 129, 146, 147, 163, 165, 166, 170, 172, 174, 175, 176, 186–89; arranged, 132, 135, 144, 183; child, 45; conventions of, 138; delaying, 133; divorce and, 135–37, 241n1; durable, 33; false, 39, 144, 157–58; first cousin, 135; hypergamous, 39; legal, 144; motherhood and, 135; multiple, 84, 85, 140; poverty and, 167; registration of, 126, 142–44; unofficial agreements for, 142. *See also* divorce; separations

marriage-scape, 123–24
married life, 173–75, 181–82; durability of, 167
Marx, Karl, 61
material arrangements, 6, 33, 38–39
maternity leave, 177–78
Mbembe, Achille, 216
media: garment industry and, 76; social, 46, 47, 48, 152
Mezzadri, Alessandra, 27
MFA. *See* Multifibre Arrangement
microfinance programs, 55, 79, 101
middle class, 9, 107, 108, 128, 130–31, 170, 177, 210, 211; categories of, 106; divorce and, 137; entertainment for, 112; ideas of, 8; old/new, 106; serials about, 50; term, 34–35, 105; upward mobility and, 109
migrants, 108, 133; female, 65; as industrial workers, 37–38; poor, 89; urban, 200
migrant workers, 17, 101, 108, 110; gendered, 25; return of, 53
migration, 7, 104, 124, 135, 152, 167, 197; family, 17; industrial work and, 42; male, 79–80; shifts in, 171; unmarried female, 100
Millennium Development Goals (MDGs), 54
Minimum Wage Board, 72
Mirpur, 1, 10, 13, 156, 172, 202, 204; garment factories in, 63; research in, 15
Mishu, Moshrefa, 208
mobility, 124, 125; class, 28, 78, 109, 196, 197, 209; male, 80; social, 105. *See also* upward mobility

modernity, 7, 42; capitalism and, 3, 4–5; colonial, 43; GDP, 197; question of, 43–51; spaces of, 10
Moral Economy of the Peasant, The (Scott), 38
moral subjectivity, 37, 38, 137
mortality rates, 45
Muhammad, Anu, 60, 61
Muhammad, Prophet, 113, 232n81
Multifibre Arrangement (MFA), 8, 55, 62, 64, 65
Muslim Family Laws Ordinance (1961), 126

Namasudras, 12
Nari Sramik (Woman Worker) (Yesmin), 20
Nasrin, Taslima, 238n17
National Public Radio, 62
necropolitics, gender and, 216
neoliberalism, 3, 7, 16, 20, 28, 55–56, 78, 109, 114, 124, 191, 210, 211, 217; in Bangladesh, 58–61; cruel optimism and, 36; cruelty of, 195; garment industry and, 200; innovation of, 57
networks, 11, 36, 49, 171; economic, 30, 137; familial, 17, 74, 183; informal, 93; kin, 182–83; social/economic, 8, 30, 100–102, 104–5
New Industrial Policy (NIP), 60
New York Times, 55
Next Collections, 88, 206
NGOs. *See* nongovernmental organizations
nongovernmental organizations (NGOs), 11, 12, 31, 41, 54, 55, 56, 59–60, 68, 91, 92, 93, 95, 96, 126, 137, 141; labor rights, 5, 10, 15, 143; legal aid, 42, 142; marital rights and, 84

Ong, Aihwa, 25, 61
"On the Issue of Bangladeshi's Upper Class and a Social Revolution" (Sofa), 45
opportunity, 29, 39, 62, 64, 85, 155, 156, 202, 210, 211; glorified, 105; unequal, 32
oppression, 32, 138, 208; capitalist, 31, 197, 201; worker, 24, 25, 27, 127, 163, 169
optimism: circumstantial, 34; dance of, 163; false, 33; instantaneous, 34; neoliberal, 78, 162, 170, 195; operation of, 32. *See also* cruel optimism
Ortner, Sherry, 16, 37–38, 105
"Our Modernity" (Chatterjee), 43
"Overtime" (Yesmin), text of, 90
overtime work, 87, 89, 90, 93

Paper Tangos (Taylor), 42, 129
Parkinson, John, 59
patriarchy, 4, 7, 9, 22, 50, 79–80, 125, 134, 163; capitalist, 76; factory-based, 25
physical movements, 11, 86, 194, 200
pink-collar workers, 25, 30
Players Unknown Battle Ground (game), 49
poetry, 127; seeing workers through, 20–22
political parties, 7, 199, 210
political subjectivity, 37, 40–41, 42
politics, 41, 56, 127, 166; crowd-based, 207; industrial work and, 200; labor, 70, 200, 207, 209; left,

206; nationalist, 106; radical, 9; trade union, 200; worker, 207–11
pollution, 4, 76, 88, 92
Posner, Michael, 70
poverty, 16, 35, 45, 48, 50–51, 65, 89, 109, 172, 195; alleviating, 54, 55, 59; household, 79, 185; marriage and, 167; rural, 81
power: discretionary, 29; economic, 67; patriarchal, 79–80; social, 168
Power to Choose, The (Kabeer), 26
precarity, 30, 70, 199, 211, 217; economic, 31, 210; emotional, 161; social, 31
pregnancy, 167, 173, 177–78; regulating, 175; terminating, 134; unwanted, 133
Prentice, Rebecca, 70
Prevention of Women and Child Repression Act (2000), 137, 146, 193
Primark, 206
privatization, 8, 55, 59, 60, 61, 138
production, 94, 116; commodity, 6, 28, 39, 113; costs, 64; global supply chain of, 28, 122; industrial, 76; social, 17
Proshika, 232n78
protests, worker, 10, 37, 68, 71–73, 169, 190, 202, 203, 205, 206, 207–8, 210
public spaces, 49, 87
PVH, 65

Quader, Noorul, 62
Quayum, Seemin, 106
Quran, 113, 136, 226n7, 232n81

Rahman, Shahidur, 26
Rahman, Sheikh Mujibur, 59

Rahman, Ziaur, 59, 60
Ramamurthy, Priti, 26
Rana Plaza factory catastrophe, 13, 14–15, 26–27, 30, 55, 67–71, 73, 87–88, 94, 96, 205, 216; aftermath of, 68; deaths at, 68
rape, 97, 98, 139, 240n6
Rasputin, 128
Ray, Raka, 106
Razzak bin Yousuf, Sheikh Abdur, 113
ready-made garment (RMG) industry, 7–8, 13, 55, 64, 200, 201
reciprocity, 17, 36, 38, 125
relations, 132, 142, 159, 160; abusive, 137; associational, 101, 102; gender, 66, 155; navigating, 146, 156–57; romantic, 138; social, 42; society, 66; toxic, 12; working, 171. *See also* sexual relations
religion, 17, 38, 47
remittances, 17, 106, 232n1
reproduction, 4, 24, 29, 105, 169; social, 17, 23, 27–28, 101, 240n10
resilience, 3, 9, 78, 197
responsibility, 17, 70, 87, 117, 138, 196; spousal, 80; taking, 80
retailers, 32, 69, 204, 206, 217
Revised Industrial Policy (1975), 59
Rezaul Factory, strike at, 202–4
rights, 6, 44, 141–42; fighting for, 2; human, 24, 26, 41, 48, 59, 206; individual, 46; knowledge of, 41; legal, 42, 56, 142, 208; marital, 84, 163; union, 65; women's, 46, 136–37. *See also* labor rights; workers' rights

254 Index

RMG industry. *See* ready-made garment (RMG) industry
romance, 8, 51, 105, 122, 130, 163
rule of law, 44, 46

sacrifice zones, 217, 242n7
Safa, Helen, 24
safety, 61, 91; improving, 69–70; issues, 13, 69, 70–71, 139
Sahanaj, 10, *86,* 130, 147, 213; activism of, 162; garment workers and, 156; Moni and, 157, 158, 159, 160; on rights, 141–42
Samsung, 108
Sandoz, 232n78
Saraka garment factory, 68, 200
Savar, 13, 15; survey results from, *82–83*
Saxena, Sanchita Banerjee, 26–27
Scott, James, 38
security, 3, 4, 46, 81, 136; employment, 29, 30, 89, 209; financial, 2, 29; industrial citizenship, 29–30; marital, 45; sexual, 124; skill reproduction, 29; social, 138, 156, 169
self-improvement, education and, 20
self-worth, 16, 38, 99, 180
Sen, Binayak, 46
Sen, Samita, 24
separations, 94, 106, 126, 136, 137, 142, 167, 170, 182
Setara, 205
sexuality, 122, 131–34, 145, 148, 175; attitudes toward, 8; discourse of, 131; female, 14, 131; impoverished, 131; regulation of, 86; social conventions around, 156

sexually transmitted infections (STIs), 131, 133
sexual relations, 7, 8, 9, 42, 47, 130, 142, 149, 159, 161, 186, 188, 194, 211; extramarital, 151, 158; female workers and, 144–48; forced, 182; illicit, 145; premarital, 131–32, 134; safe, 131, 133; unlawful, 47
sex workers, 14, 183
Shafi, Maulana Ahmed, 47
shalwar kameezes, 88, 112
sharecroppers, 35, 49, 50, 88
Sheng Lu, 73
Siddiqi, Dina, 23, 26
slums, 104, 106, 168, 183, 197; described, 102
social arrangements, 125
social attitudes, 8, 88, 163
social change, 126, 136, 166
social clause, lack of, 65
social control, exercising, 14
social conventions, 57, 122, 125, 156
social costs, 111, 136
social dynamics, 8, 100–102, 104–5
social norms, 77, 104, 161, 216
social order, 41, 106, 137, 152
social problems, 31, 211
social status, 31–32, 126, 136
social structure, marriage/divorce and, 136
social vulnerability, levels of, 171
Sofa, Ahmed, 45, 46
Solidarity International, 41, 201
Sommilito Garment Sramik Federation, 237n8
sovereignty, 7, 196, 216
Special Powers Act (1974), 205

Sramik Karmachari Oikya Parishad, 72
Standing, Guy, 3, 29, 30, 196; industrial citizenship and, 68; precariat and, 41, 60, 199
Stephen, Lynn, 166
Stern School of Business, 70
STIs. *See* sexually transmitted infections
strikes, 8, 41, 72; motivations for, 208–9; outcomes of, 202–7
structural adjustment policies, 56, 59, 65
subcontractors, 27, 61, 70–71, 116–18, 129, 168; independent, 15; safety issues and, 71
subject formations, 37–42, 197
subjectivity, 37–42, 99–100; economic, 101, 182, 191; legal, 179; moral, 101, 182, 191; political, 179, 210
Sultana, Sunzida, 98
support, 14, 167, 168, 195, 200, 203, 215; child, 142, 143; economic, 30, 36, 104, 138; familial, 16, 100, 113, 114, 116, 137, 138, 139, 156, 157, 159, 172, 180, 183, 187; social, 30, 171
surveillance, 86, 90–91, 97, 145
surveys, 15–16, 81, 84–88

tailoring shops, 115, *115,* 178
Target, 69
Taylor, Julie, 42, 129
Tazreen Fashion, fire/deaths at, 68
Tchibo, 65
textiles, 60, 61, 62, 65, 89
Tithi, 10, 130, 141, 142, 147, *153*
Tommy Hilfiger, 88

trade union leaders, 5, 18, 37, 72, 127, 178, 202, 205, 206, 209, 236n56; fake, 71
trade unions, 5, 7, 10, 26, 30, 41, 58, 116, 121, 169, 201, 208, 209–10; culture of, 199; export-processing zones and, 63; focus on, 12; gender dimension to, 200; legal aid from, 42; persecuting, 204; Rana Plaza and, 14; representation by, 63; restrictions on, 61, 71. *See also* labor unions
transformation: economic, 48; political, 211; social, 48, 125; structure of, 42
Translated Woman (Behar), 165, 195
Tuba factory strike, 208

unemployment, 16, 108, 167, 180, 223
Union Council, 222
United Nations, 54, 55, 56
upward mobility, 9, 108, 195, 196; education and, 107; middle class and, 109; women and, 81
urban living, 10, 39, 78, 85, 133
U.S. Child Labor Deterrence Act (1999), 70, 73, 192–93

Valentine's Day, 127, 175
violence, 13, 130, 148, 168; domestic, 45, 85, 102, 168, 214; gender-based, 37; impact of, 14; sexual, 42, 126, 148
vote, right to, 44

wage board, appointment of, 71
wages, 7, 10, 34, 48, 49, 70, 71–73, 108, 142, 143, 162, 204; autonomy and, 148; defrauding of, 31;

factory, 148, 182; fair, 19, 71, 73, 209; increase in, 39, 71, 73–76, 189–90, 206, 207, 210; low, 27, 64, 65, 68, 71, 72–73, 81, 89, 172; minimum, 73, *74*; nonpayment of, 41, 72–73, 208; severance, 176, 179, 184, 185, 190
Waliullah, Syed, 50, 51
Wall Street Journal, report by, 88
Walmart, 64, 65, 69
waste, industrial, 76, 91, 102
We Are the Face of Oaxaca (Stephen), 166
weddings, 36, 176–77, 179, 181
welfare, 17, 30, 45, 58, 61, 137, 143
White, Sarah, 38–39, 79, 195
white collar jobs, female-coded, 79
Willis, Paul, 196
Windy Apparel factory, strike at, 205, 206
Wolf, Diane, 25
womanhood, Islamic, 47, 135, 136
Women's Role in Economic Development (Boserup), 55
work: age and, 3; disruptions, 41, 203; domains of, 78; globalization and, 77; love and, 30–36; routines, 8; shifts in, 78–81, 171; women's, 18, 48, 57, 105; years at, *83*
workers. *See* factory workers; female workers; garment workers; industrial workers; migrant workers; pink-collar workers
workers' movements, 41, 190
workers' rights, 10, 11, 27, 48, 65, 116, 177, 209; focus on, 12; labor laws and, 200; organizations, 183–84; protecting, 201
workforce, 2, 3, 17, 23, 30, 76, 200; female workers in, 4, 28, 43; global precariat, 28
work hours, regularization of, 73–74
working class, 7, 9, 107, 128, 137, 152, 210; consumer culture and, 111; feminization of, 60; interests of, 208; term, 105
working conditions, 19, 26, 27, 183; dehumanizing, 232n1; improving, 68–69; poor, 9, 68, 73, 116; substandard/hazardous, 65; work-related diseases and, 92
workshops, 41; labor rights training, 11, 13, *13,* 37, 97, 179–80, 184
World Bank, 8, 54, 55, 60, 111; development policies of, 56; structural adjustment policies and, 59, 65; women's work and, 57
WTO, trade agreement/social clause in, 65

Yesmin, Lovely, 11, *19,* 51, 127; overtime work and, 90; poetry of, 20, 21–22, 42, 53, 90, 95–96, 128, 129, 131; romantic love and, 127; on sexual harassment, 99; subjectivity and, 99–100; trade unions and, 208
Yunusia Madrassah, clergy attack by, 232n78

Zara, 76

Lamia Karim is professor of anthropology at the University of Oregon and author of *Microfinance and Its Discontents: Women in Debt in Bangladesh* (Minnesota, 2011).

Lightning Source UK Ltd.
Milton Keynes UK
UKHW022008121122
412092UK00003B/11